WHO KILLED JOHN CLAYTON?

Who Killed John Clayton?

Political Violence and the Emergence of the New South, 1861–1893

Kenneth C. Barnes

Duke University Press Durham and London 1998

Printed in the United States of America

on acid-free paper ∞

Designed by C. H. Westmoreland

Typeset in Janson with Copperplate display

by Keystone Typesetting, Inc.

Library of Congress Cataloging-in-

Publication Data appear on the last printed

page of this book.

To my parents,

Curtis and Maxine Barnes

Contents

List of Illustrations viii

Preface ix

Acknowledgments xi

Introduction 1

1. Local Divisions and Lasting Grudges: Civil War and Reconstruction 7

2. Motives for Murder: Democrats and Republicans Compete for Power, 1872–1888 33

3. Murder and Fraud: How Democrats Reclaimed Conway County, 1888–1889 60

4. Consequences of Murder: Things Fall Apart, 1890–1893 94

5. Murder's Reward: Rule of the Fine-Haired Gentlemen 117

Appendixes 133

Notes 149

Bibliography 181

Index 195

Illustrations

1. The landscape of Conway County 8
2. Lewisburg on the eve of the Civil War 10
3. Samuel J. Stallings 14
4. Captain Thomas Jefferson Williams 19
5. The monastery farm of the Holy Ghost Fathers 44
6. W. H. Ward's plantation, west of Morrilton 49
7. The Stout plantation near Morrilton 50
8. Cotton waits for the train at Morrilton 51
9. The Conway County courthouse 55
10. Conway County in 1888 63
11. The Republican ticket in the 1888 federal election 69
12. Oliver T. Bentley 73
13. Plumerville, circa 1900 75
14. John Middleton Clayton 77
15. The house where Clayton was killed 78
16. Richard Gray 86
17. An application from Morrilton for emigration to Liberia 106
18. Benjamin G. White 118
19. Charles C. Reid Jr. 119

PREFACE

This project began when through some distant family connections, I received an audiotape of an interview of John Mason just a few years before his death in the early 1980s. Mason grew up in Conway County, Arkansas, in the early twentieth century, became a high school history teacher and principal, and throughout his life listened avidly to stories of the old days. Mason understood the significance of these stories, committed them to memory, and became a virtual griot, preserving an oral heritage of his rural community of origin. Mrs. Polly Church conducted the interview for the purposes of family history, but throughout the interview, Mason digressed into numerous asides and anecdotes. In one he told the story of the murder of John M. Clayton, a Republican congressional candidate, from the point of view of the men who committed the murder. Mason even identified the killers by name.

I grew up in Conway County in the 1960s, a time when the county had the reputation within Arkansas as the epitome of the southern Democratic machine at work. After college I left this Faulknerian atmosphere to pursue graduate study in modern European history, then a job teaching at a small college in the Chicago area. Fifteen years later, I took a position at the University of Central Arkansas in Conway, Arkansas, just down the road from Conway County. My life had come back around the circle. Getting back in touch with my extended family eventually brought me into possession of the Mason tape. I had only a passing acquaintance with the history of my own state, and the textbooks on Arkansas history said that Clayton's murderers had never been found. What began as a curiosity became a quest to solve a century-old murder mystery and then evolved into this monograph.

In some ways, this study has been an attempt to understand my own roots, the space on earth that formed me. The extraordinary sequence of political violence I found in the late nineteenth century helped me understand how sixty years later, I could grow up in a county where almost all African Americans could not vote and where authorities still used fraud and terror, when necessary, to neutralize their opposition, all in the name of tradition and civic righteousness.

The study of my own roots led me to confront the salient themes of southern history. Larger than local questions kept surfacing. How does a community create the account of its history? By examining Arkansas histories and collecting oral testimonies of Conway County residents, I discovered that the telling of history by white, educated, respectable citizens did not match the documentary evidence I was accumulating. How does the historian use and interpret this evidence? *Evidence* as a word always looks more impressive than the mixed bag of data that historians usually have at their disposal. In this case, I as author had to choose between competing versions of the truth. The cases of murder and electoral fraud described in this study were tried in federal court in 1889 and the next year were heard by the Committee on Elections of the U.S. House of Representatives. As in any trial, participants presented different accounts of the same events. In the 1800s, white judges found it difficult to take the word of uneducated black farmers over that of prosperous and prominent white community leaders. Sorting out contradictory testimony and competing versions of events involves judgments, and occasionally informed speculation, about things that are ultimately uncertain. In the 1990s, it is much easier to cast blame on dead white male elites. The problem is, of course, that the writing of history nowadays may be shaped by the forces of what is politically correct just as early white Democratic versions whitewashed, justified, or ignored white crimes.

Acknowledgments

My greatest debts for this study belong to my oral sources. The storytellers of Conway County first led me to this narrative. I especially wish to thank Polly Church, Ruth Cupit, Earl Bentley, Jane Emde, Clarkia Turney, Robert Cruce, Alpha English, Blanche McCray, Mrs. Grant Reddig, and Poindexter Fiser, who shared information about their ancestors for my story, which in some cases does not flatter them.

Librarians at the University of Central Arkansas, the University of Southern Mississippi, and the Arkansas History Commission provided much assistance in finding and using relevant materials. Special thanks go to Sandy Breeding and Karolyn Thompson of the interlibrary loan departments at UCA and USM. Meg Hacker of the National Archives Regional Center in Fort Worth helped me get the federal court case files concerning fraudulent Conway County elections. Rod Ross of the legislative office of the National Archives in Washington, D.C., after much hunting, located the four volumes of manuscript testimony concerning the Clayton murder and Conway County elections, which forms the basis of much of this study.

I greatly benefited from the critical readings of all or parts of this work by my colleagues at the University of Central Arkansas, Waddy Moore, Cathy Urwin, David Petersen, and, as always, my wife, Debbie Barnes. Besides reading the manuscript, Tom Dillard gave me numerous leads on sources from his vast knowledge of Arkansas history. An early draft of a section of this work was published in the *Arkansas Historical Quarterly*, and I thank particularly editor Jeannie Whayne for her interest and advice. I especially thank Charles C. Bolton, Mark Schantz, and Duke University Press's insightful reviewers, who read later versions of the manuscript and provided valuable comments and criticism. My friend Ralph Gallucci encouraged me to write this book even though it seemed to be an unconventional career turn. Thanks also to Valerie Millholland of Duke University Press for her support. Graduate assistants Edman Wilkes, Mick Cabe, and Sharon Allen helped with many tasks ranging from counting census entries to bibliographic work. A special thanks goes to Donna Johnson for her assistance in so many ways.

This study, like much of the writing of southern history, stands under the looming shadow of C. Vann Woodward, who spent his adolescence in Conway County. His later views would be so apt in explaining the environment of his youth. Beyond the works of Woodward, I owe a great debt to several other magisterial books, most notably Eric Foner's *Reconstruction: America's Unfinished Revolution* and Edward Ayers's *The Promise of the New South.* In my study of Conway County's thirty-year political struggle, I, like Woodward and Foner, tend to favor the powerless who take on the powerful. But Ayers forcefully cautions against the portrayal of southerners as stick figures, as simplistic cartoon characters in white or black hats. Ayers inspires an ironic sympathy with the leaders of the community, the educated, prosperous townsmen who led the Democratic party. After all, as a small-town university professor, my life is more like theirs than it is like that of rural sharecroppers. Hence comes a mystery more fascinating and elusive than Clayton's unsolved murder: just how could these pillars of the community do such horrible things?

I dedicate this book to my parents, Curtis and Maxine Barnes, who spent a lifetime in Conway County, and who in their own way and time struggled there against corruption and injustice.

Introduction

In late January 1889, in the small town of Plumerville, Arkansas, a group of leading citizens gathered around the potbellied stove in Malone's general store to plan a cold-blooded murder. They drew straws, resolving that the man who received the short straw would kill John Middleton Clayton, a Republican leader who had come to Arkansas during Reconstruction days. In the preceding fall, Clayton had narrowly lost his race for the U.S. Congress after a band of masked white Democrats stole at gunpoint the Plumerville ballot box, which contained the majority of the county's black Republican votes. When Clayton arrived to investigate the stolen election, local Democrats feared they would end up in a federal penitentiary and thus took desperate measures. On a cold winter night shortly thereafter, the man who had drawn the short straw and a partner stood for some time on the muddy soil outside the window of Clayton's room in a Plumerville boardinghouse, waiting for the perfect moment to strike. Finally, as Clayton sat down at a table next to the window to pen a letter to his children, a blast of buckshot burst through the window, ripping the curtain into shreds, killing him instantly. By the next morning, the footprints made by the killers' rubber overboots—one pair old, one new—had frozen solid in the muck.

The murder of a congressional candidate brought headlines in national newspapers for Conway County, Arkansas. Newspaper reporters, Pinkerton detectives, and state and federal officials investigated the vile crime. But because the most prominent and socially respectable citizens of the county provided alibis for one another, no assassin was ever found. Arkansas history books henceforth treated Clayton's killing, one of the most famous political murders in the state's history, as an unsolved mystery.

Detectives failed to solve the murder of John Clayton. Only careful historical analysis can explain who killed him and why. For this community, the sensational murder was just the climax of a cycle of local political violence that had begun in the Civil War. But an examination of Conway County's experience sheds light on more than just a murder; it also reveals how the use of illegal political violence was central to the fashioning and streamlining of patterns historians call the New South: the single-party system, black disfranchisement, and segregation by law. Clayton's murder crystallizes in one dramatic moment what happened throughout the South with the creation of Jim Crow law.

Political violence means the illegal use of force to keep or increase one's power. Throughout American history, the transfer of political and economic power to powerless outsiders has involved political violence. Richard Hofstadter said: "What is most exceptional about the Americans is not the voluminous record of their violence, but their extraordinary ability, in the face of that record, to persuade themselves that they are among the best-behaved and best-regulated of peoples." Contemporaries and historians have described the nineteenth-century South as a violent place, even in the best of times. The Civil War, however, made killing into a culture. After the war, weapons were everywhere; the survivors of the war had the experience and disposition to use force to protect themselves or to get their way.[1] The story of Conway County demonstrates how especially the most prominent members of the community employed political violence between 1861 and 1893. Various groups of both the privileged and the poor saw local government as the means to advance their own interests, and some were willing to use the most flagrant acts of violence to get, maintain, or extend their power.

From the beginning of the Civil War to the establishment of Jim Crow laws in the early 1890s, Conway County was in a state of turmoil and transition. In 1861 secessionist cotton planters and their hangers-on along the bottomlands of the county clashed with subsistence farmers in the northern hills who remained loyal to the Union. This rivalry blossomed into a vicious guerrilla conflict during the last two years of the Civil War. Congressional Reconstruction, which followed, became a battle between the victorious small farmers and the defeated local aristocrats and their allies, who first organized as the Ku Klux Klan and then became the revived Democratic Party. The white Unionists, joined by freedmen under the banner of the Republican Party and supported by federal laws and guns, possessed the upper hand until the end of Reconstruction. But conservative white Democrats regained power and exacted their retribution.

In the two decades that followed, Conway County, like the South in general, saw the rise of towns and a commercial economy with the arrival of the railroad and the expansion of cotton production. The planters moved to town and built big white houses, and their sons became merchants, lawyers, bankers, and physicians. But as cotton prices declined and debt and tenancy mushroomed in the 1880s, the commercial-professional-planter elite faced a larger and angrier class of the rural poor. Debt-ridden white farmers swelled the ranks of Arkansas's homegrown agrarian populist movement called the Agricultural Wheel, which ran candidates in the local elections after 1884. Moreover, a significant black migration challenged white control as the African American portion of the county's population grew from nearly 8 to 40 percent between 1870 and 1890. African Americans overwhelmingly voted Republican, allying with a white Republican holdout of Union veterans and loyalists. With the fractured white vote, Republicans swept the elections of 1884 and 1886. In this quintessentially southern county, the local GOP won through the democratic process, and the elected officials, including some black Republicans, took their offices.

By 1888, after four years of Republican rule, white Democrats in Conway County were determined to regain control of local government. In the five years that followed, Democrats used electoral fraud, intimidation of black voters, the outright theft of ballots, and even political murders to destroy their opposition of poor white farmers and black and white Republicans. Although violence against white Republicans, such as the Clayton assassination, made the newspapers, the worst violence was always reserved for the most vulnerable link in the coalition, African Americans.

Besides the political murders and lynching of blacks, the most lasting blows came through the actions of the state legislature elected in 1890. The fraudulent elections in Conway County and elsewhere in Arkansas sent legislators to Little Rock determined to rescue the state from this Republican and agrarian populist alliance of the poor. The General Assembly, in its 1891 session, wrote legislation instituting a secret ballot and poll tax. The secret ballot virtually disfranchised illiterate voters, and the poll tax further removed the poor from the voting rolls. By 1893 the Democratic Party in Conway County had won a total victory. The party was in the grasp of white townsfolk, and African American and poor white farmers had been put firmly in their place. After 1893 Democrats so thoroughly controlled the county that only occasional acts of terror were necessary to remind other groups of the Democrats' total power. With this white Democratic ruling class controlling county offices, the courts, and the newspapers, and even writing the history books thereafter, it should be no surprise that the

Clayton murder of 1889 remained such an inexplicable "mystery." However, this murder and the voluminous documentation it generated give us a window through which we can see how the use of violence reconstructed this small part of the South from a region of democracy and relative opportunity for blacks and poor whites into a land of Jim Crow.

Some of the men who engineered the Democratic victory were still running county government three decades later, in the early 1920s, when C. Vann Woodward passed through adolescence in Morrilton, the county seat of Conway County. Woodward remembers one Sunday morning at Morrilton's First Methodist Church when members of the Ku Klux Klan, dressed in full regalia, burst into the service, gave a donation of money to the minister, and then quietly left the sanctuary. The young Woodward noticed that neither the minister nor the congregation appeared ungrateful for the gift or displeased with its source. In 1924, after Woodward graduated from high school, he left Morrilton for college, and in 1928 he departed Arkansas for good.[2]

Years later, in *Origins of the New South* (1951) and *The Strange Career of Jim Crow* (1955), Woodward described a New South that arose from the devastation of the Civil War as a very different world from the Old South that had preceded it. In the place of antebellum planter elites, a new class of white middle-class townsmen pushed through economic and political changes that, by the end of the century, had impoverished white yeoman farmers and stripped away the rights African Americans had won in the Civil War. The leaders of Woodward's New South mirrored the men who ran Conway County when he grew up there. A flurry of historical studies on the late-nineteenth-century South have followed Woodward's work, most either extending or rejecting his powerful arguments, but all in some way reacting to them. If the literature has resonated with any common theme, it most surely is the difficulty in making large generalizations about a region so intensely local as the nineteenth-century South. Only careful local studies will fill the broader shapes sketched by Woodward, his proponents, and his critics.

This account of political violence in an Arkansas county addresses a void in this literature. Perhaps because of the state's location on the northern and western edge of the South, Arkansas has received little attention from southern historians. Several fine local studies have tested Woodward's views on the relationship between the agrarian populist movement and the origins of Jim Crow; however, these works have primarily examined the states of the Deep South.[3] Between 1870 and 1890, Arkansas's black population grew faster (both in aggregate numbers and proportionally) than that of any other southern state. In addition, the state's native agrarian populist movement, the Agricultural Wheel, was arguably the most widespread, radical, and politically mobilized of any in the South. Yet Arkansas in the last quarter of the nineteenth century remains virtually an unmined field for historians.[4] Conway County's story serves as a small luminary within a dark area of southern history.

This examination of one southern community aims to chart the relationship between political violence and the creation of the structures of New South politics. Some seminal works have explained how southern state governments in the 1880s and 1890s designed and implemented the discriminatory legislation of Jim Crow. On the other hand, studies of political violence during this time have largely focused on the outbreak of lynchings throughout the South.[5] However, these subjects have remained virtually separate literatures. Solving the Clayton murder will show how Democratic elites used violence to end any aspirations to power by poor white and black farmers, and indeed how legislators got to the state capitol to write the laws that made Jim Crow and the solid South.

1. Local Divisions and Lasting Grudges

Civil War and Reconstruction

Not long after John Clayton's assassination, the sheriff of Conway County received a letter purporting to be from Clayton's murderer. Signed "Jack the Ripper," the letter suggested that John Clayton had been killed to atone for crimes committed in the county twenty years before by his brother, Powell Clayton, the Republican governor of Arkansas during Reconstruction. Former rebels had regarded Governor Clayton as the worst sort of carpetbagger. They never forgave him for declaring martial law in Conway County and for arming and organizing freedmen into a black militia to keep order during Reconstruction's most tumultuous days. When John Clayton was murdered in 1889, local folks in Conway County, like the writer of the Jack the Ripper letter, suggested that the crime culminated a cycle of violence that had begun in the 1860s. Four years of warfare indeed had ruptured community and life in the county. Distinctions regarding where and how people lived and worked suddenly became matters to fight about. The war ended in 1865; the fighting did not. Thus to solve the murder of John Clayton, one must go back thirty years to understand the setting and background of Conway County.

As virtually a microcosm of the state of Arkansas, Conway County was divided by Mother Nature into distinctly different landscapes. And in nineteenth-century Arkansas, like the South in general, geographic divisions meant political divisions. One of the oldest counties in the state, Conway County was settled from each end, north and south. On the county's southern border, the shallow and shifting Arkansas River served as the highway for early Arkansans. In the three decades before the Civil War, settlers arrived by boat to exploit the rich bottomlands alongside the river. However, in the northern two-thirds of the county, rolling hills formed the prelude to the most rugged area of the Ozarks, the Boston Mountains, just to the north. In the 1840s and 1850s, many of the ridge runners, settlers who came to the mountains in search of healthy air, filtered south to settle the northern hills of Conway County. Here, like elsewhere in the Ozarks, subsistence farmers scraped together a meager living on small plots of hilly land.

In the early 1850s, the area constituted the true frontier of the

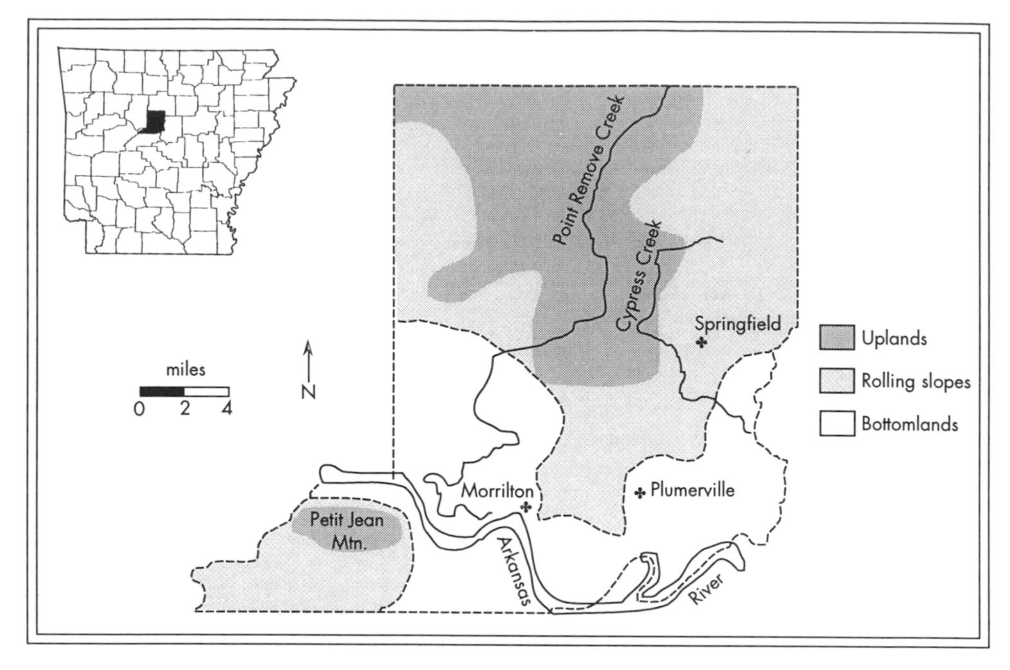

Figure 1. The landscape of Conway County. *(Courtesy of Brooks Green/Kelly Nichols.)*

South. But with rapid migration and the arrival of the cotton economy in Arkansas, the county entered the mainstream of southern life and culture. The county's white population almost doubled, growing from 3,339 in 1850 to 5,895 in 1860, and the number of slaves grew twice as fast as that of white residents. But perhaps more telling, the production of cotton grew almost sixfold, from 516 450-pound bales in 1850 to 3,170 in 1860.[1] In the early 1850s, Conway County cotton sold for more than forty dollars a bale, providing ample incentive for new settlers to stake out farms in the rich bottomlands.[2] By the mid-1850s, land in the bottoms was selling for twenty dollars per acre, and settlers with their slaves were pouring in.[3] King Cotton and black slavery had clearly arrived.

The impact of the cotton economy, however, was not evenly distributed through the county. Wellborn and Cadron, the two townships that lay beside the Arkansas River, produced 82 percent of the county's cotton in 1860, whereas the remaining eight townships together accounted for only 18 percent. Similarly, almost all of the slaves in Conway County (707 of 762) were in these two townships. In Wellborn township, where the river valley fans out into a wide alluvial plain, several families farmed plantations larger than one thousand acres. One planter, George W. Carroll, alone possessed 125 slaves. By 1860 Wellborn township contained slightly more than one-quarter of the county's improved farmland but produced nearly three-quarters of the cotton (2,339 bales).[4]

In contrast, Lick Mountain township, in the extreme northern part of the county, contained only five slaves and produced just twenty-five and one-half bales of cotton in the reported year. On their small plots of land, the hill farmers primarily grew corn to become the corn pone, hominy, and cornmeal mush that graced their tables, and to feed their livestock, which provided some animal protein. The average wealth per head of household in Lick Mountain was only one-fifth of that in Wellborn. The settlers hailed from small farms of the hilly upper-south states; 60 percent came from Tennessee alone. Although Tennessee provided the largest number of settlers to Wellborn township (19.8 percent), settlers there came from a wider arc of states stretching from Virginia to the south and west.[5]

Anchoring these widely varying landscapes were the county's only two incorporated towns in 1860. Lewisburg, on the Arkansas River near present-day Morrilton, had the reputation in the 1840s as a hard-drinking and violent frontier outpost that served as a stopping point for steamers passing between Little Rock and Fort Smith, on the edge of Indian Territory. Lewisburg became a market town and port for the cotton trade as it grew in the 1850s. On the eve of the Civil War, Lewisburg had seven stores (one constructed of brick, a first for the county), two hotels, a school, regular mail delivery, a temperance society, and a thin veneer of civilization. Near the geographic center of the county, the county seat, Springfield, served as the trading post for farmers in the northern hills. In 1860 it was little more than a clearing in the forest, with one combination store and hotel and a two-story frame courthouse.[6] Rustic Springfield and bustling Lewisburg symbolized the different characters of Conway County.

On a casual thirty-minute drive today, one can pass from the mountainous Ozark National Forest in the northwest corner of the county to the fields of row crops alongside the Arkansas River, now mostly soybeans instead of cotton. Many residents make this trip daily to work in the factories in Morrilton. But by the beginning of the Civil War, this upland and lowland division in the county, as in Arkansas and the South in general, had produced two cultures that had little in common: the

Figure 2. Lewisburg on the eve of the Civil War. A drawing by Susan Gordon, daughter of Confederate colonel Anderson Gordon. *(Courtesy of Clarkia Turney.)*

cotton planters along the Arkansas River and the poor but proud mountain farmers in their log cabins and dogtrot houses in the northern townships.[7] The tension between the commercially oriented elite and the poor farmers that emerged in the earliest days of the county's history would ignite into violence periodically until the end of the century.

The gulf between planters and subsistence farmers became politicized in the secession crisis of 1860. Sectional conflict had only begun to emerge in Arkansas politics in the 1850s. As a frontier state, Arkansas had been dominated by a clique of prominent and interrelated Democratic families who held almost every elected state office before the Civil War. Most powerful of them all was the extended Conway family, for whom Conway County was named in 1826. Opposing the Conway-led Democratic Party were the rival Whigs, who drew their strength from the small market towns across the state and planter counties of the Mississippi Delta. Whig leaders on average were actually better educated and wealthier than Democratic ones. Before 1850, Arkansas politics were the politics of personalities, the personal rivalries between the aristocrats, rather than sectional or ideological battles.

That suddenly changed in 1850 with the national debate about the extension of slavery into the newly acquired Mexican territories. Arkansas's congressman, Robert W. Johnson, who had married into the Conway family, threatened the secession of Arkansas if slavery was not allowed in the new territories. Johnson's secessionist threats alienated Democrats in mountainous northern and western Arkansas, who had few economic ties to the slave system. His harsh rhetoric propelled the small farmers to defect from the Democratic Party and ally with the Whigs, who presented themselves as the party of the Union. The Democrats usually carried Conway County handily in the elections of the 1840s, but in the congressional vote in 1851, Johnson just barely defeated his Whig opponent, John Preston.[8]

After the election, the secession issue quickly evaporated, and the old politics of family and personality returned. On the national level, the Whig Party died. Many former Whigs lent their support to the new American Party, better known as the Know Nothing Party, which organized in Arkansas in 1855. Nationally the Know Nothings held to an antiforeigner, anti-Catholic platform, but in Arkansas, where few citizens fell into either category, the party functioned as a continuation of the old Whig opposition to the Democratic Party. Whereas several national Know Nothing leaders took an antislavery position, in Conway County, the party was led by wealthy planters such as Henry Benedict and Robert H. Standlee, who each owned thousands of acres along the Arkansas River. The only political issue the county party singled out in its 1856 platform concerned the upholding of southern rights, hardly an issue of sectionalist opposition to the Democrats.[9]

After the presidential election of November 6, 1860, sectionalism quickly emerged again, and in Conway County this meant the divergence of interests between planters and subsistence farmers. The race in Arkansas boiled down to a choice between the southern Democrat candidate from Kentucky, John C. Breckinridge, and John Bell of Tennessee, who ran on the ticket of the Constitutional Union Party, a party of old-line Whigs who could not stomach the antislavery position of Lincoln's Republican Party. Lincoln did not even appear on the ballot in Arkansas. Breckinridge carried the state with 53 percent of the vote to Bell's 37 percent (with Stephen Douglas trailing a poor third with 10 percent).

The vote divided along the usual lines: Bell did well in the counties where Whigs formerly had their greatest strength, southern and eastern Arkansas planter counties, and Whiggish commercial centers such as Little Rock, Fort Smith, and Van Buren. Poor farmers in Arkansas voted for Breckinridge apparently out of traditional party loyalty rather than sectional or ideological interest. Breckinridge, the prosecession candidate, carried Conway County (by 549 to 326 over Bell) as well as most of the mountainous counties of northwest Arkansas.[10]

But with the talk of secession that followed Lincoln's election, the upland and lowland interests quickly polarized into opposing camps, replacing the old Whig-Democrat division. By December the newly elected Democratic governor, Henry Rector, first cousin of former governor Elias Conway, and Robert Johnson, formerly the prosecession congressman who had now become a senator, led the calls for southern loyalty should secession come. The lowland counties of eastern Arkansas, which traditionally had held the core of Whig strength, began clamoring for a state convention to discuss secession. The hilly and largely slaveless counties of the northwest, which generally had gone for Breckinridge in November, emerged now as the center of antisecession sentiment.[11]

With both lowland and upland regions, Conway County began to divide into competing secessionist and Unionist factions almost immediately. On December 15, citizens gathered for a public meeting at the courthouse in Springfield to discuss the secession crisis. Led by a committee of yeoman farmers and a lawyer, the meeting produced a set of pro-Union resolutions that were sent on to the state government in Little Rock and published in the Whiggish *Arkansas Gazette.* The resolutions deplored that "a sectional party" had elected Lincoln but held that the election was nonetheless constitutional. The leaders took a clear stand opposing secession and condemned fanaticism and the inflammatory speeches that were so arousing the public mind in both North and South. At least the majority of the citizens of Conway County at this public meeting resolved their support for the Union and their rights under the Constitution. However, one of these rights, their report concluded, was the right to own slaves.[12]

Five days after the meeting, South Carolina seceded from the Union. In early January, a second meeting to discuss secession was held at the county seat. This meeting was dominated by planters, who held a different view. William L. Menifee, a wealthy planter who owned over 3,500 acres in the bottomlands, gave an eloquent address against northern aggression. While he spoke, an elected committee prepared a statement, which the meeting adopted and sent on to Little Rock's secessionist newspaper, the *True Democrat.* Declaring Lincoln's election an outrage to the South, the meeting resolved to support the sovereignty of the state and its right to secede from the Union and called for a state convention to elect delegates to a general convention of southern states. Should this convention fail to secure southern rights, the resolutions concluded, Arkansas should follow the other southern states in seceding from the Union.[13]

The public meetings of December 15 and January 7, with two completely different sets of leaders, producing two contradictory sets of resolutions, indicate the political division that had taken place among the residents of Conway County in the wake of the 1860 election. At this point, opposing parties were still discussing their differences; for the next three decades, they would use force to settle their disagreements.

In a referendum in February, Arkansas voters showed similar ambivalence by calling for a convention to discuss secession but at the same time electing a majority of Unionist delegates to that convention.[14] To become Conway County's delegate, the secessionist planter William Menifee ran against Samuel J. Stallings, a young Lewisburg physician who had been one of the leaders of the Unionist meeting in December. According to Stallings family lore, the two candidates met while campaigning in the countryside, had a "cussing fight," and hit each other with their walking sticks. Stallings won the election over Menifee by a three hundred vote majority.[15] When the state convention assembled on March 4, 1861, the very day of Lincoln's inauguration, Unionists from hilly northern and western Arkansas stood practically united against secessionist delegates from the lowlands of eastern and southern Arkansas.[16] With Stallings voting with the upland block, Unionists defeated the ordinance for secession. The convention made only one concession to secessionists before delegates returned home: a clause strongly opposing northern aggression against the six southern states that had already left the Union.

The firing at Fort Sumter and Lincoln's call to arms of all remaining states in the Union ran counter to the sense of the nonaggression clause just enacted in Arkansas. But after the surrender of Fort Sumter, Samuel Stallings, Conway County's representative, still privately opposed secession and even the recall of a convention to consider the issue. He did feel, however, that Arkansas should fight in self-defense if northern states committed acts of aggression. Like many other Arkansas

Figure 3. Samuel J. Stallings, Conway County's representative to the state secession convention. *(Courtesy of Mrs. Alan Stallings.)*

Unionists, Stallings supported action in concert with the other border states.[17] When the convention reassembled on May 6, the mood in Arkansas, as in most of the border states, had swung toward secession. By an overwhelming majority, secessionists defeated a motion supported by Stallings and Unionist delegates from nine other mountain counties to refer secession to the people, a last-ditch effort to delay the inevitable. Giving up, Stallings voted with the majority as the convention hastily took Arkansas out of the Union and into the Confederate States of America.[18]

Even before Arkansas's secession became formalized, planters in Conway County began preparations for war. Under the leadership of George Carroll, the wealthiest plantation owner in the county, citizens of Wellborn township formed a vigilance committee in early May, perhaps anticipating conflict with their neighbors in the northern hills of the county, who obviously disagreed with them. Immediately after secession, a rebel army unit numbering 128 men and calling itself the Conway Mounted Rifles organized at Lewisburg, the center of Confederate support. Residents of the town and neighboring plantations gathered in Lewisburg for a rally at the Masonic hall to honor their men before they left for war. After an emotional speech by state senator G. W. Lemoyne and the singing of "A Soldier's Response to Dixie," one reporter said not a dry eye was left in the crowd. Women of Lewisburg hurriedly sewed uniforms for the volunteers.[19]

The men marched to Fort Smith, where they became organized as Company J of the First Arkansas Regiment. In the following June and July, the Tenth Arkansas Infantry organized at Springfield, with nine companies drawn primarily from Conway, Perry, and Van Buren Counties. Soon after muster into Confederate service, the regiment was ordered east of the Mississippi River, where it eventually fought in the great battle at Shiloh in the spring of 1862.[20]

The men who raised these rebel outfits and became the officers were the planters and their sons in the lowland townships. However, poor white farmers, also primarily from the lowland townships, formed the bulk of the troops. One of the great questions that still remains is why landless white farmers would go to war to defend a system that did not benefit them. Perhaps they fought out of a sense of loyalty to the "big men" of the community or to the state and region. In any case, many poor whites throughout the South and in Conway County showed their allegiance to the Confederacy by serving in the rebel army.[21] However, in the county's northern townships, further removed from the influence of lowland planters, outside the cotton economy, and isolated from a substantial slave population, white farmers showed much greater reluctance to fight against the Union. Like the mountain men of Appalachia, it seems these common hill folk most of all just wanted to be left alone.

The earliest known organized resistance to secession in Arkansas came when Unionists in Conway County and neighboring counties of the Arkansas Ozarks formed underground peace societies, as they called them, in the fall of 1861. Surviving oaths and constitutions proclaimed that the purpose of the societies was to protect members, their families, and their property from their enemies. Whether these enemies were Confederate authorities, soldiers, or merely unsympathetic rebel neighbors is unclear. The peace societies used elaborate secret signs and passwords. They even hung colored ribbons on their homes as a signal of their allegiance to the Union should violence begin. Local authorities in several counties of north Arkansas apprehended members of the societies in November 1861, tried some for treason, and impressed most of them into units of the Confederate army.[22]

In Conway County, officials took no members of the peace society into custody, and thus the names of members are not known. But the likely leader of the county's resistance faction was Thomas Jefferson Williams, a Disciples of Christ preacher, who had ties with several leaders of the society (also Disciples preachers) in neighboring Van Buren County. A small farmer and staunch Unionist in the county's northernmost township, Lick Mountain, Williams was typical of the yeoman hill farmers mobilized for the first time in their lives into political action by the secession crisis. Of mountaineer stock from Tennessee, the Williams family had moved to Arkansas in 1844, built a log house, and cleared land for a small farm. Williams's given name at birth in 1811, Thomas Jefferson, suggests the family's past attachment to the party of small farmers. However, in the 1850s, Williams named two of his sons Henry Clay and Daniel Webster, for the Whig senators from Kentucky and Massachusetts who symbolized antisectionalist loyalty to the Union after the Compromise of 1850.[23] By 1860 Thomas Jefferson Williams had emerged as a leader of the small farmers' opposition to the planters. His family would remain adversaries to the Democratic elite as the conflict continued well into the 1890s.

In April 1862, Williams organized a band of relatives and neighbors in northern Conway County to resist the Confederate Conscription Act, which made military service compulsory for men aged eighteen to thirty-five. Two new rebel companies were raised in the county that spring, one by Colonel Anderson Gordon, a planter and store owner in Lewisburg who became Conway County's most distinguished Confederate officer and war hero. Williams and his men hid out in the woods to avoid the rebel parties and agents who scoured the countryside for recruits.[24] To make matters worse for these mountain Unionists, after the battle of Pea Ridge in northwest Arkansas in early March, Arkansas's rebel army retreated south to an encampment in the northwestern corner of Conway County before the force was sent east of the Mississippi to halt General Ulysses Grant's march southward through Tennessee.[25]

Just as Williams organized his Union band in Conway County, General Samuel Curtis marched a large Union force from Missouri south along the White River into Arkansas, arriving in Batesville in early May. Williams and about seventy Union men made their way through rebel lines from Conway County to Curtis's camp and there joined the Union army. Mustered into service as Company B of the First Arkansas Infantry Battalion, these farmers from the northern hills were the first citizens of Conway County to wear the Union blue. The men elected

Thomas Jefferson Williams as their captain and his son, Nathan, as second lieutenant. They marched off with Curtis's army to Helena, a port town on the Mississippi, and six months later were discharged in St. Louis. During six months of inglorious service in the Union army, about half the men had died, mostly from diseases acquired in camp in pestilent Helena. In January 1863, the discharged remnant of Arkansas Unionists could not return to their homes in rebel territory for fear of being killed. Nor were their families safe there. Captain Williams's wife and children, fearing retribution, fled rebel-held Conway County and made the dangerous journey to Missouri to join their men. Others probably did the same, hiding out in the Missouri Ozarks near Union camps until they thought it was safe to return to Arkansas.[26]

Although Conway County provided no safe haven for the minority that had openly sided with the Union cause, otherwise the semblance of law and order prevailed for the first two years of the war. Elected Democratic officials, linked with the Confederate state administration, kept local government functioning. Events of late summer 1863 dramatically changed that situation. Union troops moved west from Helena, took Little Rock in September, and sent the governor and his staff fleeing for refuge to the rebel-held southern part of the state. Federal troops proceeded up the Arkansas River to Fort Smith, effectively cutting the state in half, with the region north of the river nominally in Union hands. On September 28, the U.S. flag was planted firmly in the soil of Conway County at Lewisburg, and General Frederick Steele established a federal garrison there, which remained until the end of the war. Conway County became an occupied territory.

During the fall of 1863, Union recruiters raised two companies in the county for a new regiment, the Third Arkansas Cavalry, headquartered at Lewisburg under the command of Colonel Abraham H. Ryan. Several of the recruits were former rebel soldiers who had deserted rather than retreat with the Confederate army to southern Arkansas. The survivors of Williams's Union company now thought it safe to return home from Missouri. On September 15, 1863, orders of General Steele authorized them to form an independent company to guard their homes and families and scout for the Union army. It appeared that the federal victory would bring safety to Union families in north central Arkansas. In fact, it did not.[27]

With the capture of Little Rock, civil government in central Arkansas disappeared. Federal control over Conway County dissolved on the edge of the Union camp in Lewisburg. During the last two years of the war, the county, like most of northern Arkansas, experienced a vicious local civil war between Union and rebel guerrillas. The surviving remnant of the Tenth Arkansas Infantry, the rebel regiment organized in Conway County in 1861, had been taken prisoner at Port Hudson, Louisiana, in June 1863, and by the fall these men were paroled and returned to their home territory. Colonel Allen R. Witt, their commander, reorganized the surviving men into a ragtag company to operate behind Union lines from their base near Quitman, in Van Buren County. From 1863 to the end of the war, Witt's men fought a guerrilla war with Williams's independent company and scouting parties of the Third Arkansas from Lewisburg. Savage killings and brigandage became commonplace as rebel and Union citizens of Conway County exacted retribution against one another. The countryside was so dangerous that at various times, both Union and Confederate families had to flee for safety to the federal fort in Lewisburg.[28]

One victim of rebel retribution was the Unionist leader Thomas Jefferson Williams. During the night of February 12, 1865, Witt's rebel guerrillas surrounded the home of Captain Williams and called for him to come out. Turning to his wife, Margaret, Williams said, "My time has come." The rebels shot him dead as he opened the door. The vendetta waged by the Williams clan against the rebels who had killed the captain would not end for years afterward. Descendants of both Union and rebel guerrillas tell the story of how the Williams men chased one of the rebel assassins, a Pate man, to Clinton, where they shot him in the hip. According to all accounts, the Williams men poured the blood out of the wounded man's boots and wore them away, leaving the Pate man there to die.[29]

When the war ended in 1865, Colonel Witt, the rebel guerrilla leader, refused to disband and surrender his arms until the federal command disarmed the Williams company, which, Witt said, had committed so many "murderous crimes and outrageous depredations." He asked Colonel Ryan in Lewisburg to bring occupation troops from outside Arkansas, not to use "men of this State who have personal grudges."[30] Ryan had good reason to fear, for the rancor ran deep, and the grudges resulting from the outrages in the northern part of Conway County lasted long.

The citizens of Lewisburg also nourished bitter memories of the two years of Union occupation of their hometown. Colonel Ryan built his

Figure 4. Captain Thomas Jefferson Williams, Union guerrilla leader in Conway County. *(Courtesy of Polly Church.)*

federal post on the highest point, with six cannon looking downward on the town while Union soldiers dug breastworks and rifle pits alongside the main streets. Ryan and several of the other officers of the Third Arkansas boarded in the Gordon house, one of the most substantial residences in the town. General Steele's Unionist newspaper in Little Rock expressed fears that the local men of the Third Arkansas stationed in Lewisburg would use their arms to "visit unnecessary suffering upon the families and friends of those who have oppressed them."

Elizabeth Howard, the daughter of a rebel family from the Conway County bottomlands, recounted how Union guerrillas ransacked their home, taking everything: food, clothing, bedding, even the pictures off the wall. By the end of the war, her family buried what corn, meat, and salt supplies they had to keep the bushwhackers from getting them. Union officials arrested her father, a prosperous planter whose two sons joined the rebel army, and kept him in prison until the end of the war to keep him from being assassinated by angry local Unionists.[31]

Atrocity stories abound in the area of occupation. Like the Howard family story, residents often told tales of Union soldiers looting the homes of rebel families and of local women cleverly hiding food and valuables from the intruders. One family recounted how Union soldiers tortured a local planter, John Kurtz, to get him to disclose where he had hidden money. They strung him up with a rope, stood him on the back of a wagon, and threatened to whip the horses into a gallop. Fortunately, the story goes, he convinced the soldiers that he had no hidden money. In another account, Ryan's men chased a deserter, a young Missouri boy fleeing toward home, until they captured him at Clinton, forty miles to the north. Bringing the unfortunate lad back to Lewisburg, they forced him to dig his own grave before shooting him above it.

With this sort of occupation, the most ardent Confederates apparently fled the area. The Hervey family took all their slaves to Palestine, Texas, to wait out the war. By one estimate, 150,000 Arkansas slaves had crossed the Red River by the middle of the war. At the war's end, Conway County contained seven abandoned plantations; only eight other counties in the state, mostly in the delta region, had a higher number of acres deserted by their owners.[32]

Despite their dislike of occupation, most Lewisburg residents seemed to have peaceably coexisted with their conquerors. Several prominent local merchants made their loyalty oaths to the Union to keep their businesses afloat. Some citizens were downright hospitable to the soldiers. Orville Gillet, an officer of the Third Arkansas at Lewisburg, kept a diary in which he spoke of frequent dances and entertainments in local homes. Another Union soldier, John Patterson, writing to his wife in Kansas, remarked that about forty of his men had frolicked at a dance in a home near Lewisburg. The dance had lasted until six o'clock in the morning, and Patterson noted dryly, "The boys says that the lades was very a comadating." The local population may have taken what advantage they could of the northern soldiers. Patterson wrote that his good friend, Tont, had come home that morning and had gone to sleep, exhausted. Tont was a great favorite with the girls, Patterson said, but it cost him a great deal of money. General Steele's *National Democrat* reported that all the single women in Conway County under age sixty were "gobbled up as soon as soldiers find them."[33]

Besides having their daughters prostituted to Yankee soldiers, local residents suffered the ravages of wartime occupation in a variety of ways. Dysentery, pneumonia, typhoid fever, and other camp diseases took a huge toll on soldiers garrisoned there. But the fevers also spread to the local population. In 1864 a smallpox outbreak ravaged Lewisburg. Twice the Union garrison was evacuated, first when several thousand rebel troops moved into the area in May and again in September 1864 preparing for General Sterling Price's raid on Missouri. The federals cleverly left behind their supplies inside houses malignant with smallpox so that the rebels would not dare to touch them. One Confederate regiment swept through Lewisburg and camped four miles north of the town. To the chagrin of local secessionists, the Confederate armies did not stay and pacify the region; they merely passed through the county, making a clean sweep of remaining food and forage as they went along. Union soldiers reoccupied the town after the rebels had gone.[34]

It is no wonder that the Lewisburg area would be the center of vengeful conservatism during Reconstruction and the bastion of the Democratic support in the county in the years thereafter. The personal and family grudges that resulted from the Civil War would be played out in years to come between Democrats and Republicans in the county. Conway County emerged from the war devastated by guerrilla violence and lawlessness in the northern hills and the ravages of military occupation along the Arkansas River. Before 1860 local residents fought their political battles through speech making and hand shaking. The Civil War taught citizens to use brute force.[35]

If the war left behind a memory of vicious conflict between rebel and Union citizens of Conway County, the Reconstruction years only intensified the rift. State government remained under the leadership of Governor Isaac Murphy, elected in a rump election in 1864 under the supervision of Union troops. A suitable candidate for governor of Union Arkansas, Murphy was the lone delegate who had steadfastly refused to vote for secession in the convention of 1861. However, on the local level and in the state legislature, conservative supporters of the Confederacy managed to regain power through the lenient policies of Presidential Reconstruction, begun by Lincoln and softened by his successor, Andrew Johnson. Colonel Allen R. Witt was elected in 1866 to the state legislature to represent neighboring Van Buren County, and J. W. Duncan, a former captain in the Tenth Arkansas Confederate Cavalry, represented Conway County.[36]

Under the noses of conservative county officials, the federal government opened a field office of the Freedmen's Bureau in Lewisburg in June 1866. Its director, U.S. Army captain William Morgan, helped freed slaves negotiate labor contracts with remaining local planters and tried to ensure that landowners did not take advantage of the new citizens. Morgan also ran a school for freedmen and took it as his job to teach the freed slaves "good morals, such as industry, sobriety, and virtue." The white men of Conway County's lowlands did not make Morgan's task an easy one. One threatened the teacher of the bureau's school, W. J. Evans, that he must stop "teaching niggers and leave the place or be killed." In early 1867, Colonel Morgan found Conway County in such a troubled state that he requested fifteen U.S. soldiers to help him restore order. He reported that a band of nearly twenty lawless white men in the area had been terrorizing the refugees and freedmen. The thugs stole the freedmen's possessions and money just after they had been paid. Several black residents had fled the county fearing for their lives. Morgan worried, however, that if he arrested the outlaws and turned them over to local county authorities, no justice would be executed. He preferred to deal with civil disorder in a military fashion.[37]

Government by Confederate sympathizers in Conway County, as elsewhere in the South, ended when Congressional Reconstruction took effect in 1867 and 1868. The Confederate-dominated General Assembly of Arkansas had refused to ratify the Fourteenth Amendment, which granted citizenship to blacks, and defied both Governor Murphy and good judgment by giving pensions to Confederate veterans. After such actions, the U.S. Congress, taking over the supervision of Reconstruction policies from the president, declared the state government of Arkansas illegal and placed the state under military control. The U.S. military oversaw the registration of black and white voters in the fall of 1867, using the Ironclad Oath, by which prospective voters had to swear that they had never voluntarily aided the Confederacy. This tactic thus excluded former Confederates from the voting rolls. By November, 934 whites and 148 blacks were registered in Conway County. The constitutional convention elected through such methods wrote a new constitution granting civil rights to blacks and enacting the most stringent voter restrictions against former Confederates of any southern state. Through a combination of fraud, intimidation, and disfranchisement, a March 1868 vote passed the new constitution and propelled Republicans into state offices. With their wartime enemies and former slaves now empowered, the conservative opposition organized to resist.[38]

Resistance became violent after the inauguration of radical Republican governor Powell Clayton in July, just two weeks after Arkansas was readmitted to the Union. A native of Pennsylvania, Clayton came to Arkansas as an officer in the Union army, married a local woman, and acquired a large plantation in the delta region just south of Pine Bluff. John Clayton, the future murder victim, had followed his brother south and helped manage the plantation until he too entered politics, joining other so-called carpetbaggers in the state legislature. Governor Clayton cut a swashbuckling figure when he arrived at his inauguration dressed for the occasion, down to his white gloves and swallowtail coat, in the July heat. An imperious man who was willing to use force to keep order, Clayton quickly became the savior for freedmen and the enemy for conservative Democrats.[39]

In Conway County, the leading Democratic families who had controlled county government since the end of the war were now swept out of office. County-level Republican meetings during the spring of 1868 had put forward slates of candidates for local offices. The governor was empowered to choose county officials to serve until the next election, and Clayton's appointees in Conway County for county judge, clerk, sheriff, treasurer, coroner, and assessor were all veterans of the Union army. With the poor farmers taking the helms of local government away from their sworn enemies, Conway County, like other counties throughout Arkansas, became the scene for a renewed civil war in the fall of 1868. The most prosperous white men in the community put on the costume of the Ku Klux Klan to combat the alliance of freed slaves and white Unionists, now united in the Republican Party.[40]

C. Vann Woodward argued that the Civil War destroyed the planter class, and that a new bourgeois commercial townsfolk replaced them. Carl Moneyhon, in his recent study *The Impact of the Civil War and Reconstruction on Arkansas: Persistence in the Midst of Ruin*, agrees with the critics of Woodward who find more continuity between the Old South and the New. The evidence for Conway County affirms Moneyhon's argument that wealth remained primarily in the hands of the same families despite the near anarchy caused by the Civil War. In 1860, thirty-two planters in the bottomlands of Wellborn township owned land valued in excess of $5,000. After the dust had settled from the war, the 1870 census recorded twenty-nine persons with such holdings; however, only five of the twenty-nine were newcomers to the county. Three had acquired wealth during the decade to move into the upper ranks. But fully twenty-one of the twenty-nine wealthiest landowners in 1870 had been leading planters in 1860 or had received their land as an inheritance from a family member in that group. In other words, the large property owners in 1870 were for the most part the same individuals or families as ten years earlier, before the war.[41]

These local elites, who had campaigned for secession in 1861 and then lost the war, refused to give up power in 1868 to their rustic neighbors who had sided with the Union. It was these men, not a Republican militia, as most southern accounts would have it, that began a renewed war in Conway County in the fall of 1868. One Republican from the northern hills of the county wrote to the Little Rock *Republican* soon after Clayton's inauguration:

> We have distinguished characters, who are taking the lead in inciting the community to lawlessness. . . . At the close of the rebellion, they returned to their homes,—making full confession of their sins, and only asked permission to live among us as peaceable citizens, and that they would go to their respective avocations and build up their broken-down fortunes. . . . Are they doing it? We think not. But to the contrary, doing everything within their power to incite another rebellion.[42]

As they began another rebellion, the former Confederates struck at the weakest element in the coalition against them: newly freed slaves.

The spark that ignited the county into racial and political violence came inauspiciously in early August 1868 when a freedman killed another black man's dog. One account suggested a political motive for the quarrel, and another said the conflict came out of the two men's "mutual admiration of a lady of color" named Nancy. Toney, the accused dog killer, had been the household slave of local Confederate war hero Colonel Anderson Gordon.[43] On August 15, Toney was brought to trial at Lewisburg. Gordon, a Lewisburg merchant and planter who had no experience as a lawyer, appeared at the trial to defend his former servant. The jury acquitted Toney, but the Republican prosecutor, Thompson, secured a retrial on a technicality. Local blacks apparently viewed Toney as a turncoat, and they were determined to see him get his due.

When court reconvened on August 21, a large crowd of African

Americans from the plantations came into town for the trial, carrying shotguns and pistols. When the court selected jurors for the case, black Republicans refused to serve with a black Democratic juror. A ruckus fueled by whiskey and angry tempers ensued in which men on both sides pulled out their weapons. The prominent white citizens present, led by Colonel Gordon, Eugene B. Henry, and Dr. Edward W. Adams, convinced the black men to surrender their arms, which they deposited at a local store. But when the freedmen came to get their firearms before returning home, they were not returned as promised. White community leaders threatened to keep the arms until after the November election, Republicans charged.[44] In any case, enraged freedmen returned to the plantations, collected more weapons, gathered in the woods outside Lewisburg, and threatened retaliation. Later that same evening, some young white men went out to a black settlement and took away firearms from three other black men.[45]

What had begun with a murdered dog escalated to a political event when white Democrats tried to disarm the local black population. The situation threatened to expand further into race war. The Democratic paper, the *Arkansas Gazette*, reported that the angry blacks held a meeting on August 23 at which they "resolved to exterminate the white people of Lewisburg from the cradle up." As rumors flew that a black mob planned to attack Lewisburg, whites in the area prepared for defense. Several hundred armed men collected in town and organized under Colonel Gordon's command. The men set up pickets on the Little Rock road east of town and sent out two men, George Bentley and Thomas Burchfield, as a scouting party to ascertain the strength and location of the black force. Just a few miles east of town, some trigger-happy black men fired on the party from the roadside. The gunshots killed the horse of young George Bentley, and he returned home vowing to his mother that he was through with the Ku Klux Klan. His companion, Thomas Burchfield, a former Confederate who had lost one arm at the battle of Wilson's Creek, fared less fortunately. He took a shot in the bowels and died a gruesome death a week later.[46]

The standoff lasted several days, with the Democrats in town and the radical Republican force in the woods. The conflict was not merely racial, for the *Gazette* reported that the armed assembly in Lewisburg contained "friendly Negroes," and the blacks in the field consorted with local white Republican leaders, particularly William R. Hinkle, whom the press called "a prominent and unscrupulous radical." To break the stalemate, a negotiating party led by Dr. Adams and including two black Democrats met the black party on August 26 and demanded that they lay down their arms. They refused to do so unless their opponents did the same. The next day, however, the black rebels gave in and surrendered their arms as requested. Although white elites experienced the only casualty, they clearly won this battle. They did make one concession: to allow blacks to use their firearms for hunting if they returned them to white hands before nightfall.[47]

While the conflict sputtered in Conway County, Republican leaders in Little Rock took political advantage of the situation. Governor Clayton issued a proclamation condemning the lawlessness in the county. In a speech on August 27, Clayton used the bedlam in Conway, Perry, and Columbia Counties as his justification for organizing the Republican state militia. The *Arkansas Gazette* charged that one of Clayton's men, Republican congressman James Hinds, who was assassinated by the Klan seven weeks later, went to the plantation country ten miles downriver from Little Rock and recruited more than a hundred former slaves to go to Conway County to "fight for their race." On the night of August 27, the steamer *Hesper* picked up the men and transported them to Little Rock, covered by canvas so that the citizens there would not see them. Then the governor apparently changed his mind. He had his black militia leave the ship while he and other politicians (and a *Gazette* reporter and several buckets of iced champagne) steamed to Lewisburg on Friday, August 28, to diffuse the crisis themselves.[48]

Clayton apparently had no confidence that he would succeed, for he had his black militia hide out in the bush near Little Rock in case he might need to call on them later. He also sent Adjutant General Keyes Danforth, the officer in charge of the state militia, to Springfield with instructions to bring to Lewisburg a column of armed Republican men from the Unionist strongholds in the northern part of the county. The crisis was already over, however, when the *Hesper* arrived in Lewisburg. For two days, Clayton's company met with citizens of the town. On Saturday he and Augustus Garland, a moderate Democratic leader and future governor, gave speeches at the Masonic hall exhorting blacks and whites in the audience to live together peaceably. Clayton scolded whites for disarming freedmen and reminded them that "the colored man possesses the same rights, privileges, and immunities—civil and political—that the white man possesses." Both whites and freedmen should look to civil authorities to keep order, Clayton concluded, and not take law into their own hands.

After their addresses, the politicians returned to Little Rock, calling the mission a great success. Clayton sent a courier north to Springfield to stop the armed Republican posse, reportedly comprising 350 men, which was advancing on Lewisburg. These local white Republicans were reluctant to abort their mission, for they had taken orders before leaving for "coffee and dry goods they were to bring back from the looting of Lewisburg." At first refusing to disband, the posse eventually decided to obey orders. Instead of the loot from Lewisburg, they each received $2.86 from the county coffers for their services.[49]

On September 10, Republicans began registering voters for the presidential and congressional elections in November. Local Democrats adopted the rituals and tactics of the Ku Klux Klan, organized in neighboring Tennessee, to intimidate new black voters into voting the Democratic ticket or not at all. The Conway County Klan functioned as the paramilitary wing of the local Democratic Party, not as a group of undisciplined thugs. To combat the Klan, the state adjutant general had commissioned officers to lead two companies of Republican militia, one of them a company of Williams men and their kin who had scores left to settle from the Civil War, the other a black unit led by a white carpetbagger officer, John L. Matthews. But one Republican in Springfield wrote Governor Clayton in September requesting him to send even more troops to the county. Without state troops to protect them until the local militia could be organized and drilled, he said, officials could not stay in the county to hold elections. Captain Matthews, the commander of the black militia company, informed the governor that a white man in Lewisburg had shot a freedman who was preparing to join the militia. A St. Louis newspaper reported the burning of black churches in the county. By the end of September, a party of rebels was "skulking in the woods," according to Matthews, and bands of mounted men, numbering from five to twenty-five, rode unabashedly through Lewisburg. The Republican registrar, Anthony Hinkle, another veteran of the Third Arkansas Cavalry and the county's delegate to the 1868 constitutional convention, had to be accompanied by the quickly organized militia as he moved about the county registering voters.

Democrats tried hard to mobilize their supporters and to woo the new black vote. In October they made plans for a political rally complete with a barbecue, an old-fashioned barn dance, and speech making by members of both races. Registrar Hinkle rather meekly reported to Governor Clayton that he had great difficulty in registering people because all the Democrats insisted on voting. Another observer reported that Democrats in Conway County were determined to vote "at all hazards" and had threatened to kill or drive out all the Union men. When the election arrived on Tuesday, November 3, the Registrar had apparently done his work well, for the Republican presidential candidate, Ulysses S. Grant, carried Conway County over the Democratic opponent, Horatio Seymour, by a vote of 434 to 309.[50]

The Democratic violence did not stop after the election; in fact, the Ku Klux Klan seemed to get more organized in November. Thomas Hooper, a Klan leader from the Lewisburg area, threatened to kill two black men unless they left the area at once. Another Klansman, Dr. Edward Adams, the Lewisburg physician who had disarmed blacks in the altercation in August, was reported "abusing Freemen after his old fashion." Matthews said that terrorized black residents feared that if they reported the abuse of white Democrats, they would become more vulnerable targets. The show of force by the Republican militia, drawn mostly from the Unionist strongholds in the northern hills and black neighborhoods in the bottoms, further angered the Democrats, and the militia was fiercely opposed in southern areas of the county. After the militia drilled in Lewisburg, Klan leader Adams threatened he would fight the militia with four hundred men if it drilled again.[51]

The most vicious cycle of racial and political violence broke out in December, climaxing Conway County's Reconstruction turmoil. Near Lewisburg, late in the evening of November 30, 1868, a party of six disguised Klansmen went to the house of two black men, Alvin and Wash Lewis, who lived with two white women (Democrats called the women prostitutes, and Republicans insisted they were the men's wives). The party broke in to the house, killed Wash Lewis, and scared away his brother. The next day, the black militia company led by Captain Matthews arrived in Lewisburg to avenge the murder. Acting supposedly on behalf of the county sheriff in Springfield, the militia arrested two men for the crime, Joe Jackson and Robert Perry. Taking the men into a cane thicket, the black militiamen stood Perry against a tree, put a gun to his head, and ordered him to divulge what he knew about the Ku Klux Klan. When Perry's answers were less than forthcoming, the men shot off his ear before he broke away and escaped.

They treated Jackson in a similar manner, finally knocking him down with a gun and shooting him. They left him in the thicket to die, but not before he was able to tell who shot him.[52]

The militia then proceeded to the house of Thomas Hooper, where they arrested the sixty-year-old man. Matthews identified Hooper as the captain of the Ku Klux Klan. Hooper had apparently crafted his Klan hood out of a folded issue of the *Arkansas Gazette*. On the night of the Klan raid against Wash and Alvin Lewis, Hooper's cap fell off when the black man's female partner hit Hooper on the head with a pumpkin crusher, revealing his name as a subscriber on the inside of the cap.[53] Matthew's squad carried off Hooper with his hands tied to his horse and a rope around his neck. His body was found the next day on the Plumerville-Springfield road with a gunshot in the back of his head. His gray horse escaped and returned home spattered with blood, causing quite a scene with his widow and children. Predictably, Matthews said Hooper had broken and run while under arrest and had thus been shot while trying to escape. But even Republican sheriff Nathan Moore in Springfield was aghast at what the militia had done supposedly under his orders.[54]

In the midst of these tit-for-tat murders, someone set fire to downtown Lewisburg. Republicans pointed fingers at the Ku Klux, noting that the arsonists wore disguises and that the blaze began in a hotel owned by Captain Matthews and another radical Republican leader and former Union officer, John Gill. Democrats countered that the fire actually consumed more of their property than that of Republicans, and that Gill and Matthews's "hotel" was actually an old vacant storehouse. The fire had spread quickly to destroy an adjacent store owned by the former rebel Colonel Anderson Gordon, two saloons, and the post office.[55]

The killings and fire prompted Governor Clayton to declare martial law in Conway County on December 8. The local justice of the peace, L. B. Umphlett, had written to the governor requesting a garrison of at least fifty men to restore order. Umphlett explained that he did not dare try to maintain civil authority, for over half the people in the area were "of the Ku Klux order." Without state troops, he insisted, those who favored the Union and the present state government would have to leave the county or be murdered.[56] Under martial law, Captain Matthews and his black militia patrolled Lewisburg, to be joined in the following week by three additional companies of white Republicans under the command of Captain John J. Gibbons. This military occupation by local Republicans with personal grudges to settle, however, only escalated the violence. On December 16, another fire broke out, consuming three stores and killing one store owner, James Casey. Democrats charged that the Republican militia, in a spree of shooting and demonic yelling, had looted the stores and then set fire to them. Casey was shot during the melee, they said, and his body was thrown into the flames. Republicans countered that the militia had restrained looters and helped to put out the fire. An inquest into Casey's death by a Republican jury blamed his murder on two local Democrats, Casey's partner in the store, Pompey Breeden, and Breeden's young son-in-law, George Bentley, both of whom had fled the town fearing for their lives. In other words, the Republicans suggested improbably that Breeden murdered his partner and then set fire to his own store.[57]

For the inhabitants of strongly rebel Lewisburg, the occupation of their town by a Republican militia must have provided a bitter reminder of the hated federal occupation during the war. Besides looking down the gun barrels of the poor white farmers from the northern part of the county who had opposed them during the war, Lewisburg residents endured the added humiliation of being subject to a company of local African Americans. Citizens of Conway County sent Governor Clayton two petitions requesting that he disband the militia and end martial law. The crisis came to an end when a deputation of citizens from the county, probably the other exiled Democrats who had fled Lewisburg such as Klan leader Dr. Edward Adams, met with the governor and pledged to abide by the law and its enforcement by civil authorities. Governor Clayton lifted martial law on December 24. Adams, however, still feared for his life should he return.[58]

The last half of 1868 had been a second civil war for Arkansas. Conway County, in particular, was a battleground between former Confederates calling themselves the Ku Klux Klan and the alliance of former slaves and former Unionists from the northern hills who temporarily wielded power. Democrats showed they were willing to use violence to regain power taken from them by Congressional Reconstruction. The alliance of white and black Republicans met violence with violence. Governor Clayton's use of military force throughout Arkansas had broken the Klan and restored order. In Conway County, the Klan itself was terrorized by armed black militiamen, a feat seldom seen in the South.[59]

Although Republicans held offices in Conway County until 1872, the remaining years of Reconstruction were less tumultuous than the turmoil of 1868. In August 1869, a small band of men stormed inside and blasted a volley of gunfire through the store owned by William P. Egan, a Union veteran from Ohio who had moved to the area two years before. But Republican authorities promptly arrested, tried, and jailed the offenders. They also indicted Eugene B. Henry, the former courier for Witt's Confederate guerrillas and prominent Democratic leader in Lewisburg, with the charge of assault with intent to kill the Republican prosecutor Thompson. Republicans apparently used their control of the courts to strike back at their enemies. Democrats would do the same later. Otherwise it appears the worst violence had subsided.

Democrats would later speak of this period as a time of stolen elections and corrupt Republican officials. The scant information about these years supports this assertion. In 1869 a county resident, John C. Gregory, complained to Governor Clayton that the Republican county clerk, William R. Hinkle, stayed drunk nearly all the time and could not keep the county books. In 1871 the Republican-controlled state legislature impeached Hinkle, charging that he had issued and appropriated to his own use several hundred dollars in county scrip, and that he had been "habitually drunk, while in the discharge of his official duties."[60]

At Governor Powell Clayton's urging, this same legislature created a militia claims commission to compensate citizens who had lost property through appropriations of the militia during martial law. Although some claimants had genuine losses, Democrats charged that many who received the most funds had never even lost "a chew of tobacco on account of the militia." The claimants from Conway County were not the victims of militia outrages but the perpetrators. Captain John J. Gibbon, the commander of the four militia companies, received $147 for his "losses" to the militia. The other three claimants were two Union veterans, William P. Egan and John W. Gill, and the Republican county sheriff, Nathan W. Moore. In all, the state spent $120,000 of the taxpayers' money on these shady dealings, with the claims commissioner himself drawing two claims.[61]

In October 1871, the Democratic party in Conway County formally organized, and in the November 1872 election, conservative Democrats won back the county. Reconstruction in Conway County had come to an end, two years before it would end at the state level.[62]

The Civil War and Reconstruction, indeed, provided a vivid and acrimonious background for the bitter political battles that were to come in Conway County. The war had divided residents into two hostile camps, a group of small farmers in the upland townships who supported the Union versus planters in the bottomlands and their poor white allies. The collapse of government and civil order then allowed these groups to prey viciously upon one another. The Reconstruction years permitted both sides to settle old scores and continue the battle to control county government. By 1868 the white upland farmers, although they did not necessarily harbor progressive racial attitudes, had allied with the county's black population, and for four years, this alliance of the poor held power. Although both conservative former rebels and Republicans willingly used violence against their opponents, the four years of Republican rule in Conway County gave Democrats the raw material to forge the public image of Reconstruction as the "bad old days." Powell Clayton, the carpetbagger governor who declared martial law and placed the county at the mercy of a Republican militia, became an icon representing the evils of Reconstruction for generations of Democrats in Conway County and throughout Arkansas. As the brutal murder of his brother, John Clayton, twenty years later suggests, the bitter memories of those days lasted long.

2. Motives for Murder

Democrats and Republicans Compete for Power, 1872–1888

Sam and Mary Moore and their ten children packed their belongings and left Fayette County, Tennessee, and moved west in January 1880. Like the Moores, black families by the scores were leaving the plantation country around Memphis for Arkansas, a place so abundant in food, the stories went, that there were molasses pools, flapjack trees, and hogs running wild with knives and forks sticking out of their backs, ready for roasting and eating. The Moores and around twenty-four other families chartered a train in Memphis bound for Conway County. After a few years living on land owned by a prosperous black farmer, the Moores realized their dream and purchased their own farm.[1]

The arrival of thousands of new black residents, people like the Moore family, provided the incentive for the spectacular political violence that followed in Conway County in the later 1880s. Sam Moore and other new black settlers could vote, and it appears that they did in large numbers. The block of black Republican votes, especially when allied with a populist movement of poor farmers, transformed the political scene. With Republicans winning control of county government in the 1880s, white Democrats resorted to violence, rather than votes, to win back the county for their party. Thus whereas the Civil War and Reconstruction experience provided a background for conflict in Conway County, the circumstances of the later 1870s and 1880s provided the motive for John Clayton's murder.

With the end of Reconstruction, Democrats thought they would rule forever. After winning county offices in 1872, party leaders set to work to consolidate their power locally and hasten the redemption of state government. Some physical changes enhanced their opportunities. The 1873 state legislature radically redrew county boundaries and created Faulkner County largely from the eastern half of old Conway. In compensation, the legislature gave Conway County some territory on the south side of the Arkansas River, mostly plantation country, formerly belonging to Perry County. The change established Conway County's present boundaries, but it only exaggerated the division between hills and lowlands. The widest band of alluvial bottomland and yet also the hilliest portion in the north remained inside Conway County. As the county moved south to straddle both sides of the Arkansas River, the county seat relocated from Springfield to Lewisburg, the Democratic stronghold, which could now claim a more central location.

In 1872 the Little Rock–Fort Smith Railroad Company built its line through the county. Taking a straight course rather than hugging the river, the line skirted two miles north of Lewisburg. As rapid growth occurred around the depot, the old river port, now the county seat, rapidly became a ghost town in the 1870s. Morrilton, the bustling new town that grew along the railroad tracks, replaced Lewisburg in 1883 as the seat of county government.

By the time Republicans lost the county in 1872, they had divided into squabbling factions, mirroring the divisions on the state level. The farmers from the hill country, whose Republican loyalties had been forged in the Civil War, had little in common with the northern whites, mostly former Union soldiers who stayed after the war. These Republican newcomers, most of whom ran businesses in the Lewisburg area, threw in their lot with the black voters of the lowland townships. Thus the county saw the classic division of Republicans into carpetbagger and scalawag factions, as their opponents called them derisively.

In the previous year, Governor Clayton had replaced the native Unionist, W. R. Hinkle, as county clerk with A. D. Thomas, a former Yankee soldier who had married a local Lewisburg woman. Thomas was already the state senator for the area; thus he served in the body that tried Hinkle for impeachment. In the November 1872 elections, Thomas used his authority as county clerk to declare invalid the votes from all the townships but his own, Wellborn township, because they lacked the proper certificate. Through such a ploy, only votes in the plantation belt and Lewisburg counted; the native white Republicans in the northern townships lost their voice. This election gave Democrats most of the county offices, with the exception of William Kearney, a northern Republican who ran for clerk against the impeached W. R. Hinkle, and Benton Turner, a Republican who was elected as representative. State senator Thomas seems to have been willing to sacrifice county offices to the Democrats in order to get Turner elected to the General Assembly. Called by one Democrat "an avowed political wrecker, and loud-mouthed supporter of all measure of oppression and extortion . . . a carpetbagger of the deepest dye," Turner introduced the controversial bill to release the indebtedness of the railroad companies and use Arkansas tax money to pay the interest on the bonds. When the native white Republicans of the county squawked about losing their votes to a technicality, they were punished by the removal of the county seat from Springfield to Lewisburg. Senator Thomas, in fact, introduced the bill for the relocation to Lewisburg.[2]

In Conway County, the opposition to white Democrats thus remained hopelessly divided. The two hostile Republican factions put forward separate tickets in the 1874 county election and accused each other of "various rascalities." Similarly, the black community was divided between a minority who supported the Democratic Party and the larger group that opposed it. At a Lewisburg rally on August 7, 1872, so-called Liberal Republicans and Democrats brought a cadre of black supporters to cheer on their speeches in favor of their fusion presidential candidate, Horace Greeley. One Lewisburg black woman was so firm in her support of Grant that she expressed her wish to "poison some of the Little Rock colored people who professed to be for Greeley." Similarly, in 1876 one black man dared to climb onto a platform at a black political meeting in Lewisburg to speak on behalf of Democratic candidates. The angry pro-Republican crowd pushed and punched the speaker off the stage.[3] Democrats did not need violent measures to keep their opponents on the run in the 1870s.

The local Democratic Party was organized and led by former Confederates Anderson Gordon, Eugene B. Henry, and Dr. Edward Adams, the very men who had sparked the troubles of 1868 by disarming blacks. Adams had led the band of Klansmen that had terrorized local blacks and begun the violent duel with the Republican militia in 1868. Taking most county offices two years before the party reclaimed government at the state level, these Conway County Democrats set to work to remove the last vestiges of Radical Republican rule.

Reconstruction in Arkansas ended in a fitting way with a violent blowout in the spring of 1874. Powell Clayton had moved on to the U.S. Senate, and his supporters used fraud in 1872 to get Clayton's candidate, Elisha Baxter, elected as governor. Baxter, the Radical Republican candidate, defeated the Liberal Republican Joseph Brooks, who had the support of Democrats, now a growing block of voters. During 1873 and 1874, however, Baxter began to express his independence from Clayton, most symbolically by refusing to sign railroad subsidies that promised to enrich a number of Radical leaders. As Baxter strayed from the Radical fold and gained support of Democrats, Clayton shifted his backing to the former enemy, Brooks. In a curious turn of events, Clayton, who had cheated Brooks out of the election in 1872, convinced a state court to oust Baxter and give Brooks the office. Democrats, who had supported Brooks in 1872, now howled as he was sworn in as governor on April 15, 1874.

The affair escalated into the farcical conflict known as the Brooks-Baxter war. Brooks's men seized the arsenal in Little Rock and barricaded themselves in the state house, and Baxter's conservative supporters made their headquarters at the Anthony Hotel, three hundred yards away. For nearly a month, Little Rock was in chaos, divided between the rival militias, or—more accurately—violent, angry, and often drunken mobs. Conway County's Democratic leader, Eugene B. Henry, organized an armed unit from Conway, Pope, and Faulkner Counties to march to Little Rock on behalf of Baxter, whom Lewisburg Democrats called the "only honest man in the governor's chair since the Rebellion." White Republican leaders John Gill and Benjamin Coblentz brought squads of blacks from Conway County to Little Rock to fight for Brooks. Several skirmishes in Little Rock and elsewhere in the state claimed two hundred lives before President Grant finally decided in favor of Baxter in mid-May. Although the Conway County Baxter men had seen no real fighting in the affair, they returned to the county as heroes. Democratic women of Lewisburg hosted a grand gala to honor the volunteers, presenting flowers to the men as they marched in procession down Main Street.[4]

The role Grant played in the Baxter victory made clear the president's retreat from Reconstruction in Arkansas. In June voters called for a convention to write a new state constitution. Conway County's Democratic organization held mass meetings later that summer to mobilize voters for the new constitution, which would formally end statewide Reconstruction and restore more power to local government. With voting restrictions on former Confederates now relaxed, in October the county endorsed the constitution by a vote of 888 to 341. By a similar margin statewide, voters passed the constitution and elected Augustus H. Garland, a Democrat, as governor of Arkansas. Democrats in Lewisburg celebrated by firing one hundred guns for the "redemption of the American people." The Democratic rallies throughout the 1870s would be festive public occasions with brass bands, ribbons and bunting, torchlight processions, and flowery oratory.[5]

Democrats used their control of offices to strike back at local Republicans. In 1877, to exact retribution for crimes of Reconstruction days, county authorities arrested John Matthews, the white Republican leader of the black militia company during the troubles of 1868. Matthews had moved to neighboring Perry County in 1872; nonetheless, Conway County Democrats indicted him for the murder of Thomas Hooper, the Klansman slain by Matthew's militia nine years before. Feeling that he could not get a fair trial in Conway County, Matthews requested and received a change of venue and was tried in Yell County, with Conway County's leading Democrat, Eugene B. Henry, serving as prosecutor.

Henry had his own scores to settle with Matthews. When the county had been under martial law in December 1868, a black militiaman had pushed the young lawyer off the sidewalk as he made his way through Lewisburg. Henry responded by knocking the black man sprawling in street. Later Matthews and his men caught up with Henry, and Matthews gave the order to "shoot the hot-headed little rebel!" Fortunately for Henry, the black militiamen showed more restraint than their captain.

By dredging up these painful memories, the legal proceedings of 1877 kept the Reconstruction battles alive. By the time the Matthews case finally came to court, however, the prosecution's chief witness, a man who claimed to have seen the Hooper murder, had died. The lawyers thought the case too weak to pursue and asked the judge to nol-pros the case, in effect acquitting Matthews. It would not matter, for a few years later, Matthews was murdered in Perryville, purportedly by the Ku Klux Klan.[6]

Republicans at the national level wearied of controls over the South and looked the other way as southern Democrats struck back at their enemies. Throughout the 1870s, Democratic authorities in Conway County prosecuted Republicans and former Union soldiers for crimes ranging from assault and battery to bigamy. The tables were indeed turned from Reconstruction days when the Republican militia had marched through the county. Now the leading local Confederate war hero, Colonel Anderson Gordon, commanded the district militia, and prominent local Democrats led the county guard.[7]

This favorable situation for Democrats changed, however, by the end of the decade. Thousands of acres of cheap land in the Arkansas River Valley came on the market in the late 1870s after the completion of the Little Rock–Fort Smith railroad. Twenty years earlier, the federal government had given a generous land grant to the railroad company as an inducement to build the line through western Arkansas. The new railroad and the promise of available land brought thousands of new settlers into the county. Unfortunately for Democrats, most were the wrong color.

Beginning around 1878 and continuing through the 1880s, the arrival of large numbers of African Americans to Conway County would challenge white Democratic control. With a general westward movement of blacks from east of the Mississippi River, Arkansas's black population nearly tripled between 1870 and 1890, with the black proportion of the state's population increasing from 25.2 percent in 1870 to 27.4 percent in 1890. Although Arkansas gained more black residents than any other southern state, Conway County's black increase was truly extraordinary. The *Arkansas Gazette* called Conway the "Kansas county" of the state, referring to the exodus of southern blacks to that state in the late 1870s. The county's black population grew from 630 in 1870 to 3,206 in 1880, a whopping increase of 409 percent, whereas the white population increased from 7,482 to 9,546, or only 28 percent. Moreover, the trend continued: the black population doubled between 1880 and 1890. As the black proportion of the county's population grew from 7.8 percent in 1870 to 25.1 percent in 1880, to a peak of 39.4 percent by 1890, the impact on voting and race relations would be profound.[8]

Land agents of the railroad companies had been scouring the southeastern states to publicize the opportunities in Arkansas for cheap land. Little Rock's *Arkansas Gazette* charged that large numbers of blacks under the "absolute control of a few Republican politicians" had been brought to Conway County "on a political venture." But no other evidence supports a coordinated effort by local Republicans to organize a mass migration. Fon Louise Gordon's recent study of the black experience in Arkansas suggests that African Americans moved to Arkansas in the 1870s and 1880s because of the more flexible racial attitudes and opportunities for political participation, education, and social advancement to be found there in comparison to Deep South states. The large number of blacks who moved to Conway County from the Deep South clearly came there inspired by these opportunities. They would later be severely disappointed.[9]

An organized movement from western Tennessee began the black migration to Conway County in the late 1870s. But in the early 1880s, it became a flood as African Americans from the plantation country of South Carolina came in a mass exodus to central Arkansas. The end of Reconstruction in South Carolina in 1877 had a devastating impact on African Americans there, much greater than Reconstruction's end in Arkansas three years before. So-called white redeemers throughout South Carolina used fraud, intimidation, and violence to take away the Fifteenth Amendment rights of blacks, who formed an outright majority of the population. By 1881 these problems resulted in the largest single mass migration in South Carolina's history.[10]

Nowhere did blacks suffer more than in Edgefield County, the center of the South Carolina exodus to Arkansas. One historian has called Edgefield in the later 1870s one of the most violent places in the South.[11] Like Conway County in 1868, throughout most of the 1870s, this region of South Carolina was in a virtual state of war between irregular white military bands calling themselves rifle or saber clubs and black militia units organized by Reconstruction authorities. This conflict mobilized thousands on both sides, and casualties mounted. Before the 1876 election, the leader of Edgefield's white planters, General Martin Witherspoon Gary, outlined his plan for the redemption of the state through a systematic program of murder, intimidation, and bribery. With this strategy, commonly known throughout South Carolina as the Edgefield Plan, the county became synonymous with the worst terror against blacks in the closing days of Reconstruction. Some thirty-five Democratic rifle clubs were busy in Edgefield County on election day in 1876 deliberately terrorizing potential black voters. Not surprisingly, white Democrats won by a huge majority in a county where they were a minority of the population.[12]

After Reconstruction ended in 1877 with the removal of the last federal troops, local blacks in Edgefield and neighboring counties immediately began efforts to leave. A group of 356 Edgefield blacks applied to emigrate to Liberia through the American Colonization Society (ACS), with one local black man begging the organization to "send us to Africa or some where else where we can live without ill treatment."[13] When the ACS was unable to accommodate them, Edgefield blacks joined with others in South Carolina to form the Liberian Exodus Joint Steamship Company. The company purchased a ship, the *Azor*, which sailed in April 1878 with more than two hundred passengers for Liberia. Lacking the necessary funds, however, the *Azor* never sailed again; the company folded shortly thereafter, and to pay for its debts, the ship was sold at auction the next year.[14]

With the Liberia emigration foiled and the situation getting no better, Edgefield County blacks began plans for a mass migration to Arkansas. After another violent election in 1880, the South Carolina General Assembly established a joint committee to revise the voter registration and election system in the state, clearly with the intent of curbing or removing the black vote. The particulars of this law were just coming to public discussion in the fall of 1881 when the Arkansas migration movement began in earnest. The legislature passed the act in January 1882.[15]

To be sure, the black migrants also claimed economic motives for their move: hopeless tenancy, the depleted South Carolina soil, which required expensive guano to fertilize, and the end of free ranging of hogs and cattle because of a new fence law. Blacks had many reasons to hope for a better life somewhere else. But their main reason for fleeing the area was clearly political. A young reporter from Charleston who interviewed the migrants explained that they had "invariable complaints that the negroes enjoy no political rights, that they cannot vote at the elections and if they do vote their ballots are not counted, that they have no representation in the government, and that their rights are in the keeping of a hostile political party." One black man wrote to the *New York Times* about the migration:

> Our people are suffering under a worse bondage in this State than they did before the war. We have no rights, civil or political, which the party in power respects. Congress gave us the right to vote, yet we are not allowed to exercise that right; or, when we are allowed to approach the ballot-box, our ballots not counted. . . . Who can blame us if we are restless and anxious to seek homes where we, and our children in time to come, can enjoy the rights and privileges conferred on us by an all-wise Providence?[16]

The unhappy blacks of Edgefield County thought their promised land would be Conway County, Arkansas.

During the fall of 1881, a black Baptist preacher named John Hammond and William Lawson, a black school teacher, organized twice-weekly meetings to plan the move to Arkansas. The crowded assemblies were open to the public; some white spectators even attended. One could become a member of the emigration club by paying dues of a single dollar. Late in the fall, the would-be migrants sent Hammond, Lawson, and a black farmer named Spencer Dearing to Arkansas to investigate and report back about the area. By mid-December the three returned from central Arkansas, reporting a great demand for labor, good wages, and cheap available land. The club took a vote and resolved to go. Hammond began collecting money to charter a train to carry the migrants from Augusta, Georgia, the nearest railway center, to Little Rock. Meanwhile, on December 20, Spencer Dearing set out with the first group of 150 emigrants, called by newspapers "a thrifty-looking set and comprised of some of the best laborers in the county." Within a week, they arrived in Conway County, Arkansas, to settle around Morrilton.[17]

During the week of Christmas 1881, the roads between Edgefield County and Augusta were swarming with thousands of emigrants bound for Arkansas. A newspaper reporter described the scene: "Here and there they would halt along the highway in their weary march and rest for awhile around brightly burning camp-fires. Nothing could be more grotesque than the scenes transpiring on the routes these poor deluded people pursued in escaping from their half-fancied wrongs to real ills of which they do not know." But contradicting his own despairing description, the reporter explained how the travelers filled "the air with the rich melody of their voices as they would join in singing some old fashioned cornfield song or in the rude choruses of their religious chants."[18]

Arriving in Augusta, the migrants gathered at the depot to wait for Hammond and the chartered train for "Rockansas," as they called the state. White newspapers reported that the train did not come and suggested that Hammond had made off with the reported five thousand dollars he had collected. According to these accounts, the crowd after several days had become large and disorderly, and local authorities eventually forced them to camp somewhere else. Eventually, most of the emigrants left for Atlanta to make their connection to Little Rock; a few returned discouraged to Edgefield.[19]

By early January, whole townships in Edgefield County stood practically vacant. Several planters reported that there was not a Negro left on their plantations. All had left for Arkansas. A Charleston newspaper suggested that five thousand blacks had left Edgefield County alone and estimated that some twenty thousand acres in the county would go uncultivated in the next year for lack of labor. The Edgefield *Chronicle*, which tried to downplay the size of the migration, estimated that only two thousand had left the county but admitted emigration fever was still spreading.[20]

Most of the black migrants to Conway County settled in the bottomlands to the north of the Arkansas River, with the largest number in Howard township, in the southeastern corner of Conway County. Howard township, created from Wellborn township in 1862, contained a wide stretch of rich alluvial soil and several wealthy planters. The township's mainly white village of Plumerville, on the railroad line six miles east of Morrilton, became surrounded by a sea of black farmers in the countryside. Just east of Plumerville, a thriving black settlement was founded, named Menifee after the secessionist family whose plantation was in the area. Today Menifee is the county's only incorporated all-black community.

In late January, one of the new settlers, N. D. Bryan, returned to South Carolina to take the rest of his family to Arkansas. He reported that most who had gone from Greenville, Laurens, and Edgefield Counties had settled around Morrilton in Conway County. A land agent met the settlers at the depot, Bryan said, and took them to some large buildings erected to accommodate the settlers until they could buy land or obtain work. Bryan said work was plentiful, with wages for farmhands ranging between twelve and twenty dollars a month, and that Arkansas soil gave higher yields than that of South Carolina, even without using fertilizer. He did admit that some migrants were unhappy and wished to return east, but most, he insisted, were very satisfied with their new homes. Another settler, Sam Raiford, wrote back to a friend in Edgefield County, urging him and other blacks to make the move, saying, "Arkansas is the best place for negroes this side of heaven."[21]

After African Americans in Edgefield and neighboring counties in South Carolina experienced political violence, terror, and the loss of basic rights in the 1870s, they viewed Arkansas as the "land flowing with milk and honey." In many ways, it was. In Edgefield County as throughout the Deep South, electoral fraud and violence disempowered blacks after the end of Reconstruction, long before legal disfranchisement came in the 1890s.[22] But in Arkansas the white Unionist minority guaranteed that the Republican Party would not go away with the end of Reconstruction. Through this viable Republican Party, African Americans participated in politics to a high degree during the 1870s and 1880s. In black-majority counties, white Democrats entered into "fusion" agreements whereby they divided county offices between themselves and black Republicans. In Jefferson County, for example, Democrats customarily named the county judge, one clerk, assessor, and state senator, and Republicans chose the sheriff, another clerk, and state representatives. Arkansas blacks served in the state legislature well into the 1890s.[23] From Reconstruction to the late 1880s, Arkansas politics were more thoroughly democratic than at any time in the nineteenth century. Ironically, however, when Conway County became the promised land for thousands of black settlers from Carolina, their presence posed a threat to conservative white control. After moving there to enjoy more rights, later in the 1880s blacks would experience a reprise of the terror they had fled.

Besides this deluge of people of color, native white southerners in Conway County had to contend with the arrival of foreign immigrants of a variety of nationalities—Italian, German, French, and Polish. Early in the decade, mostly single German and Polish workers had provided the labor to build the Little Rock–Fort Smith railroad. Some immigrant laborers stayed in the area and sent home for their families to join them. By the late 1870s, foreign immigrants, like African Americans, were taking advantage of the cheap railroad land for sale in the Arkansas River Valley.

Worst of all, from the locals' point of view, these newcomers worshiped God by way of the Roman Catholic Church. A group of German Benedictine monks purchased land and formed a Catholic settlement in western Arkansas between Russellville and Fort Smith. In February 1878, German-born Father Joseph Strub of the Holy Ghost Fathers, an order based in Paris, arrived in Arkansas looking for a suitable location for a mission colony. He claimed to have acquired a concession of land totaling about 200,000 acres along a seventy-five-mile stretch of the Arkansas River north of Little Rock. The heart of the St. Joseph colony, as it came to be known, ran right through Conway County, where Father Strub set up his headquarters on a large tract two miles north of Morrilton.[24]

By 1880 eight priests and brothers had constructed a monastery-chapel-seminary complex they called Marienstatt, after their home

Figure 5. The monastery farm of the Holy Ghost Fathers, near Morrilton. *(Handbook of the Arkansas River Valley, 1887.)*

abbey in Germany. Later that year, a group of St. Joseph of Cluny sisters arrived and built a school, a convent, and their own chapel near the railroad in Morrilton. The governor, the secretary of state, the bishop of Arkansas, and railroad officials came to Morrilton on a special train for the dedication festivities. Within a few years, the colony operated its own steam-driven sawmill, cotton gin, and corn mill, which protected the immigrant farmer population from the higher prices charged by local Protestant operators. The brothers also cultivated grapes in fifteen acres of vineyards and made and sold their own wine.[25]

Hundreds of immigrants poured into the Arkansas River Valley between 1878 and 1883. Most immigrants were Roman Catholics who had left Germany, where Chancellor Otto von Bismarck's anti-Catholic policies encouraged an exodus. Agents representing the railroads and the state were in Germany distributing propaganda about the paradise that was Arkansas. The Holy Ghost Fathers from the headquarters in Morrilton even published a pamphlet in German that described in the rosiest terms the favorable climate and landscape of the area, the cheap land, and the possibilities for quick farming profits.[26] So many immigrants answered the call that in 1880 the new arrivals had to sleep on the floor of Mr. Thies's boardinghouse in downtown Morrilton until they could be located on their farms. Besides the German settlers around Morrilton, eighty Italian families bought land directly from the railroad in 1880 and settled twenty miles north of Morrilton in a community called to this day Catholic Point.[27] The Holy Ghost Fathers claimed that attendance at mass at the Morrilton chapels had climbed to more than one thousand by the early 1880s, although such reports to the home office may have been prone to exaggeration.[28]

The Fathers, however, planned for their ministry to extend past the foreign immigrant population to the local black community. The Holy Ghost Fathers had extensive missionary operations in French Africa. Father Strub, the founder and head of St. Joseph colony, had graduated from Africa's oldest senior seminary in Senegal and had stayed in Africa until health problems forced him to leave. The Fathers wanted their colony in the Arkansas River Valley to become the center of a southernwide mission to African Americans, with the hope of eventually recruiting and training black priests for the African missions. The Fathers did not realize their dream, but they did make some substantial efforts to assist and educate local black residents.

Twenty black families from the Memphis area settled near Plumerville on colony lands in 1878, and by the next year, Father Strub wrote to his superiors that he had baptized two black girls in Morrilton. Father Strub even recruited two black postulants into the brotherhood in 1879, and a third arrived in 1883. By that time, about half of the 140 students in the school run by the sisters in Morrilton were black, a radical innovation for Arkansas, where schools were segregated by race. Protestant ministers in town, apparently fearing the Catholic influence over local children, pushed the formation of tax-supported free schools, which undercut the dime-a-month tuition charged by the sisters. The next year, the bishop of Arkansas built schools for black students in Morrilton and Conway, the county seat of neighboring Faulkner County, providing forty dollars a month to keep the schools running. A St. Joseph sister who had spent years in the African missions directed the Morrilton school, which enrolled about sixty students. The missions to Conway County blacks, however, did not achieve the desired results. The Morrilton school produced only one conversion in ten years.[29]

The sudden arrival of hundreds of outsiders with strange customs, language, and religion threatened to upset the world of white southern Democrats, who had dominated Conway County since Reconstruction. More troubling, these white newcomers made direct overtures toward local blacks. In nineteenth-century America, most Catholic immigrants became Democratic voters. In Conway County, where experience with foreigners was practically nil, the prospects were uncertain at best.

The influx of African American voters and German Catholics meant that an atmosphere of intense political competition would follow. The Democrats barely carried the county in the 1880 elections, with the Democratic candidate for governor, Thomas Churchill, outpolling his opponent, W. P. "Buck" Parks, by only 26 votes out of a total 2,146 votes cast. In the absence of a Republican candidate, Parks ran on the Greenback Party ticket, which advocated currency inflation. Although Democrats had absorbed much of the Greenback platform, Park's strong showing demonstrated that in Conway County, as elsewhere in Arkansas, small white farmers and black Republicans were beginning to link their votes in opposition to the Democratic Party. The 1882 elections were close as well. The Democrats won all local offices, but the Republican gubernatorial candidate, W. D. Slack, actually carried Conway County over the future Democratic governor, James H. Berry. The local correspondent in Morrilton attributed Slack's majority to the ethnic German vote. With some exaggeration, the correspondent said that about four hundred German-born voters, most of whom had come to the area to work on the railroad, went en masse for Slack for governor while otherwise voting a straight Democratic ticket. "So hot and bitter has been the fight for county offices," the correspondent concluded, "that the state ticket has been lost sight of."[30]

As blacks and immigrants became more of a political threat, racial violence began to break out in the early 1880s. In August 1881, a prominent white citizen in Morrilton accused a black man of "abusing" his children and a few days later gave the man a severe thrashing in the streets of the new railroad town. The incident became a brawl as blacks and whites took sides in the fight. On one day alone, August 13, the newspaper reported ten fights with whites and blacks hurling bricks and rocks at one another in downtown Morrilton. Democratic officials responded by swearing in large numbers of extra policemen to protect white property, "the colored people having threatened to burn down the town." One white citizen from Morrilton even traveled to Little Rock to ask the governor for authority to raise a militia, although the county sheriff, George W. Griffin, assured the public that he and his men could preserve the peace.[31]

Enemies of the Democratic authorities struck back that year by accusing Sheriff Griffin of seven counts of malfeasance in office. In March 1883, a jury found him innocent, and local Democrats fired one hundred guns to celebrate his vindication. However, a grand jury later began an investigation of the county accounts, which revealed that Griffin owed the county more than two thousand dollars. George M. Bentley, who in 1868 had joined the Ku Klux Klan party that had warred against local African Americans, was appointed sheriff after Griffin's suspension. But Bentley too was behind in his account by $1,300 at the time of the grand jury report in April 1884. The investigation showed that the three Democratic sheriffs who had preceded Griffin going back to 1874 all owed the county money, as did the county clerk and the prosecuting attorney. The grand jury turned the matter over to the county judge, who, in the language of the *Arkansas Gazette*, "allowed no convictions to come down."[32]

This bad publicity for Democratic officeholders in the county may have contributed to their defeat in the September 1884 election. But certainly other factors conspired to bring Republicans back to power in the county. The larger number of black voters formed a block with the Unionist townships in the northern part of the county, which still voted Republican. Emerging as leaders of the incongruous mixture that constituted the county's Republican party were a few prosperous farmers, for the most part outsiders who had newly arrived, some from the North, some of German ethnic backgrounds. For the six months preceding the election, Republican leaders published a new county newspaper, the *Arkansas Republican*, which suspended publication shortly after the vote.[33] But besides the revived Republican party in the county, a whole new political force had exploded on the scene by 1884, a class-conscious agrarian populist movement called the Agricultural Wheel.

Actually two rival agrarian groups had organized in the state in 1882. Founded in Prairie County near Des Arc, the Agricultural Wheel had more than five thousand members in Arkansas by 1884, and ten thousand by February 1885. A few months after the organization of the Wheel, farmers in Johnson County, just thirty miles to the west of Conway County, founded the Brothers of Freedom. By the time the two groups merged in 1885 under the name the Agricultural Wheel, the Brothers of Freedom was the larger of the two groups, with an estimated 43,000 members in more than six hundred lodges primarily in northwest Arkansas.[34]

The movement mushroomed as conditions for the small farmer deteriorated. The farmers cast much of the blame for their woes on merchants, lawyers, and other townsfolk, whom the farmers felt benefited from agrarian distress. A growing rift between town and rural culture became evident by the 1880s. Morrilton was a true boomtown, born around the depot in 1875 and claiming 770 residents in 1880 and 1,644 in 1890. The growth of the railroad town also meant the advance of a commercial bourgeois culture into Conway County. By the 1880s, Morrilton residents had transportation links, daily mail and telegraph services, a bank, six hotels, six churches, two newspapers, and a variety of stores selling everything from books to jewelry and, of course, groceries and supplies. The only factory in the county, a glass manufacturing plant, was located there. A dozen lawyers and as many physicians practiced their professions in the growing town. Even the planters from the bottomlands were moving into town to build fine residences and supervise their plantations from afar.[35] But as Morrilton boomed, like other railroad towns in Arkansas, life in the countryside became increasingly difficult.

In Conway County's pre–Civil War days, the rural landscape had been divided between the lowland plantations that produced cotton through slave labor and the upland small farms used for subsistence agriculture. The plantations along the Arkansas River remained. By the 1880s, one planter alone, W. H. Ward, cultivated two thousand acres of bottomland three miles west of Morrilton. He hired eight hundred hands and had a hundred tenement houses and a plantation store for his workers. But as black and white settlers poured into the county, cotton production expanded greatly on the small farms, including those in the upland areas. By 1880 almost one-third of the tilled acreage of the entire county was devoted to cotton cultivation. This shift from growing food to growing fiber was rapid and extensive for the small farmers in the 1870s, but it was by no means easy. The poorer soil of the hills produced a third less cotton per acre than in the lowland townships. This meant farmers had to work longer and harder to yield the same output. Moreover, the small farmers in Conway County put their land into cotton cultivation just as the price of cotton declined, falling 49

Figure 6. W. H. Ward's plantation, west of Morrilton. *(Handbook of the Arkansas River Valley, 1887.)*

percent between 1870 and 1880, and continuing to fall thereafter until the mid-1890s.[36] This pattern was of course true for the entire South in the later nineteenth century. Cotton dependency had so increased that by 1880 the region no longer produced enough food to feed its people but had become a net importer of livestock and grain.[37]

As small farmers turned increasingly to cotton, they embraced the infamous cycle of mortgage debt to local merchants. In 1875 Arkansas's legislature approved the system of mortgages granted on future crops. Small farmers could borrow in the spring from furnishing merchants using the expected fall harvests as collateral. Merchants encouraged small farmers to grow cotton rather than to diversify their production, for cotton was a more secure form of collateral than other crops. A farmer who sold his crop for cash without the lender's consent and without repaying his debt committed a felony offense under the new law. Farmers dubbed these mortgages on the coming year's crops "anaconda" mortgages, after the snake that squeezes its victim to death. Farmers had little cash to pay for seed, flour, and other items, but merchants readily provided credit at high rates of interest and sold items at large markups above the usual cash price. The merchant made his money if the farmer repaid his debt, and if not, the merchant could even claim the farmer's land or personal possessions. For merchants, the crop lien system was a win-win proposition.[38]

Figure 7. The Stout plantation near Morrilton. *(Handbook of the Arkansas River Valley, 1887.)*

Cotton prices often did not even cover production costs for Conway County farmers, according to the county's correspondent for the 1880 census report on agriculture, W. C. Stout, who owned a thousand-acre plantation on the Arkansas River. Local farmers, he said, fell further and further in debt as they purchased supplies on credit using their future harvest as collateral and then, after harvesting in the fall, had to pay merchants' commissions and charges for storing, handling, shipping, and insuring their bales. Stout reported that the system of advances for the future cotton crop, the infamous anaconda mortgage, occurred in Conway County "to a large and ruinous extent."[39]

As wealth flowed from the countryside into the pockets of the merchants, shippers, and railroad companies, the agrarian protest movement took off. The creedal declaration of the Brothers of Freedom, which organized lodges in Conway County, displayed a surprising level of class consciousness, much like that of Knights of Labor, the working-class movement that was flourishing in urban industrial America. De-

Figure 8. Cotton waits for the train at Morrilton in the mid-1880s. *(Courtesy of the Conway County Preservation Society.)*

claring that capitalists lived off the labors of others and amassed fortunes at their expense, the Brothers formally excluded merchants, bankers, and lawyers from membership. One Arkansas Ozarks farmer recalled that his chapter of the Brothers "developed into an order, the object of which was to oppose the town people, especially the merchant. The merchant, although necessary, was looked upon as a common enemy, and under the miserable system of business and farming which prevailed, the people had some grounds for complaint."[40] By 1884 the Brothers lodges encouraged members to break the cotton dependence and debt cycle by diversifying their plantings and by turning away from commercial agriculture back to the self-sufficiency of subsistence agriculture. Realizing that this goal might be idealistic and impractical, the central committee gave county organizations the power to contract with local merchants for reduced rates in exchange for the farmers' business. If the farmers could not persuade a merchant to grant them such a contract, they were encouraged to run their own cooperative stores.[41]

In Conway County, as in neighboring counties, the agrarian radicals went further than grassroots economic organization and advice to members. By 1884 they got involved in local politics. Conway County's Brothers of Freedom was a shadowy group about which few records exist. However, Randy Henningson has carefully examined the rhetoric and actions of agrarians in Pope County, the neighboring county to the west. The county town's newspaper, the *Russelllville Democrat*, gave weekly space to the agrarian movement. The Brothers of Freedom claimed to have two thousand members in Pope County by 1884, most of whom had formerly voted the Democratic ticket. But by 1884 the agrarians were angry at Democratic state officials, who they felt favored business interests over those of the farmer. For example, the Arkansas legislature in 1883 had passed a revenue act that gave tax exemptions to the railroads but taxed farmers' stocks for home consumption. The Pope County Brothers of Freedom, in their 1884 election platform, called for an ad valorem tax on the railroads and all capital, but which would exempt farmers' supplies of less than $100. In general, the Brothers and the Wheel picked up the Greenback agenda for expansion of the money supply and government regulation to favor farm interests.

In the September 1884 election, the agrarians fielded tickets in most of the counties of north-central Arkansas. Agrarian views found a willing audience, for the Brothers of Freedom candidates swept the county offices in Van Buren County and won several of the offices in Pope County and Perry County.[42]

In Conway County, the agrarians had ample fuel to arouse small farmers, for more than one thousand mortgages were executed there in the first nine months of 1884. One can only speculate because of the scarcity of evidence, but many of the white Republicans on small farms in the northern townships probably joined the agrarian lodges, for they symbolized protest against Democratic business and planter elites. Republicans and populists would for the next decade have a considerable amount of collusion at the state and county levels. In fact, the voting patterns in Conway County in the elections for which returns by township exist (1886, 1892, and 1894) show a great amount of variability in the populist and Republican vote. Many white rural voters apparently switched back and forth between the agrarian and Republican candidates at will. What remained fairly constant in these elections was the percentage voting in opposition to the Democratic Party.

By 1884 Conway County Democrats became well aware of the splintering effects of a third-party vote. They tried to convince voters that a vote for the farmers meant a vote for the Republican Party, reminding voters of the county's Reconstruction agony under Republican rule. It is unclear if the farmers and Republicans had a fusion ticket or completely separate slates. What is certain is that with the highest voter turnout ever seen in Conway County, the farmers and Republicans defeated the Democrats for every county office, with most of the winners appearing to be Republican. The Republican candidate for governor, Thomas Bole, carried the county over the Democrat Simon P. Hughes, himself a Grange leader of the 1870s, by only 67 votes out of 2,731 votes. The Democrats lost even despite the "disappearance" of the ballots and poll books in Washington township, which was expected to provide an easy Republican majority. The Republicans went on to carry the county in the November presidential race by a wider margin of more than 250 votes.[43]

The new Republican county officials were not well received by the Democratic old guard. Most of these Republicans had moved into the county in the 1870s and 1880s, bringing some considerable wealth with them. The new Republican county sheriff, Pleasant H. Spears, born in Tennessee and a veteran of the Union army, had come to the county in 1880. He owned more than one thousand acres of land in the northwestern corner of the county as well as his own sawmill, gristmill, and cotton gin. An accomplished violinist, Spears owned nine violins, one of which his family claimed was a Stradivarius. The 1886 election replaced Spears with J. H. (Harry) Coblentz, of a prosperous Pennsylvania family of German extraction who had moved to the county in the early 1870s by way of Illinois. Coblentz functioned as party boss until he left the county fearing for his life in 1889. Of all the Republican elected officials of the 1880s, only one, T. J. Halbrook, elected surveyor in 1886, came from one of the county's old northern Republican families that had fought for the Union in Civil War days.[44]

What made these Republican leaders most suspect and threatening in the eyes of local Democrats was surely their alliance with the county's large black population. The Republican victory in 1884 almost immediately provoked a backlash of Democratic violence. By October Morrilton's partisan Democratic newspaper, the *Headlight*, announced that a military company had been organized in Morrilton. By early 1885, reminiscent of the worst days of Reconstruction, Democrats had pulled out the costumes of the Ku Klux Klan and began night riding again.[45]

The Klan raids in Conway County appear to have been both politically and racially motivated. During the middle of a February night in 1885, a Klan posse numbering about one hundred men rode onto Sheriff Spears's farm in the northwestern part of the county. Spears employed several black laborers, and their families lived on his estate. The Klan announced its intentions to force all blacks in Conway County to relocate south of the railroad in the southern part of the county; therefore Spears must send away his laborers and their families. When Sheriff Spears refused to do so, the Klansmen destroyed the fence on his farm and vowed that it would not be rebuilt until "every nigger left the premises." The unruly mob passed on to terrorize the farm of a neighboring white farmer, a Dr. Adcock, who also employed black laborers, similarly ordering these black families to move south of the tracks. Sheriff Spears armed his black employees and prepared to resist the Klan.[46]

The Klan raids continued almost nightly throughout the month of March. One black family found a written notice posted near their home ordering them to leave the area or meet certain violence. On the evening of March 9, the Klan returned to Spears's farm and riddled the homes of two black men with gunshot. Sheriff Spears counted thirty bullet holes in one house alone. During the next week, the Klan shot up the Adcock farm and left a note ordering him to "take his Negroes and get out." The night riding continued until April 12, when in the early hours of a Sunday morning, the Klan returned to the cabin of J. W. Hawthorn, a black laborer on Sheriff Spears's farm. They poured coal oil on the house and tried to set it ablaze. Somehow failing in this endeavor, they called Hawthorn out and shot him dead.[47]

The white Republican county officials did little to help the terrorized African Americans. Sheriff Spears apologized that he could get no warrants to arrest the criminals; darkness, he said, prevented him from establishing their identities. The circuit court impaneled a special grand jury to investigate Hawthorn's killing but brought no one to justice. The Klan made sure no one would testify against them. On the evening of August 17, when the black worshipers of Zion Hill Church dismissed their evening service and started for home, they were surprised by a party of more than twenty-five heavily armed men "in full dress and regalia of the mystic KKK." The posse went to a neighboring house, where they called out a black man who had witnessed the Hawthorn killing. The Klan took the man down the road, where they "gave him some advice" and ordered him to leave the county by the end of

Figure 9. The Conway County courthouse. The barbed wire has been replaced by a wooden fence in this drawing. *(Handbook of the Arkansas River Valley, 1887.)*

the week. Finding no prosecution for these crimes or even protection from Klan terror, the black citizens of the county organized their own military company that summer to defend themselves.[48]

Among Republican officials, a siege mentality apparently settled in, fostered by the Klan raids. Although the Republican constituency was to be found primarily among the small upland farms and the black settlements in the bottomlands, the party governed the county from the courthouse in Morrilton, the white Democratic stronghold. The Republican county officials were so isolated in hostile Morrilton that in 1885 they built a barbed wire fence to surround the courthouse. The Democratic-controlled Morrilton city council tried to remove the fence as a nuisance, but the county court directed the sheriff to see that the fence stayed.[49]

During the four-year hiatus when the county's Democratic Party was out of power, it experienced a changing of the guard. None of the older, experienced party leaders would again serve in public office, with the exception of one, Morrilton lawyer W. S. Hanna, who represented the county in the state legislature in 1883 and again in 1889. A younger generation of local politicians had taken over. Most were sons of established planter families of Wellborn and Howard townships, who came of age during the Civil War and had been nurtured on memories and tales of wartime federal occupation and wicked Republican rule during

Reconstruction.[50] By the 1880s, this second generation of local elites had largely moved to town, entered business or professions, and become the type of solid bourgeois townsfolk so influential in the late-nineteenth-century South.

After 1884 these young Democrats concentrated their efforts to take back county government. They faced formidable opposition. Arkansas's two agrarian protest movements, the Agricultural Wheel and the Brothers of Freedom, had merged in 1885, keeping the name of the Wheel. The meeting to discuss the merger of the two organizations had, in fact, taken place in Conway County on December 3, 1884, at Springfield, which was the stronghold of the local farmers' movement. The Wheel continued to grow and had several chapters in the county. By the end of 1886, the farmers operated their own flour mill, corn mill, and a cotton gin in Springfield that processed that year five hundred bales of cotton.[51]

The agrarian problems of the late 1870s and early 1880s only intensified as the decade wore on. The dependence on cotton, which was already high in the county, further increased, with acreage under cotton cultivation more than doubling between 1880 and 1890. The new land put under the plow was less fertile soil, and the bales-per-acre yield of 1890 was only about half that of a decade earlier. Acreage in corn, wheat, and oats increased as well in the 1880s, but at a much smaller rate than that of cotton. With this greater cotton dependency, the number of chattel mortgages in the county continued to rise dramatically; almost 1,500 were executed in the first half of 1885 alone. The average amount of debt on each mortgaged acre in Conway County rose from $4.48 in 1880 to $6.86 in 1889, and the number of acres mortgaged yearly rose steadily from more than 13,000 acres in 1880 to more than 23,000 by 1889. Besides debt, tenancy increased as well. The proportion of families reduced to tenancy, instead of farm ownership, rose from 39 percent in 1880 to 53 percent in 1890.[52] The Agricultural Wheel, despite its intentions, had not succeeded in keeping debt or tenancy down in Conway County.

These conditions in rural precincts only intensified the discontent for both Wheelers and Republicans. On May 14, 1886, the Conway County Wheel met in Springfield and nominated a full ticket for county offices for the September election. Meanwhile, the Republican Party too had become better organized. In the fall of 1885, a Republican newspaper, the *Star*, began publication in Morrilton to provide an alternative to the Democratic organ, the Morrilton *Headlight*. The *Star*'s editor, A. F. Livingston, also received the county's lucrative printing contracts, a monopoly he would lose to the *Headlight* when Democrats regained county offices in 1888.[53] On July 10, Republicans held their "Jumbo Day" with a large, mostly black crowd and lots of oration. Presiding over the meeting was a black man named Brazelton, who, Democrats noted, had been indicted in the previous year for stealing hogs. The assembly nominated a full slate of white Republicans for county offices, but chose the Reverend G. E. Trower, a black Methodist preacher from Morrilton, as the party's candidate for representative to the state legislature.[54]

The Democrats ran a vigorous campaign for their county ticket. More than three hundred Morrilton men, led by a clique of prominent businessmen and lawyers, organized a Democratic club in August to canvass the county for the party. Although they charged that their Republican opponents were fanning racial passions and prejudices in bloody-shirt electioneering, the Democratic club certainly did the same. Just before the vote, local Democrats informed the *Gazette* that one Conway County black had uttered: "All the white people's got belongs to us. We made it for them and we have the right to ask 'em for anything they've got—even for their daughters."[55]

Even these fear-mongering tactics by white Democrats failed, and Republicans carried the county again in the September 1886 election. In the governor's race, the Republican candidate, Lafayette Griggs, won 53.6 percent of the vote in Conway County. In comparison, Democrat Simon P. Hughes polled 41.8 percent, and the Wheel's Union Labor Party candidate, C. H. Cunningham, polled only 4.6 percent of the county vote. Obviously a good portion of white voters who opposed the Democrats, probably even some of the Wheelers, reserved their votes for the Republican candidate. On the other hand, white Republicans in the northern townships were less generous in their support for G. E. Trower, the lone black Republican on the ticket for state representative, but he won anyway by a narrow margin, 1,621 votes to 1,600.[56]

The election on September 1, 1886, was not without incident. A row occurred while officials were counting the votes at Plumerville, the voting place for Howard township, where blacks outnumbered whites two to one. Two local Democrats, Thomas C. Hervey and Robert L. (Bob) Pate, while speaking to each other in low tones, approached the judges counting the votes. The two men started a scuffle in which they extinguished the lights, knocked over the ballot box, and scattered the tickets all over the room. After order and light were restored, the election judges gathered the tickets and completed the count. They found they had a hundred more votes than the poll books showed.

In the 1880s, Arkansas voters cast their vote not by marking a single ballot that contained all the candidates' names but by turning in a printed ticket that the voter received in advance from a party worker. The Democratic and Republican tickets were usually of different colors. The system made voting simple for illiterate voters, for all they had to do was present their party ticket. It also, however, made fraud very easy. For example, the Plumerville Democrats Hervey and Pate had only to slip in a number of extra Democratic tickets during the confusion they had created. Despite their crude attempt to stuff the ballot box, Republicans still carried the county. Democrats afterward suggested absurdly that Republicans won the election because of—rather than despite—this irregularity at Plumerville. The Republican judges, however, refused to certify the ballots and sent them on to the secretary of state in this incomplete state. Most likely, the Democrats simply miscalculated how many stuffed ballots they needed to win the election.[57]

It must have been especially galling for white Democratic leaders to see a black Republican represent Conway County in the state legislature in 1887. Democrats began harassing Trower almost immediately after the election. The local Democratic press revealed that the Reverend Trower had been marrying people in the county for more than a year without having official authority to do so. After this disclosure, Trower ran promptly to the courthouse to secure a certificate as a minister of the Gospel. Democrats still asked for the next grand jury to look into the matter.[58]

Trower served in the twenty-sixth session of the state legislature in 1887 but moved away from Conway County shortly thereafter. John Mason, the grandson of a leading Democrat in Plumerville in the 1880s, told a tale nearly one hundred years later suggesting that Trower was murdered by two local white Democrats. Mason correctly recounted how Trower defeated the Democratic candidate for representative, Allen Jones, the son of a prominent physician. According to Mason, two Plumerville Democrats, Benjamin White and Thomas Hervey, boarded the train carrying Trower home from serving in the legislature in April 1887. While one man kept the train stopped with his pistol pointed at the engineer, the other Democrat removed the black man. They then told the engineer to be on his way. Mason said Trower ended up "feeding the catfish at the bottom of the Arkansas River." Like many oral histories that evolve over the years, Mason's story shows a curious mixture of fact and fiction. Trower was not murdered. Shortly after his return from the state legislature, he moved to Independence County, where he served as pastor of another African Methodist Episcopal church in Batesville. Most likely, the other parts of the story are true, and as the tale was retold, a death threat transformed into a murder.[59]

The two Democrats Mason named as attacking Trower, Benjamin White and Thomas Hervey, are exemplars of the new generation of Democratic politicians in Conway County. Both White and Hervey had been on hand for the attempt to stuff the ballots at Plumerville in the preceding fall election, and they would be associated with Democratic treachery in the years to come. A farmer and physician, White was a self-made man who had moved to the area a decade earlier. Hervey, a prosperous farmer in the bottomlands near Plumerville, had old scores to settle. During the Civil War, his family had been forced to flee their plantation alongside the Arkansas River and took refuge in Lewisburg. As a young lad, he had watched his mother cook for, and wait on, Union officers who boarded in their makeshift home. Hervey and White would later be indicted, and Hervey convicted, in federal court for election crimes. But their extralegal efforts would succeed. After Democrats returned to power in Conway County, the two men alternated as county sheriff for more than a decade.[60]

The tale of the "murder" of Conway County's elected black representative may have grown taller over time. However, in the next year, Conway County Democrats demonstrated their willingness to use violence, even premeditated murder, to wrest control of county government from Republican hands. The rapid growth of the county's black population over the previous decade, combined with the growth of the Agricultural Wheel, had provoked a crisis mentality among the party's new leaders. With such motivations, they would turn to desperate measures during the federal and state elections that followed in 1888.

3. Murder and Fraud:

How Democrats Reclaimed Conway County, 1888–1889

Only once would John Middleton Clayton grab the headlines of newspapers in Arkansas and around the nation — with his death at the hands of unknown assassins in 1889. Before, he had always been in the shadow of his elder brother, Powell. Born in 1840 in Chester, Pennsylvania, John watched his brother go west to Kansas to seek his fortune while John, still an adolescent, stayed home. During the war, Powell became a brigadier general, whereas John was only a colonel. Afterward, Powell Clayton possessed one of the finest and largest plantations in Arkansas. John, with his young wife, Sarah Anne, and brood of children, followed his brother to Arkansas and managed the plantation when Powell left for Little Rock to be governor. In 1871 John rode the coattails of his brother to become representative for Jefferson County in the Arkansas General Assembly and then state senator in 1873. After Reconstruction, Powell Clayton ran the party organization for decades as the undisputed Republican boss of Arkansas, served on the Republican National Committee, and eventually received President William McKinley's appointment as ambassador to Mexico. In contrast, John was only the party manager for Jefferson County, serving five terms as sheriff between 1876 and 1886. By the summer of 1888, John Clayton had decided to step out onto a larger stage and run for the U.S. Congress. This decision would mean his death.[1]

In the 1888 elections, Democrats could not rely on democracy to keep their hold on state government or to reclaim it in Conway County. Facing the combined opposition of the Republican Party and the Agricultural Wheel, Democrats resorted to flagrant acts of fraud, terror, and even political murder to win back the county and then cover their tracks. The arrival of Jim Crow at the state and regional levels must be understood in light of local struggles in places such as Conway County. The Arkansas senate, which in 1889 wrote the state's first election bill designed to disfranchise African Americans, was presided over by W. S. Hanna, a Morrilton lawyer who had been elected to the senate through Conway County's stolen election in 1888.

The Democrats' opposition had only strengthened since the last election. In early 1888 a new migration of African Americans to Lick

Mountain township swelled the number of potential Republican voters in Conway County. E. D. Bush, who as a soldier had served with the Union men from Lick Mountain during the Civil War, financed and personally led the migration of these black families from Georgia in February 1888. The former Unionists of the Center Ridge area had purportedly invited Bush to bring the African Americans to the community. After the initial migration, word passed back to Georgia, and more families came later.[2]

The Wheel had continued to grow in 1887 and 1888 and threatened to siphon away more white Democratic votes. By late 1887, the Wheel had its own newspaper in the county, the Conway County *Tribune*, and Democrats could expect the Wheel's Union Labor Party to attract more votes than it had in 1886. The Wheel claimed more than 75,000 members in the state in 1888, with more than a half million nationwide. The farmers put forth a full ticket for state offices under the Union Labor Party, which had organized nationally in the previous year as a coalition of agrarian populists, the Knights of Labor, Greenbackers, and other working-class groups. The state Republican Party, still led by the Reconstruction governor, Powell Clayton, chose not to nominate a gubernatorial candidate. Instead, Clayton asked Republican voters to support C. M. Norwood, the one-legged Confederate veteran, whom the Wheel nominated for governor. With a Republican-Wheel fusion ticket, Democrats faced the biggest threat to power at the state level since Reconstruction. In most counties of north-central Arkansas, Republicans and Wheelers probably followed suit and presented local fusion tickets. The Union Labor candidate for president, A. J. Streeter of Illinois, who came to Arkansas to stump for the Wheel ticket, said leading Democrats had boasted to him that they would carry the state "fairly if they could, but violently and fraudulently if they had to resort to such measures to seat their candidates."[3]

In Conway County, Democrats campaigned vigorously for the 1888 election, setting up Democratic clubs in each township. They held gala rallies and brought in distinguished politicians as speech makers, including Governor Simon P. Hughes, James P. Eagle, the Democratic candidate for governor, and J. H. Harrod, chairman of the state Democratic Party. With some probable exaggeration, the *Gazette* reported that five thousand people gathered for a monstrous assembly in Morrilton on the eve of the September election. Two thousand men marched in line in a torchlight procession headed by a brass band. William M.

Fishback, who four years later became governor of Arkansas, spoke for two hours, insisting to the large crowd that the Democratic ticket "will carry this county."[4]

The speeches, hoopla, and brass bands would not be sufficient to win this election. Shortly before the September election, the county Democrats formed an armed militia company. Two weeks earlier, Governor Simon P. Hughes had sent the Democratic Club in Morrilton two boxes of guns and two thousand rounds of ammunition by train from the statehouse in Little Rock.[5] Led by W. J. Stowers, a Morrilton banker who had recently moved from Oxford, Mississippi, the seventy-five-member militia company paraded almost daily in the streets of Morrilton in the days preceding the election. Democrats insisted that they had formed the militia to protect the property of citizens against threats by blacks to burn down Morrilton if they lost the election. Besides the Democratic militia drilling in the streets, men on all sides carried guns as they went about their business. In the stores in Morrilton, muskets could be seen leaning next to counters. The anxiety became intense in the days leading up to the election.[6]

Early on the morning of the election, as a white Republican election judge, George W. Baker, made his way to the polls in Morrilton to begin the election, he was accosted by his neighbor, Jesse Winburn, a local paperhanger, who appeared uproariously drunk. A Democratic constable who just happened to be at the scene carted both men off to the city jail. As soon as the two were behind bars, Winburn sobered up dramatically. With election judge Baker behind bars, Stowers's Democratic militia, awake and organized as 7:35 A.M., promptly marched to the courthouse to take control of the election. By a voice vote, the militia replaced Baker and the other Republican election judge, an African American named Green Roberts, with Democratic judges. The militia announced to the Republican sheriff and clerk that no other polling place would be opened "under penalty of death if need be." The Republican officials yielded to the well-armed militia and encouraged their mainly black constituency to vote quietly and return home. However, the Democrats would not tolerate even this. When Henry Haynes, the editor of the local Republican paper, the *Star*, tried to distribute ballots outside the polling place, the Democratic militia beat him severely. Sheriff Coblentz finally took Haynes into custody for his own safety. Not surprisingly, when the votes were counted, Wellborn township went Democrat by a six to one margin. With a more regular

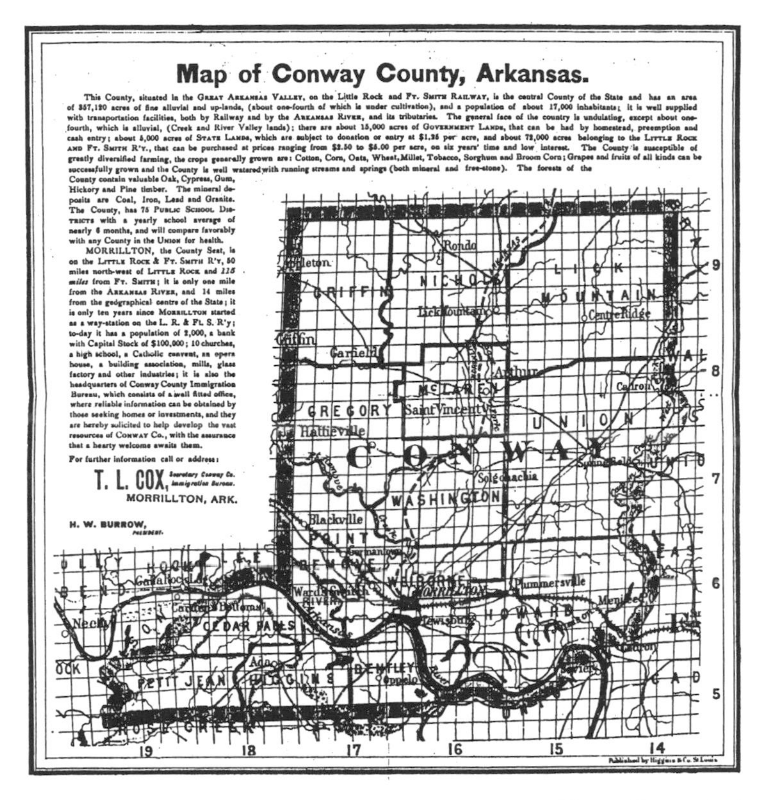

Figure 10. Conway County in 1888. *(Courtesy of Arkansas History Commission.)*

election process two years before, Democrats had carried the township by only a slight majority.[7]

Meanwhile, similar shenanigans occurred in Plumerville, where black voters outnumbered whites by a two to one margin. Democrats gathered early at the polls and voted to replace the black Republican election judges, who had lawfully been appointed earlier in the summer by the Republican county judge, G. H. Taylor. When the two black judges arrived at eight that morning, they found that the election had already commenced and that they had been replaced by two local Democrats. Democrats explained that they had taken this action because the black judges arrived too late. Now, with three Democratic judges counting the votes (Thomas Hervey, Benjamin White, and Bob Pate, the same three men who had tried to stuff the Plumerville ballots in the 1886 election), the Democrats were sure to win. By seventy-six votes, they carried the overwhelmingly black township, which had gone Republican two years earlier by a five hundred vote majority. One can assume the 1886 elections were counted more fairly, for the Republican county judge had appointed election judges from both parties for each precinct, taking as Democratic judges the men recommended by the chairman of the county Democratic Party, Carroll Armstrong. The Democrats would not continue this practice by appointing Republicans as election judges when they regained control of the county.[8]

Republicans screamed that the Democratic victory in Conway County and Arkansas in the September 1888 election came through fraud and intimidation. The Wheel candidate for governor, Charles M. Norwood, even filed a contest after the election saying that he had been counted out of votes in Conway and several other counties. With the combined Republican and Wheel votes going in his direction, Norwood lost the election by less than fifteen thousand votes to his Democratic opponent, James P. Eagle. The Democratic-controlled state legislature eventually agreed to hear Norwood's case if he would put up a $40,000 bond to cover the cost of the investigation. He withdrew his contest.[9]

In Conway County, Democrats wildly celebrated their victory by firing hundreds of guns, singing songs such as "Good-Bye Republicans, Good-bye," and listening to speeches by Captain Stowers of the militia and Carroll Armstrong, chairman of the county Democratic Party. Armstrong, a Morrilton lawyer, was the stepson of George Carroll, who had been the county's wealthiest plantation owner with 125 slaves before the Civil War. On the night after the election, Democrats held an even more elaborate rally at which they ceremoniously "buried" the Republican Party. In a grand torchlight procession in Morrilton, several hundred celebrants marched to the cemetery in the east end of town. They followed behind a team of oxen pulling a buggy that contained a mock corpse representing the Republican Party. With accompaniment provided by the Morrilton Glee Club, the Democrats interred the corpse face down. Captain Stowers preached the eulogy from the biblical text "Take Up Thy Bed and Walk." Organizers had even sent out invitations to the funeral in true mourning style, with a heavy black band around the paper with the following words:

> Funeral notice. The public is requested to attend the burial of the Republican Party at 9 o'clock this evening. The procession will start from the corner of Railroad Avenue and Moose Street. Pall Bearers — Col. Downem Quick, Major Hardworker, Capt. Ed Got There, Gen. Give'm

Thunder, Prof. Big Luck and Brother Solid Black. Chief mourners—Polly Ann Hindtit, Mary Jane Muchlabor, Much Midnight Caucus, Isaac Griefstat, Lum Hawkspit, Nath Saymuch, and a long procession of distant relatives and sorrowing friends.[10]

Despite this grim effort at levity, the campaign for the federal election in November became even more vicious than the September one. In the second congressional district in central Arkansas, the Wheel-Republican candidate for governor, Charles Norwood, had actually polled three thousand more votes than Eagle, his Democratic opponent. Thus Democrats feared that the Democratic incumbent in Congress, Clifton R. Breckinridge, would lose his seat to his Republican challenger, John Clayton, who was supported as a fusion candidate by the Wheel. Clayton was a hated name for the Democrats of Conway County. They had never forgiven Governor Powell Clayton for declaring martial law and using black militiamen to police the county during Reconstruction. They viewed John Clayton, who had served as speaker pro tem of the Reconstruction state senate, as the lackey of his brother.

In the 1888 congressional race, both Democrats and Republicans saw Conway County as a key battleground. Throughout the month of October, Democrats held rallies, complete with torchlight processions, music, speech making, and bandanna drapery decorating buggies, horses, and houses. Breckinridge and Clayton, traveling together on a joint canvass of the second district, arrived in Morrilton on October 30 to address a large crowd. The event culminated in a grand rally the next evening when hundreds of men from the Democratic clubs of Springfield and Solgohatchia marched miles overland carrying torches to Morrilton. Outside of town, they met up and marched through the streets to the shouts of a rowdy home audience.[11]

Besides traditional campaign tactics, Democrats made clear their willingness to go beyond the law to win. At one rally in 1888, W. J. Stowers, the captain of the Democratic militia, told the following anecdote: "There was once a man who had a son; he had kept him and taken care of him until he got old enough to take care of himself, and then he said, you go out and make your living, son, and go to work, and make money, and my advice to you is to make money honestly, but, he says, if you can't, make money." The application of this story was not lost on the Democratic audience.[12]

Democrats also tried to intimidate black voters. Soon after the September election, the newly elected Democratic county sheriff, Marcus D. Shelby, and the chief Democratic speech maker, E. B. Henry, cornered the Reverend Harry Miller, a black minister, behind a tavern in Morrilton. They accused Miller of dismissing black church members who had voted Democratic or for a split ticket. It does not appear, however, that black leaders needed pressure tactics to secure black votes in Conway County. Another black preacher, James Pope, summed up the black attitude toward the Democratic Party in Conway County when he said, "Well, you know, the colored people all look on the Democratic ticket to be a sort of slave ticket."[13]

Republicans campaigned vigorously as well. The *Arkansas Gazette* charged that the national Republican League had spent several thousand dollars in Conway County to defeat Breckinridge. In the last days before the election, black Republicans made the rounds through the county to get out the Clayton vote. A secret circular reportedly passed around the area, charging that Democrats had stolen the September election, and exhorting Wheelers to vote for Clayton. Just the day before the election, Mason W. Benjamin, a prominent Republican leader and former Reconstruction officeholder from Little Rock, arrived in Morrilton to confer with local Republican leaders and help mobilize the black vote. Word that he was coming had preceded him, and an angry mob armed with clubs met him at the train station. As Benjamin made his way off the train, the crowd hooted at him, jostled him, pulled out handfuls of his beard, and knocked him to the ground. Finally a lead ball propelled by a bean shooter struck the Little Rock Republican just above the eye. Although Sheriff Shelby and his deputy, Oliver T. Bentley, were in the crowd, no arrests were made.

The Morrilton *Headlight* justified the attack; one editorial argued that when Benjamin stepped off the train, "it seemed that memories of 1868–74 fired the people and they were hardly responsible for what they did." Badly shaken by the events of the day, Benjamin had the pellet removed by a local physician, Dr. Robert J. Adams, the son of Dr. Edward W. Adams, the Klan leader during Reconstruction. Benjamin then took the next train back to Little Rock. When he died of heart failure two weeks later, at the age of fifty-one, Republicans called it a murder, charging that Benjamin's death was brought on by the nervous shock from the mob attack in Morrilton.[14]

When the federal election day arrived on November 6, 1888, it quickly became a fiasco. Because of the charges of vote fraud in the

September state election, Republican federal judge Henry C. Caldwell in Little Rock chose a local white Republican, Charles Wahl, as a federal supervisor to watch the election and returns at the Plumerville polls. Russian born, Wahl was just the type of representative of the federal government guaranteed to provoke a hostile reaction—a newcomer, ethnic, and Republican. To counter this move, the new county sheriff, Marcus Shelby, a former Mississippian who had been a prosperous Morrilton retailer, swore in more than a dozen Democrats from Morrilton and Plumerville as deputy sheriffs to ensure "a fair election and an honest count." One of Shelby's deputies had been involved in the ballot stuffing incident two years before in Plumerville. Several deputies went to the polling places at Springfield and Solgohatchia, two areas with strong Wheel support. But Shelby sent the largest number to Plumerville, where the majority of the county's African Americans voted.

These deputies and a crowd of white Democrats appeared on the scene when the polls opened at Plumerville at eight that morning. The two lawful black Republican judges, Ransom Hays and Enoch Armstead, who had been removed in September for being late to the polls, arrived before daybreak this time. The white Democratic judge was Thomas Hervey, the man who John Mason claimed had killed the black legislator in the previous year. The Republican county judge had appointed Hervey the summer before to ensure a bipartisan administration of the election. However, he had issued the appointment while on vacation and had recommended that Hervey be confirmed by the voters present at the opening of the polls. Accordingly, one of the black judges nominated Hervey, and the assembled voters confirmed his appointment by voice vote. Hervey then announced that this procedure was an attempt to question his authority, and that the voters should also elect the other judges. By this ruse, he nominated two white Democrats as judges, William T. Hobbs and William Palmer, and put them to a voice vote. He called for the affirmative but not the negative and declared the black Republicans ousted from the election.[15]

Hays and Armstead objected to these proceedings as unlawful. When they insisted on taking part in the election, the Democratic deputies prevented them from doing so. Accompanied by Charles Wahl, the federal supervisor, the ejected judges went down the street to open a second voting place at an African American barbershop. Three of the deputies, Charles C. Reid Jr., James Lucas, and John O. Blakeney, followed the black judges and told them to desist in their actions or they would be put in the "calaboose." These deputies, it might be noted, were not low-class Democratic thugs but the most prominent citizens of Morrilton. Reid, the son of a Morrilton lawyer, had himself recently graduated from Vanderbilt University and had started his own law practice just two years before at the age of nineteen. Lucas was a prominent businessman, and Blakeney edited the Democratic Morrilton *Headlight.* Intimidating the black judges through force, show of arms, and rough language, they wrested from them the second ballot box they had prepared. Elijah Chism, the owner of the barbershop, said Lucas came at him with a hatchet. Under such threats, the black judges finally closed their polling place, but they stayed outside the other one all day, passing out Republican and Union Labor ballots. In his role as federal supervisor, Wahl returned to the house where the Democrats were running the election.[16]

With a Republican federal supervisor present, merely running the election would not be enough for Democrats. Their deputies loitered around the polls for most of the day, intimidating black voters. Late in the afternoon, a local Democrat, Charles Ward, came inside for a whispered conversation with Tom Hervey, leading supervisor Wahl to suspect a plot was afoot. When the polls closed at 6:00 P.M., Wahl accompanied Hervey as he carried the ballot box to the local hotel, Simms's boardinghouse, where the two took their supper. The whole time, Wahl watched the ballot box like a hawk, he said later. They returned to the polling place after seven, finding there William Hobbs, one of the Democratic judges elected that morning. Hervey left the ballot box with Wahl and Hobbs and excused himself to get paper and additional light to commence the counting of votes. As he left, he told Wahl, "If anything happens to it [the ballot box], I will give you to understand, I am not responsible for it."

Hervey went to Smith's drugstore, where some of the deputies and other local Democrats had gathered. After Hervey had been absent about a half hour, a voice called at the door of the polling place, asking if the vote count had begun. Wahl answered no, and turned to Hobbs, saying the voice sounded like that of Oliver T. Bentley, the county sheriff's chief deputy. Moments later four white men wearing rubber slickers burst into the room with pistols in their hands and handkerchiefs covering their faces. They forced Hobbs and Wahl to turn toward the wall as they seized the ballot box and poll books and carried

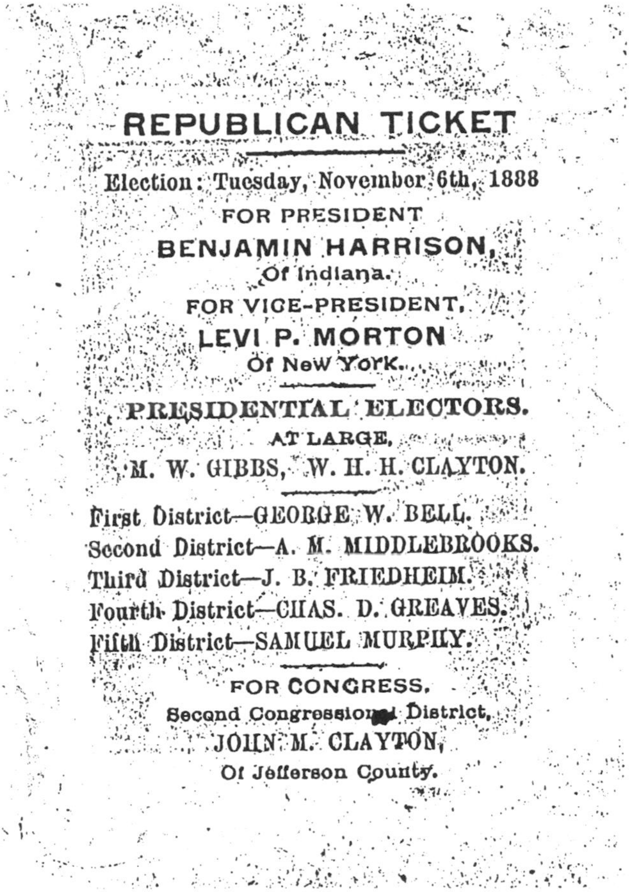

REPUBLICAN TICKET

Election: Tuesday, November 6th, 1888

FOR PRESIDENT

BENJAMIN HARRISON,

Of Indiana.

FOR VICE-PRESIDENT,

LEVI P. MORTON

Of New York.

PRESIDENTIAL ELECTORS.

AT LARGE,

M. W. GIBBS, W. H. H. CLAYTON.

First District—GEORGE W. BELL.

Second District—A. M. MIDDLEBROOKS.

Third District—J. B. FRIEDHEIM.

Fourth District—CHAS. D. GREAVES.

Fifth District—SAMUEL MURPHY.

FOR CONGRESS,

Second Congressional District,

JOHN M. CLAYTON,

Of Jefferson County.

Figure 11. The Republican ticket in the 1888 federal election, actual size. The original was red. *(National Archives.)*

them away. As the masked men grabbed the box, one uttered, "God damn you, turn it loose or I will blow your brains out. We will show you how Conway County goes."[17]

Just before the ballot box theft, on what was a miserable, rainy night, a posse of about eighteen Morrilton Democrats had ridden the six miles to Plumerville. One member of the group, Warren Taylor, later testified in federal court that just before seven that night, the posse stopped a hundred yards short of the railway depot in Plumerville while five of the group rode on into town. The five men who entered town were prominent Morrilton business and professional men: George and Oliver Bentley, Walter P. Wells, William T. Wood, and Charles Reid

Jr. Other witnesses testified they saw the men at Smith's drugstore, where Hervey and local Democrats had gathered. Oliver Bentley's voice was identified at the door just moments before the ballot box was stolen. Then, about thirty minutes after they went into town, the five men returned, just after the time the ballot box was stolen, and the entire party rode back to Morrilton.

According to young Warren Taylor, the ballot box came back to Morrilton with the posse. On arriving in Morrilton, Taylor said, Oliver Bentley and Walter Wells took the box to Wells's store, where they burned its contents in a woodstove. Other members of the Democratic posse disputed Taylor's testimony and denied in court any knowledge about the ballot box. All admitted, however, the abrupt and mysterious ride to Plumerville on the rainy night of November 6. They insisted the posse had gone to Plumerville to protect the town against black violence. When they found that the town was peaceful, the men said, they returned to Morrilton.[18]

The theft of the Plumerville votes secured the desired effect. John Clayton, the Republican candidate for Congress, lost the election by a mere 846 votes, only two-tenths of one percent of the total vote. Governor Hughes certified the results, ignoring the probable five hundred majority of Republican votes from Howard township that had been stolen, as well as election irregularities in several other counties in the second congressional district. Although no hard evidence exists to make the case, one wonders if the Conway County ballot box theft was part of a coordinated state-level Democratic plan to use fraud to carry the election. On the day of the election, Benjamin White, one of the Plumerville men who had tried to stuff the ballot box in the 1886 election, was in Little Rock for a meeting of the state Democratic organization, the Old Hickory Club. He rode on the train there and back with the chairman of the Arkansas Democratic Party, J. H. Harrod, of nearby Conway.[19] Directions could have been telegraphed from Little Rock to party leaders in Morrilton on election day, which would explain the sudden ride in the soaking rain to Plumerville shortly before the theft of the ballot box.

The election of November 6 was marked by flagrant fraud throughout Arkansas.[20] In the race in eastern Arkansas's first congressional district, William H. Cate, the Democratic candidate, defeated his fusion opponent running on the Union Labor ticket, Louis P. Featherston, through apparent ballot box stuffing in various precincts. Featherston, who was state president of the Agricultural Wheel, promptly announced his intentions to contest the election. Similarly, John Clayton cried foul and began preparations to appeal his defeat to Breckinridge. Clayton hired a Plumerville man named Alexander to collect names of citizens in the township who had voted for him, and Alexander obtained names of more than 450 such voters. The Republican Party of Arkansas issued a $1,000 reward for information about the ballot box theft. Conway County Democrats quickly became aware that irregularities in a federal election posed a greater risk than had their manipulation of the state and local election the previous September. On November 12, a week after the election, Enoch Armstead, one of the black election judges, filed affidavits with the federal court in Little Rock against the Democrats who had ousted him and Ransom Hays and against the three deputy sheriffs who had forcibly removed the ballot box from their possession. Democratic deputies Reid and Lucas were even held in jail for nine days, bail being initially denied.[21]

Democrats desperately feared a federal investigation, especially because Republicans had won the presidency and a majority in the U.S. Congress in the November election. In Conway County, Democratic leaders began to do what they could to cover their tracks. Warren Taylor, the young member of the Democratic posse who turned on his fellows, testified that Oliver Bentley, Walter Wells, and William Wood together planned the story they all were to tell about their night ride to Plumerville on November 6. Taylor and Wood were supposed to say that they rode to Plumerville but did not enter town. Bentley and Wells, two of the party who went into Plumerville, were to swear that they were playing billiards at the Speer Hotel in Morrilton that night and did not go to Plumerville at all. According to Taylor, Bentley and Wells threatened that any man who told the real story would be killed. The Democratic Club of Conway County farcically issued a reward for the thieves and put Oliver Bentley on a committee to investigate election fraud in the county. Democrats also began the ludicrous rumor that black men had taken the box because they feared that Democrats would take it first. While in the black men's possession, said the Democrats, the box became so mutilated that the Negroes had destroyed it entirely.[22]

In a more lethal fashion, Democrats covered their tracks by removing any hostile witnesses. Deputy sheriff Oliver T. Bentley appears to have been the mastermind behind the ballot box theft and the cover-up of evidence. The Republican supervisor Charles Wahl and Democratic judge William Hobbs both testified that Wahl had identified Bentley's voice at the door just before the ballots were stolen, at which time Bentley claimed he was six miles away playing pool. Oliver Bentley knew he was the chief suspect for the ballot box theft, and that knowledge made him a dangerous man.

One of the county's new generation of young Democratic politicians, Bentley had grown up under the shadow of the Civil War and Reconstruction and seen two of his sisters married off to Union officers in the army of occupation. When he was an adolescent, he and his widowed mother moved into the household of his Yankee brother-in-law from Pennsylvania, who had married Bentley's sister, Adaline, when she was fourteen. An unlikely candidate to be either a political boss or a Democratic tough, Bentley in his early thirties was a small, wiry man with piercing blue gray eyes. He had eccentric habits: he kept a coded diary; slept in his clean clothes, ready for the next day; and, his grandson remembers, always ate his dessert at the beginning of a meal.[23]

Oliver's older brother, George Bentley, had fought in the Reconstruction militia war of 1868 as a young man of twenty-one, had served as interim county sheriff in 1883, and in 1888 was town marshal of Morrilton. By late November, however, either George Bentley's Democratic loyalties or his resolve began to weaken. Or perhaps his conscience got the better of him. He opened communications with the Pinkerton Detective Agency and began negotiations to become a government witness about the ballot box theft. Warren Taylor said the posse pondered among themselves whether George Bentley would actually turn state's evidence. Taylor thought he would not, he said. Oliver Bentley apparently concluded otherwise. On the morning of November 27, Oliver Bentley shot and killed George in the presence of a single witness, William Wood, also one of the five men who, with the Bentley brothers, had entered Plumerville on the night of the election. Bentley and Wood told the same story, that Oliver Bentley was examining a Smith and Wesson revolver in Wood's saddle shop in Morrilton when the gun accidentally discharged, shooting George Bentley in the head, killing him instantly. Sheriff Shelby and the coroner ruled the death an accident. But George Bentley's grandson recalls being told how his grandfather was shot "accidentally" five times by his brother.[24]

Figure 12. Oliver T. Bentley. *(Courtesy of Robert Cruce.)*

Just two weeks later, on the evening of December 16, someone tried to kill Charles Wahl, the other chief witness in the federal prosecutions, as he played cards with some Plumerville Democrats. Wahl had come into Plumerville that day to mill some grain. It was raining hard, and he decided to remain and play poker with some local men. Accounts of the evening differ. Democrats testified that Wahl "pranced around town all afternoon," visiting at least a half-dozen persons whom he asked to join him in a poker game. Wahl and other Republican witnesses said local Democrats, chiefly Dr. Benjamin White, begged Wahl to stay overnight and join them in a card game. In any case, Wahl and White drank whiskey at Simms and Pate's saloon (co-owned by Bob Pate, the perpetrator of election fraud in the 1886 and 1888 elections) and then went to the house of Adam R. Bradley, a Plumerville physician, where they played poker until late in the night. Besides Bradley and White, the other players were John Simms, owner of the local saloon and hotel, and S. N. Landers, the town marshal of Plumerville. Near midnight, Wahl and Ben White changed seats at the playing table, placing Wahl near a glass door leading outside. About fifteen minutes later, a shot came through the glass door, grazing Wahl's neck and head and shooting off part of his ear. When he gathered his senses, Wahl quickly ran away from the house, without letting either of the two physicians present, Dr. Bradley and Dr. White, dress his wound. He fled to the house of Alexander, who had been canvassing the area for Clayton, where he stayed until daylight.[25]

Leaving his family behind, Wahl went the next day to Little Rock, where he stayed as a refugee rather than returning home. Alexander left Arkansas out of fear for his life. Wahl later sent for his family and moved permanently to Jefferson County. He had his poker companions and a few other men charged in federal court with attempting to assassinate a federal witness. The county sheriff charged no one for attempted murder. However, a Conway County grand jury did indict Charles Wahl for gambling on the night of December 16, illustrating the state of justice in the county. None of the Democrats with whom he played poker that evening, including the town marshal of Plumerville, were charged. Wahl pleaded guilty and paid a ten-dollar fine in absentia, rather than risk his life in returning to the county to contest the case.[26]

Clearly Democrats involved with the election fraud on November 6 feared they might end up in a federal penitentiary for their crimes. Fear probably turned to panic when the defeated congressional candidate, John Clayton, announced his intentions to come to Conway County in late January to investigate personally the circumstances of the stolen election. Tom Hervey had reportedly boasted in the presence of a half-dozen people that if Clayton came to Plumerville to take depositions, Hervey and his friends would "send him back in a wooden overcoat." With such rumors passing around, the former Republican county judge, G. H. Taylor, traveled to Little Rock to speak with Clayton and his lawyer in the contested case, John McClure, a Republican leader who had served as chief justice of the Arkansas Supreme Court during Reconstruction. Taylor advised Clayton to take his depositions in Morrilton, fearing he would be killed if went to Plumerville. If he did

Figure 13. Plumerville around the turn of the century. Simms's Hotel is to the rear left. *(Courtesy of Helen Mozingo.)*

go there, Taylor insisted he should take an armed guard. McClure thought Taylor exaggerated the danger. How could Democrats dare such a radical move, he argued, especially after the Republican president and Congress had been elected in November? Clayton felt that coming to Plumerville under the watch of armed guards would intimidate black voters and they would not come out to testify.[27]

Clayton unfortunately did not listen to good warning. Accompanied by Aaron W. Middlebrook, a black deputy sheriff from Pine Bluff who had been on the November ballot as a Republican presidential elector, Clayton traveled to Conway County on January 25, 1889. Clayton went on to Morrilton to confer with local Republican leaders while Middlebrook stopped off in Plumerville and took Clayton's bags to the only hotel in town, Simms's boardinghouse. Middlebrook told Mrs. Simms that he brought the bags for a man who would follow later, and she gave him a room. Middlebrook deposited Clayton's things and went on to the black settlements to announce their plans. However, when Clayton arrived later that evening, John Simms, one of the members of Wahl's poker game, refused to give Clayton a room. Saying his wife was ill, Simms referred Clayton instead to a widow, Mrs. Mary Ann McCraven, who took on boarders on the outskirts of town.

Oral evidence suggests Clayton was intentionally placed where an assassin could get at him. Mrs. McCraven's house, a one-story structure on the edge of town, certainly provided more access to a gunman than Simms's hotel, a two-story structure on the main street of town. Although Simms turned away Clayton, he provided a room for Carroll Armstrong, the chairman of the Democratic Party of Conway County, who served as Breckinridge's on-site attorney during Clayton's investigation. Simms later testified that he refused Clayton a room because his wife was ill, and that he took in Armstrong because he was already lodged there. This was an apparent fabrication, for Armstrong admitted that he did not get to Plumerville until the day *after* Clayton had arrived. In fact, Clayton was already in Plumerville by the time Armstrong received the telegram in Morrilton informing him he should go to Plumerville to assist with the depositions.[28]

Sensing hostility and danger in the community, Middlebrook told Clayton he would not stay in Plumerville and tried to convince Clayton to return with him to Pine Bluff. Clayton refused. But as a sign that he recognized an imminent threat, Clayton slept in the middle room of Mrs. McCraven's house, a room that was actually a large, windowless hallway. Clayton stayed for four days, taking statements in Mrs. McCraven's side bedroom–parlor from more than one hundred voters, almost all African Americans, who said they had voted for Clayton. W. D. Allnutt, a Morrilton lawyer and notary, assisted Clayton in recording the depositions. After Clayton's questions, Democratic chairman Carroll Armstrong cross-examined the voters on behalf of Congressman Breckinridge.[29]

While Clayton took depositions in Plumerville, Oliver T. Bentley began negotiations with Harry Coblentz, the former Republican county sheriff, for a settlement whereby Clayton would receive the stolen votes in exchange for dropping the federal indictments. In making the compromise proposal, he conferred with Carroll Armstrong, Walter Wells, and Charles Reid Jr., the young lawyer indicted for his actions on November 6. These Democrats agreed to testify to a five hundred vote Republican majority in Howard township, the site of the stolen ballots, if the federal prosecutions were dropped. Coblentz brought this offer to Clayton in Plumerville, who referred Coblentz to John McClure and Republican leaders in Little Rock. After two days of talks in Little Rock, Republican leaders agreed to the deal. Coblentz told them, "You have saved Clayton's life." But McClure stubbornly

Figure 14.
John Middleton Clayton.
(David Thomas, *History of the University of Arkansas.)*

refused to withdraw the $1,000 reward for the ballot-box thieves. Coblentz left Little Rock on the morning of January 29 and stopped off the train in Plumerville to confer with Clayton before returning to Morrilton. But when Coblentz brought the terms back to Morrilton, Bentley backed out because the reward had not been rescinded. On the night after the deal fell through, Clayton was murdered.[30]

The plan to kill Clayton apparently had already been drawn up and was waiting for the word go. A group of Democratic conspirators held a secret meeting around the coal stove in A. D. Malone's general store in Plumerville. The men drew straws, and the man who received the short straw had to kill Clayton. John Mason said his grandfather, Cyrus McCullough, was one of nineteen men who drew straws. McCullough was one of the Plumerville Democrats indicted in federal court for conspiring to kill Charles Wahl. Mason said his grandfather pulled a long straw, but he knew who drew the short one.[31]

The plan was put into action on the night of January 29, 1889. After Clayton and his companion Allnutt had eaten dinner, they retired to Mrs. McCraven's bedroom-parlor to discuss the events of the day. Another boarder, E. H. Womack, a traveling pottery salesman from Saline County, sat working on some accounts at the table next to the north

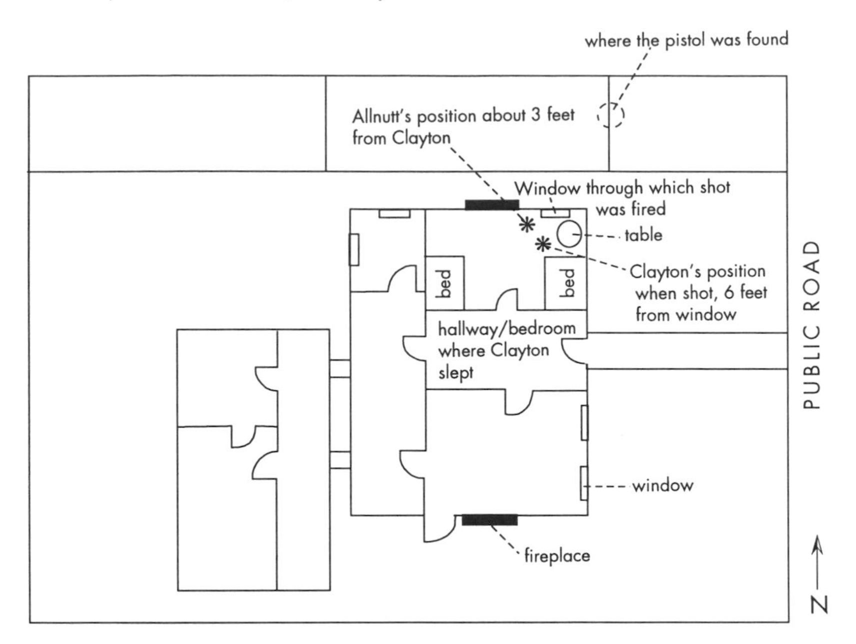

Figure 15. The house where Clayton was killed, floor plan in 1889. *(Courtesy of Randy Everett.)*

window in the room. In the window hung some thin calico curtains, which did not quite meet in the middle. For some time, the murderers stood outside the window, apparently observing as Clayton paced back and forth with his hands in his pockets, speaking to Allnutt. Womack got up from the table to go to bed. Clayton had just taken Womack's seat at the table, intending to pen a letter to his children, when the fatal shot came through the window. The blast of buckshot almost severed his head from his body, splattering blood and brains all over the floor and ceiling. The explosion extinguished the only lantern in the room. The light from the fire in the fireplace dimly illuminated Clayton's form. His chair and his body had fallen backward; his legs hung suspended over the front of the chair. His companion, Allnutt, tried to race out of the room but was so terrified, said Mason, "that he could not find the knob to the door. This lawyer would jump to the top of the door and slide down hunting for the door knob."[32] (For transcripts of eyewitness accounts of the murder, see appendix A.)

John Mason's version of this scene obviously came from the perspective of the killers peering in through the window. Mason said a man named Pate drew the short straw and that he took his brother with him when he stood outside the window and killed Clayton. After comparing Mason's account to the documentary evidence, it appears that the two men were Bob and Charles Pate. Powell Clayton testified before members of the U.S. Congress in 1890 that he believed some twenty-five men in Conway County knew his brother was to be killed, and he singled out as suspects Oliver Bentley and Bob Pate. The Clayton family never had enough hard evidence, however, to charge either man with the crime.

Robert L. (Bob) Pate had a history of political treachery and longstanding scores to settle. He descended from a prosperous Lick Mountain farm family that had moved to neighboring Van Buren County during the Civil War to escape the hostility of their Unionist neighbors. From their home in Clinton, the Pates engaged in a running feud against the federal guerrillas in northern Conway County, especially the Williams clan. Bob Pate claimed that during Reconstruction, Clayton's militia had burst into his house, slapped his sister, cursed his mother, rifled through trunks, and committed other outrages. The grudges lasted for years after the war. By 1888 Pate co-owned a saloon in Plumerville with the hotel owner, John Simms. Described by a New York *World* reporter as a long room "with a cheap wooden bar, a dirty mirror, half a dozen whiskey bottles, an assorted collection of flies, and about two inches of caked dirt on the floor," Pate's bar was the hangout of local white men.

Pate first emerged in political affairs when he attempted to stuff the ballot box in Plumerville in 1886. Two years later, he became one of the Democratic election judges who managed the improbable Democratic victory in predominantly black Howard township in September 1888. In the November election, Pate was among the Democratic cadre at Smith's drugstore that was involved, at least in complicity, with the theft of the ballots. He even organized the poker game at which Charles Wahl was shot, after Wahl had been tanked up on whiskey from Pate and Simms's saloon. Just after Clayton's murder, three black men had run into the McCraven house; one of them was so overcome by the sight of blood and gore that he fainted, and his companions carried him outside to revive him. The black men claimed that they saw Bob Pate, holding a gun, standing with a companion about twenty-five feet away. Pate asked them, they said, if the man inside was dead yet.[33]

Oliver Bentley, the other primary suspect, may have initiated the conspiracy and the drawing of straws. He had already shown himself capable of murder. But it is reasonable to presume that Mason's account is correct, that Bob Pate and his brother Charles stood outside Clayton's window that night, and that one or both of them fired the fatal shots. Interestingly, John Mason's grandfather, Cyrus McCullough, presumably the source of Mason's account naming Pate as the murderer, provided an alibi for Bob Pate when he was investigated for the crime. McCullough swore that he had been with Bob Pate in Pate's saloon at the time of the assassination.[34]

Bob Pate was among the crowd of both white and black onlookers that gathered at Mrs. McCraven's home when word spread that Clayton had been killed. Carroll Armstrong heard the gunshot as he sat chatting with some other men at Simms's hotel but thought nothing of it, he said: "Plummerville being a whiskey town, shooting at night or any other time is no uncommon occurrence." After a local physician pronounced Clayton dead, Armstrong and Allnutt pulled the body to the side of the room out of the pool of blood on the carpet. Folding a blanket for a pillow under his head, they covered his body and sat up through the night. Fearing another shot might come through, Allnutt placed a blanket over the window, which now had a round hole through the pane. Armstrong sent dispatches via telegraph to Clayton's family, the governor, and county authorities in Morrilton. Sheriff Shelby was collecting taxes at Cleveland, in the remote northwest corner of the county, and did not get to Plumerville to investigate the crime until late the next day. By the time the sheriff arrived, Clayton's twin brother, William H. Clayton, had already arrived from Little Rock (he was in town on business) and removed the body. William Clayton later complained that Plumerville residents snubbed him and refused to give him assistance with his brother's body. He told reporters: "I was impressed with the belief that the great majority of the citizens of the town were accessories to the crime before or after the fact." As an additional affront, the widow McCraven presented William Clayton with a bill totaling thirty-one dollars for damage done to her carpet by the blood from his murdered brother.

On the morning after the murder, the legal officer presiding at the murder scene was Deputy Sheriff Oliver T. Bentley, who should have been the leading suspect for the crime. To examine the body and the physical evidence, Bentley convened a coroner's jury that included Bob Pate and his barkeeper, Bert Walley. Outside the window of the room where Clayton was killed, they found powder marks on the window casing and the tracks of two men wearing rubber overshoes, one pair old, one new. The tracks had frozen overnight in the mud. The jury's verdict was death at the hands of unknown persons.[35]

Clayton's assassination intensified the already growing political tempest in Arkansas. The governor and the state legislature, in session in Little Rock, condemned the crime and issued a five thousand dollar reward for Clayton's murderer, at that time the largest reward ever offered for a criminal in Arkansas. Democrats and Republicans throughout Arkansas condemned the murder and eulogized Clayton, a man more loved in death than in life. John Clayton's wife had died a few years before, leaving him a widower with six young children, two girls and four boys. All now bemoaned the plight of the orphans, three of whom went to live with their uncle William H. Clayton in Fort Smith, and the other three with Powell Clayton in Eureka Springs, a new resort town in northwest Arkansas. John Clayton's congressional opponent, Clifton Breckinridge, even noted that he and Clayton had become friends in the course of the campaign as they rode in the same coach, ate at the same table, and even slept in the same bed during their travels. More than five thousand mourners turned out for Clayton's funeral at the Methodist church in Pine Bluff. A special train was chartered to transport mourners from Little Rock.[36]

With national headlines on Arkansas's political violence, the Democratic Party faced the problem of embarrassing publicity. On February 11, a resolution was presented to the U.S. House of Representatives that the Committee on Elections take testimony regarding the contested Arkansas election and assassination. The Kansas House of Representatives, then in session in Topeka, passed a resolution condemning the gross frauds and violence against Republicans in Arkansas and called for Congress to restore order in the state even if doing so meant imposing martial law. The Democratic senator from Arkansas, James K. Jones, defended his state and party in an article for the influential *North American Review* entitled "Was Clayton's Murder a Political Crime?" He answered his own question with an emphatic "No!" He concluded that the crime resulted not from any Democratic conspiracy at the state or local level but from "the act of some poor wretch moved by considerations wholly personal to himself." But even the two partisan Democratic statewide newspapers, the *Arkansas Gazette* and the *Arkansas Democrat*, suggested that the party leaders of Conway County had planned, or at least covered up, these political crimes.[37]

Democratic leaders indeed wanted to convince the public that Clayton's killing was the work of a lone killer addressing a personal grievance, not a political assassination. During the remainder of 1889 and 1890, Governor Eagle and Congressman Breckinridge cooperated with Conway County sheriff Shelby in working out a bizarre and elaborate theory that the murder had been committed by Thomas Hooper Jr. of California. In the summer of 1889, an Indiana man named Jared Sater, evidently in an attempt to claim the reward money, wrote to Sheriff Shelby accusing Hooper of the crime. Hooper's father, Thomas Hooper, was the Klansman murdered during Conway County's Reconstruction troubles by Captain Matthews's black Republican militia company. After his father's death, Thomas Hooper Jr. moved to California, where (according to Sater, who knew him in the West) Hooper nursed a bitter grudge against the Republican governor. Democrats suggested that Hooper returned to Arkansas to murder Powell Clayton and, not finding him, killed his brother instead. Hooper died in December 1889, before anyone from Arkansas actually traveled to California to investigate Sater's allegation. Not until May 1890 was Hooper's widow finally summoned to testify and establish that Hooper had actually been at home in bed, sick with the dropsy, during the month of January 1889. But for the better part of a year, the Hooper theory of the murder occupied Sheriff Shelby's time and the attention of the Democratic press. To a man, when asked to explain the Clayton murder, Conway County Democrats always presented the killing as a retaliation by some unknown private party for the crimes committed by Powell Clayton's Reconstruction militia.[38]

Sheriff Shelby also received two mysterious letters claiming to be from the assassin, signed "Jack the Ripper," who had recently committed a new round of sensational murders in London. Fitting nicely with the Hooper theory, the letters confessed to killing John M. Clayton by mistake, thinking he was his brother, Powell Clayton. Jack's motive, the letters claimed, was to get revenge for crimes committed by Clayton during the Reconstruction days. One letter bore a Southwest City, Missouri, postmark, near where Bob Pate was alleged to have relatives. It strains credibility to imagine that a killer would mistake John Clayton for his brother Powell, as the letters claimed. But Oliver Bentley, incredibly, told a reporter from the New York *World* that he did not even know Powell Clayton had a brother named John Clayton until the night he was killed, this despite the hotly contested race of the previous fall. Rumors of two mysterious strangers seen north of Plumerville on the morning of Clayton's murder also circulated to provide support to the theory that the killer or killers came from outside the county.[39]

Despite these attempts to deflect the scrutiny away from the most likely suspects, others looked to Conway County to find the guilty parties. Public town meetings in Plumerville and Morrilton in the days after Clayton's killing had denounced the crime, and local Democratic leaders declared they would do all they could to bring the perpetrators to justice. But even the state's leading Democratic newspaper, the *Arkansas Gazette*, suggested that the folks in Plumerville knew who had murdered Clayton, and that Sheriff Shelby knew the identity of the four men who had stolen the ballot box. African Americans in the Plumerville area reportedly wanted the murderers hung, "but they shook their heads and said, 'It will never be done.'" Both the *Arkansas Gazette* and the *Arkansas Democrat* took a strong stand, suggesting that elected officials in Conway County were trying to cover up, rather than solve, the crime. The papers pointed out that Sheriff Shelby retained Oliver Bentley as his deputy during the investigation even though Bentley was a chief suspect for both the ballot box theft and Clayton's murder. According to one report, the papers lost hundreds of subscriptions because of the strong stand they took against the political crime and cover-up. The *Arkansas Gazette*, however, radically changed its editorial stance toward the Clayton case in late spring when a large portion of its stock was purchased by leading Conway County Democrats, including Sheriff Shelby, Tom Hervey, J. L. Lucas, W. H. Ward, W. J. Stowers (the captain of the Democratic militia), and sixteen other prominent citizens of Morrilton.[40]

On Monday, March 4, 1889, Circuit Judge George S. Cunningham impaneled a grand jury in Morrilton to conduct the formal investigation of the Clayton murder. Cunningham had studied law in Ann Arbor, Michigan, before returning to his native Yell County, Arkansas, to practice law and enter local politics. He had served as a Democratic representative to the state legislature in 1878. Despite his Democratic loyalties, Cunningham gave a stinging lecture about political crimes to the jury and local citizens who attended the opening of the circuit court. Cunningham labeled Clayton's death a political assassination and advised the jury that the guilty men would be found among the powerful and influential men of the community. As if making a stump speech for populism, Cunningham said: "Political assassinations do not originate in the minds of men in the humblest walks of life. Men who earn their living by the sweat of their brows, whose lives are poems of honor and industry, do not find it in their minds and hearts to conceive assassination; but it is conceived and planned by more influential, fine-haired gentlemen who pretend to be respectable."

Judge Cunningham instructed the jury that the guilty parties should be caught and hung, regardless of their standing in the community. He went on to chastise citizens of Morrilton for their disgraceful behavior in the heckling and beating of M. W. Benjamin in November, for the stealing and stuffing of ballot boxes, and for their flagrant disregard for the law and the rights of African Americans. (For the full text of Cunningham's charge to the grand jury, see appendix B.)

Despite Judge Cunningham's pointed advice, the grand jury brought forward no indictments for either the ballot box theft or Clayton's murder. One of the members of the jury afterward circulated the story that the jury had known the identity of the murderers, but that they had fled the state. Justice failed, the juror explained, because the state treasury lacked the funds necessary to apprehend the criminals. With five thousand dollars of reward money at stake, this story rings out as a particularly ludicrous attempt to steer suspicion away from the guilty parties.[41]

With state and county officials dragging their feet, William H. and Powell Clayton hired the Pinkerton Detective Agency to investigate the killing. From February to April, a Pinkerton detective named Albert Wood gathered evidence in Arkansas, the Claytons paying him eight dollars a day plus expenses. Local residents eventually drove the detective out of Plumerville, and he took testimonies thereafter at his room at the Capital Hotel in Little Rock.

Detective Wood almost cracked the case. Charles Wahl, the federal supervisor who had nearly been murdered the preceding December, brought Gus Christenberry, a Plumerville man, to meet Wood in Little Rock. Christenberry had formerly provided one of Bob Pate's alibis for the time of Clayton's murder. Apparently Christenberry confessed to Wood that rumors had circulated in Plumerville all day on January 29 that Clayton would be killed. Christenberry said that he had given a pistol to Charles Pate around supper time. Also that evening, Charles's brother, Bob, had met privately with Oliver Bentley near the Plumerville depot, and Bentley had returned to Morrilton before the murder was committed.

Detective Wood also interviewed chief suspect Bob Pate, who evidently acknowledged he had met with Oliver Bentley near the depot earlier on the evening of Clayton's murder. However, after Detective Wood made his report and left the state to pursue other cases, the Plumerville Democrats disavowed all these statements. During the federal investigations that followed, Oliver Bentley swore that he had not been in Plumerville on the day of Clayton's murder. Christenberry denied making a confession to Wood or even meeting the Pinkerton detective. Bob Pate testified under oath that detectives had been hired to follow him, and that they drugged him and got him drunk. He could not recall anything he had said to Detective Wood, Pate later said.[42]

One cannot be too certain in the maze of this contradictory testimony. The most plausible theory would be that late in the afternoon of January 29, after the compromise settlement fell through, Oliver Bentley rode to Plumerville to inform Bob Pate that the plan was on and quickly rode back to Morrilton. Bentley admitted he delivered a legal notice at about sundown to a lawyer who lived on the Plumerville road and thus was seen riding toward Plumerville on his claybank horse. While the dirty work was being done in Plumerville, Bentley and the leading Democratic men of Morrilton had firm alibis. Bentley, Walter Wells, Charles Reid, and the rest of the courthouse gang attended a dance at the Morrilton Opera House, a public place where all could be seen. One Democrat who testified to Bentley's whereabouts at the time of the murder noted that he remembered it particularly because Oliver Bentley had not made a habit of going to dances. Because of the existing suspicions that he stole the ballot box and murdered his own brother, Oliver Bentley knew that he would need a firm alibi. Two weeks after Clayton's assassination, Oliver Bentley had his expensive horse killed, the easily distinguishable yellow clay–colored steed he purportedly had ridden to Plumerville on the night of November 6 and again on January 29. Bentley's story was that the horse had suddenly lain down and died outside Morrilton.[43]

When the Pinkerton detective Wood left Plumerville for the safety of Little Rock, he hired a local black man, Joseph W. Smith, to continue the investigation in the area. Smith had stood as an independent candidate for county sheriff in the previous election. On Saturday

Figure 16. Richard Gray, constable of Howard township. *(Courtesy of Blanche McCray.)*

morning, March 30, Smith sent a message to Detective Wood indicating he had found a man who could reveal the identities of both Clayton's murderer and the thieves in the November election, and that he planned to bring the man with some other witnesses to meet Wood in Little Rock. (For the full text of Smith's letter, see appendix C.) About sunset that same day, on a dusty road about a mile north of Plumerville, three white men on horseback overtook Joe Smith as he made his way home to his wife and five children. One of the party, eighteen-year-old David Richmond, shot Smith in the left side, killing him instantly. To leave no doubt, Richmond fired a second time, shooting Smith directly in the head.[44]

As with Clayton's killing, Democrats tried hard to convince people that Smith's murder was not politically motivated. The Democratic newspapers made the crime out to be petty violence by some rowdy teenagers. In a speech to the U.S. House of Representatives, Congressman Breckinridge charged that Joe Smith was drunk, had verbally abused young Richmond, and had assaulted him with a rock. A Morrilton physician claimed he found a bite mark on Richmond's body. According to the *Arkansas Gazette*, the investigation found that Joe Smith was "insolent, quarrelsome, overbearing, quick to take offense, and a turbulent and troublesome man in the community." Richmond admitted he fired on Smith because he was tired of his "slack jaw." They made much of the fact that Richmond's father was a Republican in Scott County. Actually, however, Richmond had admitted that he was a Democrat and that he had left home at the age of sixteen. His father knew nothing of his whereabouts until hearing news of the killing.[45]

The constable of Howard township, Richard J. Gray, a well-educated mulatto physician and a leader of the black community, had tracked down Richmond, arrested him, and turned him over to the county sheriff. Sheriff Shelby put Richmond in jail in Morrilton but told Gray he did not think the murder "amounted to much." Gray thought differently; Joe Smith was his cousin. Three days after Smith's murder, Gray traveled to Little Rock to speak with Governor Eagle about the case and the situation in Conway County. Gray reported that Richmond's friends had threatened him. In fact, Constable Gray said he had met Oliver Bentley in the street in Plumerville on the night Smith had been killed and that Bentley had made it clear that certain death awaited anyone who got on the track of Clayton's killer. Gray got no satisfaction from either the governor or the local authorities. The county grand jury refused to indict Richmond for murdering Joe Smith, instead ruling the killing a justifiable homicide. In true Conway County–style justice, however, Constable Gray was indicted for "breach of peace" because he used insulting and abusive language to David Richmond when he arrested him.[46]

During the months following Clayton's murder, Morrilton and Plumerville were overrun by reporters and detectives trying to solve the crime. Besides the Pinkertons hired by the Clayton family, other detective agencies put men on the case in hopes of claiming the $5,000 reward offered by the state. Strangers arrived in Plumerville announcing they were looking for work; men posing as salesman passed through hoping to find some evidence that would solve the case. One man, an incognito detective from Cincinnati, obtained work in Elijah Chism's barbershop, thinking it would be an excellent place to listen in on the local gossip. After the would-be barber nearly cut the throats of two or three customers, the townsfolk became suspicious of his identity. Local authorities accused him of stealing some razors from his employer; he was found guilty and sentenced to work on the county poor farm because he had not the money to pay his fine. The unfortunate detective finally telegraphed to Cincinnati and obtained money for his release.[47]

While the investigation of Clayton's killing progressed in 1889, the

Conway County election cases came before the federal court in Little Rock. In February, under Judge John McClure, Clayton's lawyer in the contested election case, the court first tried Robert Watkins, a Plumerville man and employee of Dr. Ben White, for stealing the ballot box. While staying at the Baker Hotel in Little Rock in January 1889, Watkins had overindulged in red-eye whiskey and boasted to his drinking companions that he stole the ballot box in Plumerville on November 6. He said he and Bob Pate drove off in a buggy with the box and burned it south of town near the Arkansas River. One of the persons in the Little Rock bar who heard Watkins tell this tale signed an affidavit, and Watkins was brought to trial. However, numerous witnesses from Plumerville testified that they saw Watkins in the company of Charles Pate elsewhere at the time of the theft. The judge finally acquitted Watkins, deciding that "the only thing proved against Watkins was that, when tanked up on Little Rock Sunday liquor, he was capable of some remarkably good fiction."[48]

In the April term, the court under Federal Judge Henry Caldwell heard the charges against the election judges and the deputy sheriffs who had ousted the black judges for the November election. After several hours of deliberation, the jury acquitted William Palmer and William Hobbs, the two Democrats who had replaced the black judges, Armstead and Hays. But the jury found Thomas C. Hervey, the original judge who had orchestrated the affair, guilty as charged and fined him $100 plus $114 in court costs.[49] In a separate trial, the jury acquitted John O. Blakeney, the editor of the Morrilton *Headlight*, but returned a guilty verdict for deputies James Lucas and Charles C. Reid Jr., the young Vanderbilt-educated lawyer. Charles Reid's face paled, and his mother lowered her head and cried as the verdict was read. The handsome twenty year old, who had graduated from Vanderbilt on his nineteenth birthday and had been admitted to the Arkansas bar four months later, became a convicted criminal. Two weeks later, however, in a surprise move, Judge Caldwell set aside the guilty verdicts on Reid and Lucas and discharged them from custody. This reversal most certainly saved Reid's career. He would go on decades later to serve five terms in the U.S. House of Representatives.[50]

During the April court session, young Warren Taylor, in front of many citizens from Conway County who had traveled to Little Rock for the federal trials as either witnesses or onlookers, gave his testimony explaining how the Plumerville ballot box was stolen. Taylor, a drugstore clerk in Morrilton, was a member of the Democratic posse that rode to Plumerville on election night. He named eighteen men in the posse, mostly prominent businessmen in Morrilton, and detailed the circumstances of the theft. On the basis of his deposition, the federal grand jury indicted Taylor and twelve other members of the posse on three counts of election fraud. After telling his story, Taylor promptly fled to Eugene, Oregon, saying his life had been threatened by Oliver Bentley and Walter Wells. In 1890 he testified before Congress in Washington, D.C., that he wished to return to Conway County but feared that if he did, Sheriff Marcus Shelby would shoot him.[51]

One man indicted a second time based on Taylor's testimony was Charles C. Reid, the young lawyer previously tried for bullying the black election judges. Reid created quite a sensation in federal court when he refused to answer the grand jury's question as to whether he had ever spoken with Oliver Bentley about the theft of the ballot box. The judge ordered Reid into custody until he gave an answer. By the next day, Reid, the legal boy wonder, had crafted an ingenious response. He said Bentley had made all his statements about the stolen ballots to him in his role as Bentley's attorney. Thus Reid was legally bound to confidentiality. A legal ruse perhaps, but his position indicated both Bentley's involvement in the theft and his own knowledge of the matter.[52]

Besides settling the two Conway County election cases and indicting the Democratic posse for stealing the ballot box, the federal court's April 1889 session charged four Plumerville men, William Palmer, Cyrus McCullough, William Durham, and Dr. Benjamin White, for conspiring to murder Charles Wahl, the federal election supervisor. Their trials were slated for the following November. When the court adjourned in early May, a Democratic crowd in Morrilton held a big "blowout" to celebrate the Reid-Lucas-Blakeney decision, meeting the train at the station to welcome their men home.[53]

By May 1889, however, Morrilton was no longer a safe place for Republicans. On Saturday, May 4, reports circulated that Oliver Bentley and the former Republican sheriff, Harry Coblentz, had argued on the streets of Morrilton and that Bentley had tried to kill Coblentz. Republican and Democratic leaders visited Coblentz that afternoon and begged him to leave Morrilton on the next train to avoid another fight with Bentley. The mayor even offered him a bodyguard to the train. At first Coblentz refused to go. But that evening, he boarded the train, leaving behind his wife and children. The mayor assembled a patrol of fifty men that night to keep order in town, fearing threats by blacks to burn the town. Coblentz had previously given young Warren Taylor the money to escape to Oregon. After boarding the train on May 4, Coblentz too moved west, to Tacoma, Washington, joining the growing number of Republican refugees who fled the wrath of Conway County Democrats.[54]

By late summer 1889, Circuit Judge George Cunningham, who had delivered the stinging charge to the grand jury in March denouncing the Clayton assassination and political treachery in Conway County, had resigned from his post in the Fifth Judicial District of Arkansas and moved to Guthrie, Oklahoma. Reports circulated in northern newspapers that Judge Cunningham left the state because of death threats from angry residents of Conway County. The *Arkansas Gazette* labeled these reports as vicious lies and printed a letter from Judge Cunningham explaining that he resigned early and moved because of ill health, specifically nervous dyspepsia. Conway County Democrats accused Cunningham of selling out to the Claytons and suggested that he traveled west with William H. Clayton to get first choice of property in the opening of Oklahoma.[55] It is not at all clear, however, why Oklahoma would better serve the judge's health than Arkansas.

In November the final Conway County cases came before the federal court in Little Rock. Both Warren Taylor and Harry Coblentz were subpoenaed and traveled at government expense from the West Coast back to Arkansas to testify. When Coblentz was changing trains in St. Louis, he ran into a Morrilton man, Thomas L. Cox, who had formerly been the superintendent of the town's public school. In late 1889, Cox worked as the Arkansas agent for an east coast publishing company. The two men exchanged greetings, and then Cox entered the telegraph office to send a message. Coblentz suspected that Cox was sending word to the Democrats in Morrilton announcing his arrival. Fearing he would be met at the depot by a violent Morrilton mob, Coblentz telegraphed the U.S. marshall in Little Rock and requested an armed guard. When he arrived, federal deputies escorted him to his hotel and then to court the next day.[56]

The Little Rock hotels in late November were again filled with witnesses and spectators from Conway County as the court took up the cases against the men alleged to have attempted to assassinate Charles

Wahl and the Democratic posse charged with having stolen the ballot box. John McClure, Clayton's lawyer for the election appeal and Republican stalwart, served as prosecuting attorney. In the ballot theft case alone, the prosecution called forty-five witnesses, and the defense summoned fifty-nine. For each piece of incriminating testimony, primarily by Plumerville African Americans, white Democrats swore under oath a directly opposite account. For example, one black witness, John Ford, testified that he saw Oliver T. Bentley in front of Smith's drugstore in Plumerville just before the ballot box was stolen. Then a dozen well-dressed Democrats swore that Bentley was at the courthouse in Morrilton at the time of the theft. When another government witness said he saw Walter P. Wells in Plumerville when the ballots were stolen, the prominent citizens of Morrilton, one after another, testified that they were with Wells at that time playing billiards at Morrilton's Speer Hotel. With this kind of contradictory testimony, juries in all the cases brought forward the "not guilty" verdict. The white neighborhoods of Morrilton and Plumerville were ablaze with bonfires and torches and loud with church bells, cowbells, shouts, and cheers in the victory celebrations that followed.[57] In the black neighborhoods, one can imagine, people felt differently.

The investigations had not entirely ended, however. In April 1890, a subcommittee of the U.S. House of Representatives Committee on Elections came to Arkansas to investigate the contested congressional race and the Clayton murder. John McClure, in his role as Clayton's lawyer, had kept pressing the contest forward even after Clayton's death. McClure represented the contestant, the slain Republican candidate, and W. S. McCain and J. H. Harrod, the chairman of the state Democratic Committee, appeared on behalf of Clifton Breckinridge. For two weeks, the committee, composed of five congressmen accompanied by their stenographers, took depositions in Little Rock concerning Clayton's assassination and the election irregularities at Plumerville and other locations in the second congressional district. (For a sample of the revealing testimony made before the committee, see appendix A.) Hundreds of people from Conway County were called to Little Rock to testify. To reconstruct the stolen ballot, the committee asked the voters of Howard township to come to Little Rock and declare how they voted in the November election. The congressmen even paid citizens two dollars a day plus mileage to make the trip.

The hearing took place in the federal court building in Little Rock.

The chairman of the committee, Republican congressman John F. Lacey from Iowa, said the committee feared for their lives if they took the depositions in Plumerville or Morrilton. But even the U.S. courthouse could be a violent place. Chairman Lacey reported that the men from Morrilton and Plumerville brought their pistols into the courtroom inside "little satchels swung over their shoulders." On one day near the end of the proceedings, Carroll Armstrong, the head of the Democratic Party in Conway County, approached the bench and accused the hearings of slurring the names of the good people of the county. He specifically referred to John McClure as a vile slanderer. In a fit of anger, McClure jumped from his seat and punched Armstrong in the face. Armstrong grabbed at McClure's long and full beard. For the next two minutes, bedlam prevailed. The large crowd of black spectators dashed out of the courtroom, fearing a violent reaction by the white Democratic crowd. Finally marshals restrained Armstrong and McClure, and court resumed.[58]

The congressmen returned to Washington on May 9 to prepare their report. Warren Taylor traveled to the nation's capital to give his eyewitness account to the Committee on Elections. He had told the congressmen he would not appear before them in Arkansas because Democrats there had threatened to kill him if he returned to testify against them. Congressman Breckinridge, Powell Clayton, and John McClure also gave additional testimony in Washington as the committee's deliberations dragged on. In August the Committee on Elections finally submitted to the House its report. Declaring that Clayton had actually won the election in November 1888, the report recommended that the seat be vacant on account of Clayton's death. Chairman Lacey and Republicans on the committee gave a stinging recitation of the fraud and "bulldozing" in Arkansas that had secured Breckinridge's election. Breckinridge frequently jumped to his feet to deny Lacey's charges. Nonetheless, the Republican-controlled House passed the committee's recommendation on September 5, 1890, by a vote of 105 to 62. After serving almost the full term, Breckinridge lost his seat in Congress. He began to campaign almost immediately to regain his seat in the November election.[59]

The U.S. House of Representatives had declared that the Wheel-Republican coalition actually did win the congressional seat for Arkansas's second district in 1888. Although the decision came too late to make much of a difference, it was a moral victory for Arkansas Republicans and their ally in this election, the Agricultural Wheel. In the previous March, the Committee on Elections had similarly unseated William H. Cate, the Democratic representative for Arkansas's first congressional district, ruling that Cate had actually lost to the Wheel's candidate, Louis Featherston, after accounting for election fraud. Unlike John Clayton, Featherston survived to occupy the seat. With the 1888 elections, Arkansas Democrats had faced the most formidable test of their power they would experience between Reconstruction and the 1960s.

The experience in Conway County had been even more dramatic, for it involved the Democrats taking the county back after four years of Republican rule. To do so, Democrats circumvented democracy in two elections, stole the ballot box and poll books, committed three politically motivated murders, and attempted another. Between 1888 and 1890, public officials and prominent white citizens in the county busied themselves to camouflage their crimes and solidify their control.

4. Consequences of Murder

Things Fall Apart, 1890–1893

In August 1890, W. D. Leslie of Menifee, in southeastern Conway County, begged the American Colonization Society to give him passage to the African republic of Liberia, saying:

> We do here By disire to know if you can let us know if you will make some arrangements for a bought a hundred families to embark the ship next May, making a bought one thousand people. We want to leave here as soon as we can for the times gets no better here for the negro race and we want to get out from . . . the land of slavery and how happy we will be when we get on that old ship and our song will be I am going home to die no more. . . . there can be no worse a plase in the world than this place.

Another prospective emigrant wrote from Germantown, on the other side of the county:

> The colored people of this country are very poor and we wood like to know . . . weather we wood be treaded as bad over in liBery as we ar in the U.S. Ar tha any White People over in liBery? if there is none ar going there. . . . We have a hard time to get along here. Works hard and when we make our living we are robed of it, we ar call every thing by the white people but still tha want our labour. But dear sir if that is a negro country and we can be free and speak our own mind, make our own laws then we ar redy to come at once.[1]

These poignant letters suggest the immediate consequences of the Clayton murder for the black residents of Conway County. African Americans, who had formerly possessed and used political power, were utterly defeated by the fraud and violence of the late 1880s. By the early 1890s, they were looking to escape not just Conway County or Arkansas but white America.

The ambitious challenge to white elite control by small black and white farmers, which had proved so effective in the 1880s, was eroding on all sides by the early nineties. Several factors came together to solidify their defeat. First, blacks failed to receive strong support from their white Republican Party leaders at either local, state, or national levels. Second, the alliance of Republicans with the Wheelers, although never a close one, fell apart as the 1890s progressed. Finally and most effectively, the continued use of terror and electoral fraud by white Democratic Party leaders shut out black and poor-white participation in politics. For the county's African Americans, escape to Africa, or anywhere outside the South, became an attractive and reasonable alternative.

White leaders of the Republican Party stood neither united nor strong in support of African Americans, who provided the majority of the party's votes in Arkansas. Conway County's elected Republican officials had not used their legal power to protect black citizens when the Republicans controlled county government between 1884 and 1888. They did not organize an armed militia to stop Democratic terror, as Powell Clayton had done effectively during Reconstruction. Republican federal judge Henry Caldwell had been amazingly lenient in his dealings with, and sentencing of, Democrats prosecuted for election fraud in 1889. Former governor Powell Clayton had dominated the state Republican Party from Reconstruction until his retirement from the Republican National Committee in 1913. Although Clayton had always been committed to the full participation of African Americans in the party, other party leaders in Arkansas had different ideas. Judge John McClure, who had championed John Clayton's election contest even after his death, had formed an all-white Republican club in Little Rock in 1888, suggesting that blacks had become a liability for the party. The Republican Party must choose, McClure said: it would become all white or all black. Clayton and black Republicans reacted immediately and suppressed the movement for a lily-white party organization. The ambivalence on the race issue remained, however.

On the national level, any Republican support for a fusion alliance of poor blacks with agrarian populists ran counter to the prevailing ideology of the party. Nationally, Republicans in general stood for the interests of corporations, railroads, and wealth, whereas Democrats tilted more toward labor and poor farmers. The Republican-controlled House of Representatives and its Committee on Elections had taken great interest in the Clayton murder and contested election because the removal of Clifton Breckinridge meant one less Democratic vote in Congress. But the House and the committee made no efforts to pursue justice against wrongdoers or to protect terrorized blacks in Conway

County. The party that supported forceful strikebreaking of the steel industry in Homestead, Pennsylvania, would not intervene dramatically for blacks and poor whites in the South.[2]

While Republican support wavered, the black coalition with the farmers' movement became more precarious. With their fusion ticket, Republicans and the Wheel had come close to taking the major state offices in 1888. In fact, the Wheel candidate, Charles Norwood, would probably have won the governor's race had not election fraud prevented him. So again in 1890 the farmers and the GOP formed a coalition in the governor's race to unseat Democratic governor Eagle, backing N. B. Fizer, a Methodist preacher on the Union Labor ticket. Likewise in Conway County, Republicans and Wheelers tried to ally under a common Union Labor ticket, unlike in 1888 when each group had put forward its own slate of county candidates. Governor Eagle and candidate Fizer appeared in Morrilton on Friday, August 1, in a speech-making stop. The next day, Fizer's supporters, the coalition of white and black Republicans and mostly white Wheelers, met at Solgohatchia in Washington township to nominate their county ticket. The campaign concluded with the usual political sideshows. Democratic rallies employed the music of a German brass band, and a Union Labor event in Springfield just before the election saw a solemn procession of men carrying stalks of corn and farm implements.[3]

But the alliance opposing the Democrats quickly began to divide along racial lines. African Americans became incensed at the Solgohatchia meeting because the fusion ticket included only one black candidate, T. C. Snipes, for state representative. The county's African American newspaper, the *Clarion*, edited by W. J. Jordan, a saloon owner in Plumerville, had already called for at least three black places on the ticket. The Democrats reported that when blacks protested at Solgohatchia, they were threatened with violence and driven from the meeting. Black Republicans called their own meeting for the following Saturday, at which they paid their respects to the "white long-haired radicals in the north end of the county" (it is not clear if this was the Democratic or African American term for the white populists) and then proceeded to select a straight Republican ticket. This Republican ticket included three black men, Snipes for representative, Dr. Richard Gray for circuit clerk, and C. J. Smith for county judge, but white men for the four other county offices.[4]

Although coalition attempts faltered, black and white Republicans appeared ready to use force if necessary to keep Democrats from stealing the election as they had two years before. Democrats had no monopoly on violent tactics. In March 1890, Union Civil War veterans and their sons established chapters of the Grand Army of the Republic (GAR) and Sons of Veterans in Center Ridge, a staunchly white Republican village in northern Lick Mountain township, the area that had been the focus of Union support in the Civil War. Democrats charged that these chapters were merely fronts for Republican clubs that held secret meetings to plot violence against Democrats. According to the *Arkansas Gazette*, the clubs had passed resolutions threatening to shed blood if their party did not win. John Blakeney, editor of the Morrilton *Headlight*, reported that the Republican clubs had received a shipment of two cases of Winchester rifles from "up north." One hundred Springfield rifles were also received, reportedly by the African Americans of Menifee. White citizens would not have known about the guns, Blakeney said, had not the black man who had collected the purse skipped town with the money. Democrats charged that A. G. Gratten, a prominent black Republican and landowner from Menifee, had declared in a speech at Springfield that blacks would burn Plumerville and Morrilton if Republicans did not carry the election.[5]

It was, however, Democratic violence that won out in the elections in September 1890. George W. Small, a Center Ridge Republican and organizer of the GAR and Sons of Veterans camps, had traveled to Little Rock to get the Union Labor ballots for the election. The party had the tickets printed in St. Louis to prevent Democrats from tampering with them. On Saturday, August 30, he returned with the ballots, accompanied by J. B. McLaughlin, a well-known Union Labor orator. On their arrival in Morrilton, the men were met by an angry Democratic mob, lined up in military fashion on both sides of the depot. Democrats had apparently organized a party rally to coincide exactly with Small's appearance. When the train stopped, the mob entered Small's coach, tumbling over the seats to get to him. They caned Small senseless and pulled McLaughlin backward over the seats, tearing off his collar, soiling his clothes, and severely wrenching his shoulder. By one account, Carroll Armstrong, the county Democratic chairman, orchestrated the affair. Leading the assault were James Lucas, Walter P. Wells, and Oliver T. Bentley, still the deputy sheriff, who took Small's valise containing the seven thousand Union Labor tickets.[6]

Bentley and the courthouse gang evidently did not fear any reprisal in this brazen attack and theft, for they would not come under the jurisdiction of the federal court. Tickets were printed to replace the stolen ones, and the election was held a few days later. Both sides charged the other with illegal actions in the election. According to the Democratic press, members of the Republican clubs in the northern part of the county massed at the polls with their guns and intimidated Democratic voters, keeping their turnout low. At Springfield, Republicans reportedly brought in blacks from Faulkner County to vote. Black Republicans, the *Gazette* reported, threatened violence against disloyal members of their race who voted Democrat. They slipped into the home near Morrilton of George Griffin, a black man known to be a member of the Democratic Club, and choked him while he was eating his supper. In Howard township, a black church turned out its own members for voting Democratic in the election. However, despite these allegations of Republican threats and use of force, Democrats counted the ballots, and they won the election. Bob Pate, for example, served as an election judge for Howard township. The Democratic state senator, a Confederate veteran and Morrilton lawyer, William S. Hanna, reportedly said the Democrats were determined to have the county even if the Republicans outvoted them two to one. Governor Eagle and the state Democratic ticket carried the county by a majority of 353 votes.[7]

The November election brought similar fireworks. Clifton Breckinridge's race for his old seat in Congress must have served as a galling reminder to Republicans of the earlier stolen election and assassination. In early October, Breckinridge made a campaign swing through the northern part of Conway County, speaking in Springfield on the morning of October 6 and in Center Ridge that evening. One might question Breckinridge's thinking in coming to Center Ridge, the hotbed of white Republicanism in the county, much less sleeping there in a hotel run by Frank Stobaugh, a Union veteran of Williams's independent company in the Civil War. Democrats from elsewhere in the county apparently planned to attend his address to lend him moral support in this village where Republicans outnumbered them ten to one. However, rain prevented many Democrats from coming, and the crowd listening to Breckinridge in the local church was largely Republican. The *Arkansas Gazette* suggested that many of them had been members of Powell Clayton's militia in Reconstruction days.

About halfway through Breckinridge's speech, a man's head appeared at a window behind the speaker's podium. Later an explosive noise rang out and startled the audience. The candidate finished his speech and returned to the Stobaugh hotel for the night. But on his way, a blow from a slingshot struck R. L. Norman, a local Democrat who was walking with him, and knocked him to the ground. The Little Rock papers proclaimed it an attempt to assassinate the former congressman. Center Ridge residents denied the assassination story, saying that the explosive sound heard during Breckinridge's speech was no more than a young boy striking a match. A few weeks later, two Center Ridge Republicans, Frank and Galloway Williams, grandsons of Thomas Jefferson Williams, the local Union Civil War martyr, were indicted on the charge of attempting to assassinate R. L. Norman with a slingshot. While authorities were at it, they found a charge under which to indict George Small, the Center Ridge Republican whom they had beaten the month before. He was charged with obtaining goods under false pretense, harkening back to a land deal he had transacted the year before.[8]

As the polls were closing on election day in November, a band of Republican men from Center Ridge, led by the "Williams gang," marched two by two into Plumerville armed with their Winchester rifles. When they passed the house where Clayton had been killed, they fired several shots, striking the house and the fence in front. Mrs. McCraven no longer lived in the house; it was then occupied by a Mrs. Peel, the widowed sister of Charles and Bob Pate. The Republican mob proceeded to the polling place, where they and about a hundred African Americans remained with their guns until the results of the election were called. With this armed scrutiny as the votes were counted, Breckinridge's Republican opponent, Isom P. Langley, carried Conway County by almost one hundred votes. Breckinridge, however, won the majority in the district and regained his seat in Congress.[9]

The 1890 elections were the last true multiracial elections in Conway County until the passage of the Civil Rights Act of 1964. The next meeting of the state legislature in 1891 busied itself with measures to curb black voting power and even to institutionalize racism in Arkansas. As a symbolic gesture, the legislators voted to remove the portrait of George Washington behind the speaker's rostrum and replace it with one of Jefferson Davis. This set the tone for the 1891 legislature.

As one of its first measures, the Assembly passed a statute that mandated separate railroad coaches and waiting rooms for blacks and whites, the beginning of enforced legal segregation in Arkansas.[10]

With this as its overture, the legislature went on to pass a secret ballot law specifically designed to disfranchise illiterate black and poor white voters. In the early 1890s, Democrats throughout the South began to recommend the "Australian," or secret, ballot system, whereby a single ballot printed by the state contained the names of all candidates but listed no party affiliation. Illiterates would thus not know which candidate to vote for. In the previous legislative session in 1889, the overwhelmingly Democratic state senate under the presidency of W. S. Hanna, Conway County's senator, had passed both a secret ballot and a poll tax measure. Neither bill came to a vote in the House, where Republicans and Union Labor had about one-third of the seats. However, in 1891 both chambers approved a secret ballot bill that removed all party symbols on ballots. The bill prohibited party workers from assisting illiterate voters in marking their ballots; only election judges could render this aid. This provision would not help illiterate white populist or black Republican voters, however. The new election law made sure Democratic officials kept control of the choice of election judges. The governor, auditor, and secretary of state chose three election commissioners for each county, who then chose the judges for each precinct. The law gave no guarantees that the judges would be of varying political parties. In fact, the Assembly voted down an amendment offered by a Union Labor legislator from Faulkner County that proposed a $100 fine for county commissioners if they failed to name persons of different parties as election judges and clerks. With Democrats always winning the top three state offices, the party could control the appointment of election officials even in black belt counties of the Arkansas delta, where the Democrats might be in the minority. Thus the secret ballot, usually considered a safeguard of the democratic process, was turned against the practice of democracy in Arkansas, as in other southern states.[11]

As if the secret ballot were not enough, the 1891 legislature also passed a poll tax measure that obviously aimed further to reduce the black and poor white farmer vote. This measure, however, required a constitutional amendment and did not become law until passed by a voter referendum in the 1892 election. Before adjourning, the House voted down a bill to repeal the hated anaconda mortgage law of 1875.

The Arkansas legislature had instead chosen another way to neutralize the threat of the rural poor: taking away their votes.

During the campaign for the September 1892 elections, Arkansas Democrats composed the following song, sung to the tune of "The Bonnie Blue Flag," the former national anthem of the Confederacy:

The Australian ballot works like a charm,
It makes them think and scratch,
And when a negro gets a ballot,
He has certainly got his match.

Chorus:
Hurrah! Hurrah! for Arkansas Hurrah!
And when we elect old Grover, [Grover Cleveland]
We will make them kick and paw.

They go into the booth alone,
Their ticket to prepare,
And as soon as five minutes are out,
They have got to git from there.
(Chorus)
They then next to the Judge applies,
With a little tale of woe,
And of course his ticket is well prepared,
Which someone is bound to know.
(Chorus).[12]

The Democrats of Conway County, one might expect, sang right along in tune. As early as November 1890, the Morrilton *Pilot*, the new Democratic paper in town, had urged that the upcoming legislature require ballots to be of uniform size and color and that voters make out their own tickets without any assistance. Throughout the summer of 1892, the *Pilot* editorialized in favor of the poll tax amendment coming before voters in September. One editorial reminded readers that the Populist third party opposed the new law and was "Therefore in favor of 600 to 700 voters in Conway County, mostly Negroes, walking up to the polls and voting without paying one single cent of tax to the support of the government."[13]

Despite these attempts to diminish the voting power of the poor, the agrarian movement in Conway County remained strong and well organized. It turned increasingly toward nonpolitical means to protect the interests of the small farmer, both black and white. Arkansas's Agricultural Wheel had merged in 1889 with the Texas-born Farmers' Alliance, and the People's Party was the movement's political arm. A Fourth of July rally of the Conway County Farmers' Alliance in 1891 attracted one thousand people to the Damascus Church, ten miles northeast of Morrilton. By this time, African Americans began organizing their own Alliance lodges in the county, perhaps beginning to forsake their loyalties to the Republican Party, which had not protected their interests.[14]

At the county Alliance meeting in Morrilton on August 12, 1892, the farmers adopted a resolution opposing the introduction of politics into their organization. The farmers then went on to declare their support for several specific economic measures to improve their situation. To inflate their selling prices, they unanimously called for farmers to reduce their cotton acreage by 25 percent and to use their own cottonseed for fertilizing purposes rather than selling it at giveaway prices. The Alliance members chose their own man to weigh cotton in Morrilton, the selling and shipping point for most Conway County cotton, and later built a platform for weighing cotton near the depot there. The meeting also expressed its unqualified support for the so-called subtreasury plan, drawn up in 1889 by Texas Allianceman Charles W. Macune. The subtreasury concept called for the federal government to provide credit directly to farmers through farmers' cooperatives and to facilitate marketing of crops through "subtreasuries," local government warehouses that would pay the farmer directly for produce.[15] The plan would thus remove the furnishing merchants, buyers, and commercial banks from the agricultural system. The commercial class of Morrilton would lose its economic, if not political, control over the small farmers of the county.

Even though farmers concentrated on economic measures and resolved against politicking, the 1892 election brought them again to political action. A good number of white former Republicans had joined the farmers' movement. In 1891 William Taylor, former Republican county assessor, was president and assistant lecturer for the county Alliance. T. J. Halbrook, the former Republican county surveyor and an officer in Center Ridge's GAR chapter, had a prominent role in the movement by 1892. Staunch Republicans in Lick Mountain township such as Web Williams and John Kissire, the son and son-in-law of Civil War Unionist hero and martyr Thomas Jefferson Williams, were strong Alliance men.[16]

Although most white Republicans apparently supported the Populists, black Republicans defected from the fusionist ticket. Eventually Republicans and the Alliance put forth separate tickets in the 1892 election. In July, at their county convention in Springfield, Conway County's agrarian stronghold, the Populists condemned both Republican and Democratic parties for purchasing votes and corrupting voters. They demanded *real* democracy that would follow the will of the majority. By unanimous agreement, the convention directed the party's candidates to vote against the poll tax amendment and to work to repeal the new election laws. Members of this mainly white agrarian third party obviously saw clearly that election reform aimed to disfranchise them as well as black Republicans. Four of about fifty delegates to the meeting were black men, but the Democratic press noted that all the "colored brothers had back seats" except for one, J. H. "Shell Oats" Hall, who the correspondent charged had made himself very conspicuous and tried to pass as a white man.[17]

The Farmers' Alliance and Republican opposition to the Democrats failed on election day. Through a combination of fraud and the legal exclusion of blacks with the new election law, the Democrats solidified their hold on county government. Charles Reid's young law clerk, Charles Jacobsen, who was only eighteen, clerked the election. Years later he admitted that he had voted even though he had been three years shy of legal voting age. "Votes were needed," Jacobsen said. Democratic candidates Dr. Benjamin White and Walter Wells, both of whom had been indicted in 1889 for stealing the ballot box, won the offices of county sheriff and circuit clerk. Charles Pate, who according to John Mason was one of the two men who had stood outside Clayton's window the night he was killed, became the constable of largely black Howard township, replacing Dr. Richard Gray, the mulatto physician.[18]

The secret ballot law obviously worked well for Arkansas Democrats. J. Morgan Kousser has demonstrated how the secret ballot reduced overall voter turnout in Arkansas by 17 percent between the gubernatorial elections of 1890 and 1892. The decline in voting would come disproportionately from African Americans. According to the 1890 census, 55.8 percent of Arkansas blacks were illiterate, compared to only 13.4 percent of whites. The new election laws reduced the proportion of blacks voting in the gubernatorial elections in Arkansas from 71 percent in 1890 to 38 percent in 1892. The white vote also declined less dramatically, from 75 percent to 67 percent. Using the secret ballot system, Democrats even carried black-majority counties such as John Clayton's home region, Jefferson County, which had gone Republican for decades.[19]

It is impossible to determine the exact impact of the secret ballot on voter turnout in Conway County because of the probability of deliberate miscounting by Democratic election judges and clerks. For example, in Howard township, black Republicans had previously outnumbered white Democrats by five hundred votes in 1886 and again with the "recreated" stolen ballot of the 1888 race. But the published vote for the township in September 1892 had the white Democratic candidate for state representative polling more than five hundred votes, whereas his black Republican opponent had only eight. Similarly, the township "officially" polled more than five hundred votes for the poll tax amendment and only 107 against. It strains credibility to imagine that the former Republican black voters would so radically forsake their party and color loyalties, or that Menifee and Plumerville blacks would vote for a poll tax. But there were not five hundred white voters in the township to cast these votes.

The federal election in November probably more accurately shows the impact of the secret ballot on voting numbers. The total county vote in the November congressional election was only 56 percent of what it had been two years earlier (1,960 as compared to 3,367), even though the latter was a presidential election. In 1890 the fusion candidate carried the county over Congressman Breckinridge, although the Democrat narrowly won the district election. But in 1892, with the much smaller, and apparently much whiter, voter turnout, the Democratic candidate carried the county handily. In the presidential race, the Populist candidate polled 11 percent of the vote, with the greatest number coming predictably from Union township, where the Alliance had its greatest strength. President Benjamin Harrison, the Republican candidate, won 31 percent, with most of these votes coming from the white Republican townships in the northern part of the county. The Democratic candidate, Grover Cleveland, won only 48 percent of the county's vote, but he easily carried Howard and Wellborn townships, where the majority of the county's African Americans lived. In fact, these two townships with the greatest number of black citizens had the highest proportion of Democratic votes cast of all the townships in the county. In the 1892 congressional election, only fifty-one Republican votes were cast in predominantly black Howard township, which had polled more than six hundred Republican votes in 1886 and 1888. Thus the new law appears to have left the white Republican and Wheel-Alliance vote intact but removed almost all of the black vote from the Democratic opposition.[20]

Just before the September 5 election in 1892, the Morrilton *Pilot* printed the lyrics of a song written by a woman from Solgohatchia named Sallie Lee. Entitled "Goodbye Third Party Goodbye," the song began, "The Democrats have come and come to stay." So prophetically true were these words. After the Democrats removed the black vote in the 1892 election through intimidation, fraud, and the secret ballot, the only opposition remaining was the minority of poor white Alliance men and Republicans whose loyalty had been forged in the Civil War. The poll tax instituted after 1892 only further reduced the black and poor white vote. During the 1894 campaign, the county Farmers' Alliance tried to register Populist voters but gave up and did not even bother to field a slate of candidates for local offices. One Morrilton Democrat rued, "There was not opposition enough to the Democratic ticket to make the election interesting." Indeed, the exciting days of political violence were over. In Conway County, as elsewhere in Arkansas, the Democrats would no longer need to stuff ballot boxes or steal them at gunpoint as they had in 1888, for they would no longer contain large numbers of black Republican votes.[21]

By the early 1890s, the dire situation for African Americans in Conway County fueled the back-to-Africa emigration movement. In the weeks following the murders of Clayton and Joe Smith in 1889, several black men in Morrilton corresponded with the American Colonization Society in Washington, D.C., about their desire to emigrate to Liberia in west Africa. Abner Downs wrote, "We are having a great deal of trouble in our Town and Community, three colored men have been killed within the past four months. So I am going to try by Gods help to go home." Another Morrilton man, Anthony Lipscomb, wrote requesting passage and suggested that "a great many of us would make the trip in the Spring." Lipscomb, his wife, and their five children were approved by the society, closed up their rented farm near Morrilton after the fall harvest, and moved to Little Rock in January 1890 to await their departure. They left for Liberia the following June.[22]

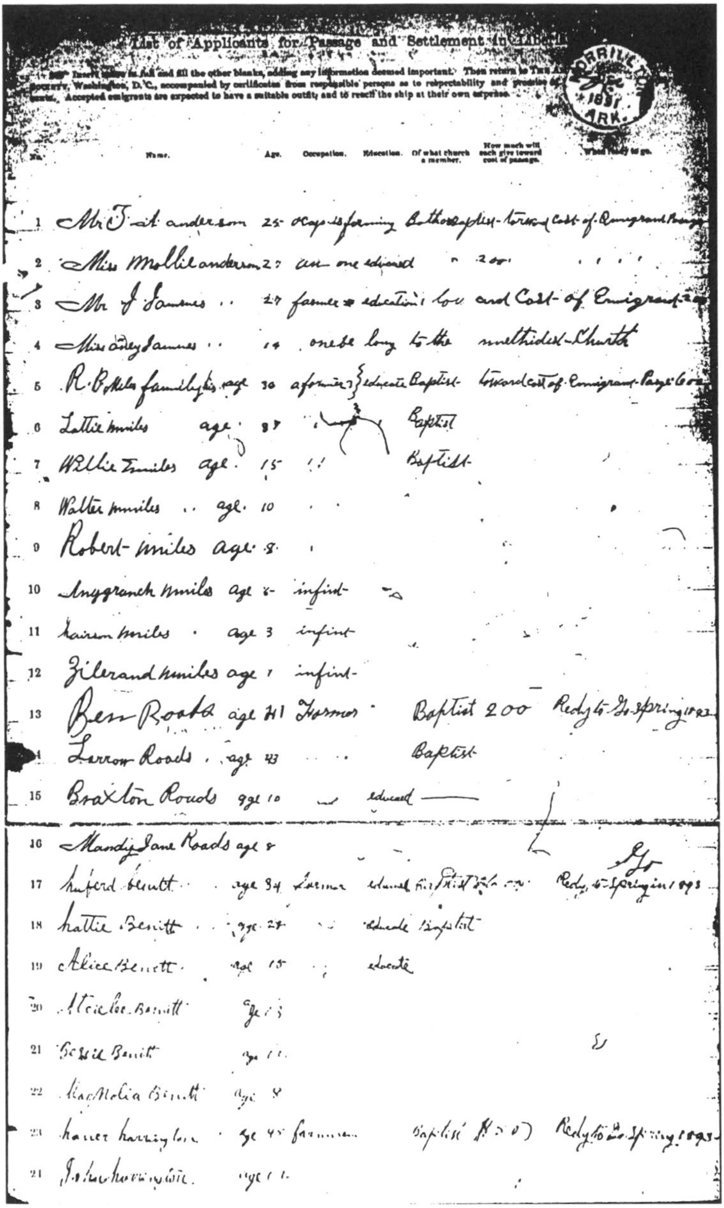

List of Applicants for Passage and Settlement in Liberia

Insert names in full and fill the other blanks, adding any information deemed important. Then return to The American Colonization Society, Washington, D. C., accompanied by certificates from responsible persons as to respectability and promise of emigrants. Accepted emigrants are expected to have a suitable outfit, and to reach the ship at their own expense.

MORRILTON 1891 ARK.

No.	Name.	Age.	Occupation.	Education.	Of what church a member.	How much will each give toward cost of passage.	When ready to go.
1	Mr J. A. anderson	25	farming		Baptist	toward cost of Emigrant passage	
2	Miss Mollie anderson	27		one educated		200	
3	Mr J. James	27	farmer	education		and Cost of Emigrant	
4	Miss ardey James	14			one belong to the methodist Church		
5	R. Bookers family his age	30	a farmer	educate	Baptist	toward cost of Emigrant Passage	
6	Lattie Smiles age	27			Baptist		
7	Willie Smiles age	15			Baptist		
8	Walter Smiles age	10					
9	Robert Smiles age	8					
10	Anygranch Smiles age	6	infint				
11	Kairen Smiles age	3	infint				
12	Zilerand Smiles age	1	infint				
13	Ben Roads age	41	Farmer		Baptist	200	Redy to Go Spring 1892
14	Larrow Roads age	43			Baptist		
15	Braxton Roads age	10		educated			
16	Mandy Jane Roads age	8					
17	Luferd Benitt	age 34	Farmer	educated	Baptist		Redy to Go Spring in 1893
18	hattie Benitt	age 28		educate	Baptist		
19	Alice Benitt	age 15		educate			
20	Alcie Lee Benitt	age 13					
21	Bessie Benitt	age 11					
22	Magnolia Benitt	age 8					
23	hanes harrington	age 45	farmer		Baptist		Redy to Go Spring 1893
24	John harrington	age 11					

Figure 17. An application from Morrilton for emigration to Liberia through the American Colonization Society in 1891.
(Library of Congress.)

The American Colonization Society (ACS), established in 1816 to repatriate free blacks to Africa, had founded the Republic of Liberia and settled 13,000 blacks there before the Civil War. By the 1870s and 1880s, the society's work had slowed to sending about 50 to 100 emigrants a year to Liberia.[23] In 1890 and 1891, racial oppression in states such as Arkansas caused a wave of hysteria about migration to Liberia. The ACS was besieged with letters from poor southern blacks wishing to emigrate. More requests came from Arkansas than from any other state, and from Conway County more than from any other county within Arkansas. It is no surprise that African Americans in Conway County would think of flight to Africa. A decade earlier, South Carolina blacks, especially in Edgefield County, had begged the ACS to send them to Liberia, and one shipload sailed there aboard the *Azor.* When the great majority of applicants were turned away, their dream shifted instead to Arkansas. With this Arkansas dream now gone sour, Liberia appeared all the more attractive.

By the spring and summer of 1890, African Americans were forming emigration clubs in Morrilton, Menifee, Germantown, and Plumerville. In April W. K. Fortson, the corresponding secretary of the Menifee club, promised that 100 families, numbering 1,000 settlers, wished to emigrate. By October he guaranteed that 1,500 would go. The Germantown club, on the west edge of the county, assured the society of another 1,000 emigrants. A Morrilton club promised 500 to 600. Local blacks wrote desperate letters asking for information, maps, and application materials. As the society sent copies of its newsletter, *The African Repository,* and circulars and application forms, information spread further into black neighborhoods causing the demand to increase.[24] Prominent members of the black community, often schoolteachers and preachers, led the movement. One Morrilton correspondent bragged that blacks there were forming their emigration company "from among our better class farmers and mechanics." The Reverend James Dargan, who led the Morrilton group, owned 160 acres of bottomland and his own five-room house in town. The society asked emigrants to pay their own way to New York and part of the $100 cost to transport and settle each colonist in Liberia. But for the most part, the leaders wrote on behalf of poor sharecroppers who could pay little toward their passage.[25]

In their application letters, some complained of low wages, debt, and miserable economic conditions. But clearly political and racial oppression constituted the primary motive for emigration. In the minds of Conway County blacks, Liberia acquired the mystique of a holy land for a people in bondage. William Jones wrote from Morrilton asking the ACS "to aid us trying to get back to our ancestry land we are in the South oppress on every hand and we found out that this is a white man's country, and we can't do any good among them." W. D. Leslie of Menifee said the members of his club were "tired of this place. I hope to the time come when . . . we can get on and leave the U.S.A. and go to our land where we can have our free and own government. . . . here we get no part in the government whatever even our women and children and young men are greaving on the count of their education is doing them no good here." From Solgohatchia came the report that "the colored people are greatly disturbed all over this country of the political conditions." Finally, John Jimison wrote poignantly to the society for passage to Africa, saying, "we do not want to spend twenty four months longer in America, we have long thought it was not our home and now it is provenn to us more and more every day of our lives here around Plummerville, Ark. . . . We are oppressed here and we know no other place on earth to apply for help."[26]

By the end of 1890, hundreds of Conway County blacks were expecting to leave shortly for Liberia. Some were selling their land and possessions and sending money to the society, making ready for their migration.[27] In January 1891, word came from Washington that the next shipment could take only forty-five emigrants from the Morrilton club. The Reverend Dargan had the onerous job of selecting the emigrants from the long list of people who had applied. He planned to lead the expedition but gave up the places of his wife and ten children to others, for he said, "so many are in worse shape than I am." He planned to bring his family over later in the year. On February 9, the Morrilton group finally boarded the train bound for New York to catch the steamer *Liberia* for the voyage to Africa.[28]

The departure of Dargan's company merely inspired others to want to go. Letters from Conway County kept pouring in to the office of the society's secretary, William Coppinger, in Washington. Requests for information and application materials came from other parts of the county, from Springfield, Solgohatchia, and Lick Mountain. Additional clubs were formed in Morrilton, Menifee, and Plumerville.[29] The Reverend W. A. Diggs of Plumerville said, "The greater part of the colored people wants to remove to the Republic of Liberia from my district." Several families were so desperate to escape that they set off for New York even though they had not been approved for migration.[30]

On May 7, the emigration movement suffered a setback when James Dargan returned from Liberia. He had apparently stayed only a few days before taking the steamer straight back to New York. Once home, Dargan reported that the society's circulars and recruitment information had lied, and that colonists were forcibly and inhumanely treated once in Liberia. Dargan said the country was no place for an American person to live; in fact, it was "not fitting for a horse to live much less of a person." He insisted he left the other Morrilton colonists "holering and cring wanting to come back, they wouden let them." Correspondents from Conway County asked Secretary Coppinger if Dargan was speaking truth or falsehood. They wondered if he had even been to Liberia. Most prospective emigrants decided Dargan was lying when letters finally arrived from other settlers, disputing his account and quashing the furious rumors spreading throughout the county. The desperate letters of application from Conway County and donations toward passage on the society's few vessels resumed as before.[31]

Desperation turned to bitter disappointment later in 1891 when residents in Plumerville and Menifee received word that there was no space on the spring voyage to Liberia. Many had already sold their property and sent in their money, expecting to go, and they had already made arrangements with the local railroad company for transportation to New York. Although they desired to leave because of the horrible conditions in Conway County, the emigration hysteria made them victims again. In November 1891, W. M. Wilson of near Menifee had put up his seventy-nine-acre farm for sale, along with farming tools, twenty hogs, two mules, one cow, a Mitchell wagon, and four hundred bushels of corn. He estimated his farm was worth $1,000, but he was only offered $200 for it. One correspondent complained there were no buyers for all the property blacks were trying to sell. They could sell only to whites, who would buy only at rock-bottom prices, if that. Now, after selling property for less than value and giving up leases for rented land, the would-be emigrants found themselves with nowhere to go.[32]

Blacks in Morrilton were more fortunate. Word came from the society that forty of their group would receive space on the next voyage. But just days after authorizing the Morrilton emigrants to proceed to New York, Secretary Coppinger caught pneumonia and died on February 11, 1892. He had handled all the details and arrangements for the migration, and things were near chaos when the Morrilton blacks arrived in New York City to catch their steamer. Matters were complicated by the unexpected and unauthorized arrival of two hundred blacks from Oklahoma and thirty-four from McCrory (Woodruff County), Arkansas, who, like the Menifee and Plumerville applicants, had been deferred to a later, unspecified date. As the authorized emigrants, the Morrilton contingent set sail on the *Liberia* on March 10, arriving in Monrovia about three weeks later.[33]

After Coppinger's death and the fiasco of desperate poor blacks descending on the ship in New York, the executive committee of the ACS reevaluated its program and decided to scale back the numbers of poor black emigrants and instead send a smaller number of skilled and educated colonists. This bad news reached the emigration clubs in Conway County, where hundreds of blacks anxiously awaited word for their approval to emigrate. Although letters continued to arrive from the county begging for passage to Africa, the new acting secretary, J. Ormond Wilson, wrote back saying the society could not help the applicants and that they should stay at home. Those who had sent money asked for it to be returned. W. D. Leslie, a club leader in Menifee, expressed the opinion of his people: "We had just well have our money back and go sum wheres else, for it a show thing we are not living here." Adding to the misery of poor blacks and further encouraging many to leave the county was severe flooding of the Arkansas River in late spring 1892, which destroyed their crops and removed them from their homes for several weeks. On top of all this, a wave of terror against blacks spread across Arkansas in the first months of 1892 with lynchings in Texarkana, Varner, Little Rock, and Perryville, just a few miles south of the Conway County line. After the Texarkana lynching, angry whites made buttons out of the cedar stump where the black victim's body was burned.

Hundreds of Arkansas blacks, unable to leave America, left instead for the Oklahoma Territory, where the federal government provided more protection for black citizens. Two Plumerville men said that when the poor colored people of their area found out they could not go to Liberia, they were off to Oklahoma in droves of fifty and sixty: "We must go somewhere for voyage for they are linching and threating all the time." A Morrilton correspondent who described such conditions asked the society not to publish his name, fearing he "may be hung for Example to other poor black men."[34]

The official position of the white community toward the emigration movement was to ignore it. The Morrilton *Pilot*, like the *Arkansas Gazette*, chose not to report the departure for Liberia of the forty colonists in February 1892, although the story made the *New York Times*.[35] Despite the violence and the exclusion of blacks from politics, whites apparently did not want them to leave the county. More than 1,300 African Americans of Conway County made formal application to the ACS to become Liberia colonists, and their departure would have constituted a huge dent in the local labor force. Whites wanted blacks to preserve their appropriate station in society, not leave it.[36]

Sensing white hostility, the emigration clubs throughout the county called themselves Young Men's Associations to disguise their true purpose. Several correspondents feared the white postmaster in Plumerville had opened their letters to the society or confiscated mail, and they asked Secretary Coppinger to send their mail instead to the post office in all-black Menifee. In neighboring Conway (Faulkner County), five miles east of Menifee, one emigration leader, the Reverend James Harris, asked the society to send mail to him in envelopes, not bearing the stamped return address. Harris wrote to Washington that he feared his mail "was seized on the way, as the whites are doing all they can to prevent the movement." One correspondent even theorized that James Dargan had conspired with local whites to plan his Liberia trip and dramatic return to Morrilton in May 1891 with the explicit intention of wrecking the county's emigration movement. As one applicant for passage to Africa said, "We are call every thing by the white people. But still they want our labour."[37]

Their dream of emigrating to Liberia showed how defeated African Americans really were in Conway County in the early 1890s. The experience constituted a second failure for the vast majority who tried to emigrate to Liberia but failed to get a space on the boats. Some Menifee blacks were defrauded of their contributions when their leader received back the money from the ACS but then skipped town. Many blacks had sold their property at prices far below value. Those who bought property and possessions at fire-sale prices emerged as the prime beneficiaries of the whole affair.

For the more than one hundred settlers who left Conway County for Liberia, the results must have been a mixed blessing. On their arrival, most traveled by canoe about fifteen miles up the Mesurado River from Monrovia (there were no roads) to Johnsonville, a new settlement being hacked out of the jungle. Many died of malaria and other fevers during the first year. Although the Liberian government gave each family twenty-five undeveloped acres, the settlers first had to clear land to build a house and plant crops. Most planted coffee trees, the leading cash crop of the area, which required several years of maturation before yielding any income. Despite the difficult work, one of the settlers, N. M. Rogers, later wrote back to his family in Morrilton that he would not return to Arkansas even if "some one would give me a place there and stock to work it." Rogers said one of the things he liked best about Liberia was that "there are no white men to give orders; and when you go in your house, there is no one to stand out, and call you to the door and shoot you when you come out." Rogers encouraged the rest of his family to come at once to Liberia: "This is the colored man's home, the only place on earth where they can have equal rights, when you get a start it will last you until death."[38] (For the full text of Rogers's letter, see appendix D.)

By 1893 the back-to-Africa movement had virtually ended. The white men who earlier had terrorized blacks and stolen their votes to engineer the victory for the local Democratic Party now ran the county. The newly elected county sheriff, Dr. Ben White, planned to put to rest the disturbing events of recent years by bringing closure to the Clayton murder. That spring, a one-legged career criminal in Montana by the name of Charles N. Landers accused another scoundrel, Frank Hickey, of killing Clayton. The accuser, Landers, had a history of petty crimes and fallacious lawsuits in several states before he made this particular accusation, apparently to claim the $5,000 reward. At the time of the Clayton killing, Landers worked as a telegrapher at the railroad depot in Malvern, Arkansas. Afterward, he moved to Montana, where he ran a restaurant and hired Hickey as his cook. The two apparently became partners in crime, cracking safes and committing a variety of petty offenses. Unfortunately for Hickey, the two men had a falling out; while under the custody of a Montana sheriff, Landers accused Hickey of murdering John Clayton. When Montana authorities passed on word of the accusation to Arkansas, Sheriff Ben White traveled to Butte, Montana, to bring both the accused and the accuser to Morrilton for trial. As one of the inner circle of Democrats who engineered the violence in Plumerville in the 1880s, and with Bob Pate as his deputy sheriff, White spent a good amount of the county taxpayers' money in 1893 to pursue a story he must have known from the beginning was false.[39]

Irony abounded in the proceedings, which began with Hickey's preliminary trial on April 12, 1893. The hearing was before Oliver T. Bentley, the justice of the peace for Wellborn township, despite the fact the crime had been committed in Howard township. Hickey's lawyer for the hearing was Charles C. Reid Jr. These three, Sheriff White, Judge Bentley, and Attorney Reid, had themselves been under federal indictments in 1889 and were thus suspects in the murder they purportedly were trying now to solve.

When Landers came to the stand, he testified that he accompanied Hickey and another man named Flannery to Morrilton, where the two men were hired to kill Clayton for a fee of about two thousand dollars. Hickey and Flannery carried out the deed, Landers continued, while he used an outdoor toilet on the edge of Plumerville. Landers hypothesized that Hickey killed Clayton for the money, and that Flannery's motive was revenge. According to Landers, Flannery had served a term in the Arkansas penitentiary when Powell Clayton was governor and had sworn thereafter to kill Clayton. Flannery thought they were killing Powell Clayton, Landers said, when they mistakenly killed his brother, John. Landers testified that the man who hired Hickey to kill Clayton was Charles Pate, who had conveniently been killed two weeks before the trial and was thus unable to deny the charge. Landers specifically pointed out that the man was *not* Charles's brother, Deputy Sheriff Bob Pate, whom Landers identified in the crowd of onlookers in the courtroom.[40]

Landers's story was riddled with contradictions and impossibilities. At Hickey's trial in the fall, the members of the jury found Landers's testimony unbelievable. His lawyer presented numerous letters showing that Hickey was actually serving a term in an Oregon prison at the time of the Clayton murder. After just a few minutes of deliberation, the jury brought forward a verdict of not guilty against Frank Hickey.[41] His accuser, Landers, a professional swindler and con man, did not stop with this attempt to get easy money. A year later, Landers fell through a hole on a railroad platform at Sherman, Texas, and sued the train company. Landers could apparently on command pop his one leg out of joint to make it appear broken. He had used the ploy before to wage lawsuits in Indiana and Montana. By 1894 the Morrilton *Pilot* suggested: "If the people of Sherman would hang Landers to a convenient lamp post they would perform a public service and rid the country of a notorious crook."[42]

Even though Landers's story has all the markings of a fabrication, it reveals some interesting points about the Clayton murder. Landers lived in Arkansas when Clayton was killed and knew the outline of the story. His brother, J. S. Landers, lived in Greenbrier, only fifteen miles away from Plumerville, and may have shared bits and pieces of local gossip. Landers apparently tried to weave into his story as many plausible details as possible to make it sound convincing. The motive of revenge against Powell Clayton and mistaken identity fitted nicely with the Jack the Ripper letters and the Hooper theories much published by the Democratic newspapers in 1889. But Landers also pointed the finger of ultimate guilt directly at the Pate brothers, particularly Charles F. Pate. One suspects that the word about the Pate brothers' connection with the Clayton killing had circulated fairly widely, perhaps even to Greenbrier, for Landers to include their names in his story.

Accusing Charles Pate of murder instead of his brother Bob was also a safe move for Landers, for doing so pinned ultimate guilt on a dead man. On April 4, 1893, just a week before Sheriff White brought Landers and Hickey to Arkansas, Charles Pate was killed by an angry black man named Flannagan Thornton. As the elected constable of mostly black Howard township, Pate was arresting Thornton for disorderly conduct when the man shot him in the bowels. Pate died a few hours later. Thornton said Pate had shot at him first, and he merely defended himself. The black man, however, would never get a trial to determine his guilt or innocence.

Two weeks after Pate's death, Thornton was lynched by a white mob in Morrilton. His attorney, William L. Moose, who feared his client could be guaranteed neither personal safety nor a fair trial in Conway County, requested, and was granted, a change of venue by the circuit judge. But when Moose asked Sheriff White to send Thornton away *that* night, White refused and merely laughed at Moose's fears about a possible lynching, despite an emphatic statement earlier by the Morrilton *Pilot* that if Thornton were caught, "he will be treated to a dose of hemp." At eleven o'clock that evening, a group of about twenty-five disguised men broke in to the county jail, overpowered a black jailer, and removed Thornton. They hung him from the sign in front of

Black's store in downtown Morrilton and fired five shots into his body to make sure he was dead. When the sign collapsed and Thornton's body fell to the ground, the mob dragged Thornton by the neck to Sandlin's store next door, where they strung him up a second time, leaving his body there to be found the next morning. One man testified that after hearing pistol shots, he went out on the street and found Sheriff White and his deputy, Bob Pate, just moments after the lynching. They claimed to be hunting for the perpetrators of the deed.

Only one person was prosecuted for the Thornton lynching, the black jailer on duty when the crime was committed. The district's prosecuting attorney, Jeff Davis of Russellville, the later governor of Arkansas famous for his racism and demagoguery, ordered the jailer arrested and charged with being an accessory to the crime. Davis later boasted that when he had run for prosecuting attorney, he had said: "I told the boys around Morrilton, Russellville, and Plumerville, that if they elected me, I would fill the penitentiary so full of niggers their feet would be sticking out the windows."[43] With Davis in charge of the prosecution in combination with the racial climate in Conway County, Thornton's fate was set the moment he pulled the trigger to shoot a white man.

On the day after the lynching of Thornton, rumors circulated that blacks in Conway County were arming themselves for a march on Morrilton. Sheriff White apparently became so jumpy that when a construction train pulled into town in the middle of the night, making a considerable noise, he mistook it for an impending race riot. He at once summoned and armed some sleepy white citizens to form a cordon of pickets to defend the town. In their haste to quell the disturbance, one of the deputies accidentally discharged his shotgun, with the load entering the fleshy part of Sheriff White's leg.[44]

The mob who broke in to the county jail to get to Thornton must have passed right by imprisoned murder suspect Frank Hickey. It is no wonder that the Democratic gentry would fear an uprising of African Americans. The lynching occurred simultaneously with this travesty of a murder trial, presided over by Judge Oliver T. Bentley, the man who Republicans believed had actually planned the crime.

The brutal lynching of Flannagan Thornton provides a gruesome but fitting conclusion to this narrative about the creation of the New South in Conway County. Thornton, a black man, had struck back against an elected white official, one of the courthouse gang of Democrats that had themselves ruthlessly used violence to win public offices. He got for it not a trial but a swing on the end of a rope. This lynching, like all lynchings, resonated with symbolic value. A lynching demonstrated that the caste system was beyond challenge, that tyranny stood behind terror. No black man in Conway County was safe if he rose up against white authorities.[45]

Three decades later, on the night of December 9, 1922, the story of this lynching repeated itself. Less Smith, an African American, had shot a white deputy sheriff as he tried to arrest Smith on Main Street in downtown Morrilton. Before Smith could get a trial, a white mob burst into the jail, took the black man east of town, and hung him from a tree until dead. A high school boy watched the mob go past, knowing what they were going to do. That boy was C. Vann Woodward.[46]

5. Murder's Reward

Rule of the Fine-Haired Gentlemen

Plumerville, once a thriving town bustling with activity twice daily when the train arrived, is now a town slowly dying. A few large Victorian homes, some still inhabited by the old families, give testimony to a more prosperous past. But the entire business district that lay down by the tracks, including Malone's general store and Simms's hotel, has disappeared. Trains no longer stop here; they just whistle as they pass through on their way somewhere else.

By the early 1990s, one hundred years after the murder of John Clayton, the house where the deed was done stood crumbling with faded white paint peeling from the weathered boards. A rusting automobile sat immobile in the yard strewn with empty beer cans. Muddy holes with standing water interrupted the weedy grass, in summer becoming pockets of dust. But recently the owner has spruced up the house, covering it with a veneer of light blue vinyl siding. The residents of the neighborhood have heard stories that a crime once took place here. By the 1990s, the murder of John Clayton has become only a bit of vague, colorful folklore.

Those who governed Arkansas and wrote its history long ago covered up, and then dismissed, the killing of John Clayton as an unsolved mystery, just as the bright plastic siding today conceals the decaying remains of the house where he was murdered. But the long-term consequences of the murder and the events that accompanied it were nonetheless profound. Through methods of violence and fraud, Democrats returned to power in Conway County; they would never lose it again. To the date of this writing, no Republican has ever since been elected to a county office in Conway County. The Clayton assassination indeed set the pace for the following century of politics and race relations in the county.

The very Democrats who planned and executed the fraudulent elections, and conspired to commit political murder, went on to dominate county government for the next two decades. Oliver T. Bentley, the mastermind of Democratic political treachery, became justice of the peace for his township, mayor of Morrilton, and, from 1894 to 1900, county judge. Except for one two-year term, Thomas Hervey and Ben

Figure 18. Benjamin G. White, Democratic conspirator and later sheriff of Conway County. *(Morrilton Pilot, 1 September 1892.)*

White alternated as county sheriff between 1892 and 1912. After his career as sheriff, Hervey—the Democrat found guilty in federal court for election fraud—went on to serve as county judge from 1916 to 1919.

Besides their control of local government, Conway County's Democrats became the model politicians for turn-of-the-century Arkansas. Charles C. Reid, the young Morrilton lawyer whom a federal jury had found guilty of electoral fraud, was elected to replace Jeff Davis as prosecuting attorney for the four-county judicial circuit from 1894 to 1898. Afterward, he went on to serve five terms in the U.S. House of Representatives, representing Arkansas's fifth congressional district from 1901 to 1911. The young Democrat, whose political career started with a felony conviction for political crimes in Conway County, spent a decade in the U.S. Congress. After leaving Washington, he had a distinguished career as a professor of law at the University of Arkansas. Reid's law partner, William L. Moose, later served as state attorney general. Reid and Moose's young law clerk in the early 1890s, Charles Jacobsen, at age nineteen was named as Jeff Davis's assistant prosecuting attorney for Conway County in 1893 during the Hickey and Thornton cases. He went on to become Davis's campaign manager and chief lieutenant to the governor. Jacobsen was a Sidney Carton figure, silently doing the work of the governor's office while Davis traveled

Figure 19. Charles C. Reid Jr., Democratic conspirator who later became a U.S. congressman. *(Courtesy of University of Arkansas, Special Collections.)*

around the state giving rousing speeches. Finally, Carroll Armstrong, the Confederate veteran who led the Democratic Party of Conway County during these turbulent years, by 1894 had received his promotion to chairman of the central committee of the state Democratic Party. Morrilton's staunchly Democratic newspaperman and former mayor, Robert Leigh, won the state printing contract in 1891, the first time it was ever awarded outside of Little Rock. The state Democratic establishment thus well rewarded Conway County for its effective work for the party. The county served as an appropriate training ground for Arkansas's New South politicians.[1]

These fine-haired gentlemen, using Judge George Cunningham's words when he lectured the Conway County grand jury, may have lost the Civil War, but they won in the political struggle of the 1880s and early 1890s. As in the South in general, the county's Democratic establishment from Civil War days had been dominated by planters in the rich bottomlands. The sons of these planters would be more successful than their fathers. Oliver Bentley, Tom Hervey, Carroll Armstrong, and Walter Wells, Conway County's Democratic leaders, all were born shortly before the Civil War to prosperous, slave-owning planters in the bottomlands.[2] C. Vann Woodward's assertion that the planter class died after the Civil War, that the Old South and the New South were discontinuous, does not entirely ring true for Conway County. This county's experience supports Woodward's many critics who emphasize planter persistence and a continuity between Old South and New. This second generation of white elites continued the struggle against the small farmers that their fathers had begun in 1861. Unlike their fathers, who lost the war, the sons were victorious; they destroyed any pretensions to power by the coalition of poor farmers, black and white.

But on the other hand, Woodward was right. The sons of the antebellum planters, such as Bentley and Armstrong, were a different sort of men than their fathers; they had taken up businesses and professions. They were joined in leadership of the local Democratic Party by other middle-class townsfolk: lawyers, physicians, store owners, a banker, a newspaperman, a hotelier. Those who still farmed, such as Tom Hervey and Ben White, by the 1890s were moving from the bottomlands into town. The victors in this power struggle were these white men of Morrilton and Plumerville, the towns along the railroad, with daily mail, telegraph communication, and electric streetlights.[3] These men wore store-bought clothes, lounged in the lobby of the Speer hotel playing billiards, ate tinned oysters in the back of the drugstore, socialized at dances at the opera house or within clubs such as the Knights of Pythias, and attended the rapidly gentrifying Presbyterian and Methodist churches.

Their opposition, who lost in this power struggle, was an extraordinary though tenuous alliance of the rural poor, white Republican mountaineers, farmers on small plots of hilly land, and African Americans farming as tenants, sharecroppers, or day laborers on the big estates. These were men who wore homespun, who had never played billiards or eaten tinned food or a meal in a hotel, men whose evenings were illuminated by kerosene lanterns instead of electricity, men whose families attended the Baptist, Disciples of Christ, or AME churches, or not at all.

Contemporaries were aware of the widening gulf that separated townsfolk from country farmers. Alice French, who lived on a plantation near the Black River in northeastern Arkansas, wrote two articles in 1891 for *Atlantic Monthly* contrasting town life with rural life in Arkansas. After describing the rusticity of rural Arkansas folk, she painted a quite different picture of those who inhabited the growing towns.

> To speak frankly, the large-town man [she defines a large town as one that had more than one thousand inhabitants; Morrilton's population was nearly two thousand] has in a great measure come into the current of modern civilization. Even when he does not belong to the more educated class, he is a vastly more civilized being than his brother of the same rank in the country or the village. He is more alert, more impressionable, he talks better English, he reads the newspaper, he would like the Arkansas legislature to vote a generous appropriation for the World's Fair. In short, he is of the New South.

Mrs. French told the educated American reader that the Clayton assassination had unjustly given the entire state of Arkansas a bad name. Yes, Conway County had the reputation of "harboring more of the 'tough' element than any other county in the state," French continued, "But I suspect that were one to go to the wild Conway towns he would find them, like some other towns I have known under the same reproach, very mild mannered indeed."[4]

The portraits of Oliver Bentley, Benjamin White, and Charles Reid (included as illustrations with this text) do not suggest a group of toughs but instead well-dressed men of polite society. As historians of the South have shown in general, the end of democracy and the calcification of racist ideology in Conway County were the work of the county's "best" citizens and are associated with forces often considered progressive — town culture, commercialism, professionalism, and modern technology.[5]

With the fine-haired gentlemen of Arkansas controlling the courts, newspapers, and education, it is no surprise that Clayton's assassination remained unsolved. Generations of Arkansans would be schooled on state histories that presented the Clayton murder as a curious mystery.[6] Indeed, a calculated Democratic interpretation of the stormy events of the late 1800s began right away. In his classic study *The Strange Career of Jim Crow*, C. Vann Woodward says, "The twilight zone that lies between living memory and written history is one of the favorite breeding places of mythology." Clayton's lawyer, John McClure, the Republican stalwart nicknamed "Poker Jack" by his opponents, called attention to Democratic mythmaking as it was happening in the 1890s. In a speech to the Lincoln Club in Little Rock in 1891, he declared:

"The ghost of Reconstruction, and Clayton's militia has done yeoman service for the democracy for sixteen years, like Fox's Book of Martyrs, and the further they get away from it, the more terrible it is made to appear." By 1889 Conway County Democrats, for example, were saying Clayton's black militia in 1868 had ravished white women in the presence of their husbands, a new twist to the Reconstruction woes theme calculated to provoke an emotional reaction. The crimes committed in the New South of the last few years, McClure insisted, were creating a new set of myths. Like the Paris Commune's views of the crimes of Danton and Marat, McClure said, Democratic leaders of the New South saw the theft of ballot boxes and even political murders such as that of Clayton as "an excess of patriotism," not criminal actions.[7]

Among the descendants of the prominent white Democrats in Conway County, an ennobling myth still today surrounds the events described in this study. To keep alive the memory of the Lost Cause, old-timer rebel Colonel Anderson Gordon and Carroll Armstrong organized a chapter of the United Confederate Veterans in Morrilton in 1892.[8] But in a more informal way, stories about the old days have circulated and recirculated like a game of gossip chain, with each telling more flattering to the family of the tellers. Accounts of the Clayton murder and ballot box thefts abound. But generally the stores describe election engineering and the killing of Clayton as desperate attempts by prominent white citizens to "rescue" county government from the hands of blacks and carpetbaggers. John Mason's extraordinary oral account of these events, though rich in detail, confuses the 1880s with Reconstruction. The theft of ballots and Clayton's killing, as Mason told the story, were last-ditch efforts of local white citizens to end Reconstruction domination by the Republican Party. Similarly, Eleanor Wood Moose's account, published locally in 1976 but based on her conversations with actual participants in the 1920s, declared that Clayton's killing ended the carpetbaggers' domination of Conway County. The circle of conspirators who planned the assassination around the old coal stove in Malone's store, she said, "risked not only their lives but their immortal souls to save their community and their state. We at this late date may question their judgement," she concluded, "but never their courage or their patriotism."[9]

It should not surprise that stories told by these descendants of Conway County Democrats flatter their ancestors. More interesting is how such tales have reconstructed history to make the Democratic triumph of 1888 to 1889 the end of Reconstruction. These histories eliminated the twenty years of multiparty, biracial democracy in Arkansas that followed Reconstruction's end in 1874. They forgot or ignored that Republicans won the county elections in 1884 and 1886 through a fair vote of all adult male citizens. Although Woodward and his followers tend to draw a neat dividing line between Old South and New South, these oral accounts, with all their errors, have correctly recognized the continuity between the Civil War and the political struggles of the late 1880s. The storytellers understood somehow that the conflicts unleashed in 1861 did not end until Democrats finally "rescued" the county through such extraordinary means in 1889.[10]

In 1904 a former leader of the Agricultural Wheel in Arkansas, W. Scott Morgan of Hardy, published a novel entitled *The Red Light: A Story of Southern Politics and Election Methods.* Morgan tried to combine a conventional turn-of-the-century sentimental romance with an exposé of Democratic corruption in Arkansas. With thinly veiled pretense at disguising people and places, Morgan described how the Democratic conspirators in a desolate county seat near the Arkansas River called Morriston planned and then executed the theft of a ballot box in a lonely town called Hummersville. When the Republican congressional candidate, John M. Claiborne, who lost the election, came to Hummersville to investigate, he was murdered by a blast of buckshot shot through the window of his boardinghouse. The man who planned all the Democratic conspiracy was, in Morgan's account, Bentley Murdoch, a man with "dark, sinister features," which bore "the unmistakable stamp of crime." Evidently Morgan had never seen a picture of baby-faced Oliver T. Bentley. W. Scott Morgan's "fictional" tale comes closer to the truthful story of Clayton's murder than any other written account, yet the book failed to make it into the collection of any library in Arkansas.[11]

So much for the winners in the battle; but what happened to the losers? The Wheel-Alliance movement of Conway County and Arkansas, by its antimerchant, antilawyer, antitown rhetoric, by opening its organization to black farmers, by specific measures to bypass merchants and create a countereconomy, and most of all by efforts to take and use county and state government, displayed radically class-conscious ideas and actions. But after the new election laws, the farmers' movement faded rapidly in Conway County just as it was reaching its zenith elsewhere in the United States. The Populist Party did not even field a local ticket in the 1894 election. In the congressional election that fall, Conway County gave the smallest percentage of votes (8.66 percent) for the Populist candidate of any county in the district. Many voters were doubtless disfranchised by the restrictive election laws. The Populists still tried to register as many of their voters as they could, a local correspondent informed the *Gazette*. But when an unspecified "confusion" arose, the reporter said, the Populists "gave up in great disgust and are feeling as badly whipped as they are."[12]

Kousser's study of suffrage restriction shows that the secret ballot law and the poll tax curtailed the white vote in Arkansas by almost 20 percent, from 75 percent voting in the 1890 gubernatorial election to 56 percent in 1894. In Conway County, the gubernatorial vote declined by 21 percent between 1890 and 1892, and a further 23 percent between 1892 and 1894. After the secret ballot and poll tax "reforms," 44 percent fewer residents of Conway County were voting. Not just African Americans in the county were disfranchised by these electoral "reforms."[13] Kousser may have overestimated, however, the extent to which disfranchisement targeted poor whites. The lower percentage of whites voting after 1892 may have resulted from a growing apathy, a recognition that the battle was already lost. Conway County's agrarian Populists appear to have been pragmatists, willing to vote even for Republican candidates, instead of Union Labor candidates, if they had a greater chance of defeating their Democratic opposition. It is very difficult to assess Populist electoral strength in the Conway County elections because the Populists had so frequently placed Republicans on their tickets.

The white Republicans of the county, whose party loyalties had been forged in the Civil War, increasingly joined with the Farmers' Alliance in the 1890s. The party leaders of the 1880s had largely fled the county, fearing for their lives after the debacle of 1888 to 1889. Harry Coblentz, the party boss, had fled to the state of Washington after his fight with Oliver Bentley. Charles Wahl moved his family to Jefferson County. W. P. Allnutt, the Republican who witnessed Clayton's depositions and ultimately his death, by 1890 had relocated to Clarksville, in Johnson County. The white Republicans who remained were the small farmers of the northern hills around Center Ridge. With their camp of the GAR and Sons of Veterans, the minority of Union veterans and their families kept their allegiance to the Party of Lincoln long after the agrarian movement had died. In 1920, when Republican candidate Warren G. Harding won the presidential election, one longtime resident of the area could hear the celebrations in Center Ridge from five miles away. The area's last surviving Union soldier, Frank Stobaugh, who had served as drummer for Captain Williams's independent company, led a ritual parade every Memorial Day in Center Ridge. Wearing his Union uniform and beating his old drum, he headed a small procession of Union veterans to the local cemetery. He continued the tradition well into the 1920s, even when he was the only one left, with his grandson following behind him carrying the U.S. flag.[14]

Republican allegiance in the northern townships could not outlast the Great Depression. Conway County, as elsewhere in Arkansas, was hit hard in the 1930s by drought and deflated prices for farm products. With New Deal federal assistance doled out locally by the Democratic county officials, Republican loyalties waned rapidly. Three generations in the Bird family illustrate the transition that took place. In 1862 George T. Bird of Springfield joined Captain Jeff Williams's company of Union men in the northern part of the county, and he was killed by rebel snipers in 1864. His son, William T. Bird, who ran a general store near Springfield, identified himself as a Republican in the county history published in 1890. During the Great Depression, however, Williams's son, William M. Bird, voted for the Democratic Party, posted a large photograph of Franklin Roosevelt in the family store, and even joined the new Ku Klux Klan.[15]

In the next decade, a country boy named Marlin Hawkins from formerly Republican Center Ridge began his career in county government. As county sheriff from 1951 to 1978, Hawkins built arguably the most formidable Democratic county machine in Arkansas. To many observers, the county became the epitome of the one-party South, perhaps even a caricature of the image of the backward southern fiefdom run by an overweight sheriff with a thick Dixie drawl. Sheriff Hawkins's Conway County was an area the American Automobile Association warned visiting motorists to avoid. Ironically, the county's wealthiest citizen, Winthrop P. Rockefeller, the New York Republican who moved to Petit Jean Mountain in the 1950s, would help rebuild the Republican Party in Arkansas and became in 1966 the first Republican governor in Arkansas since Reconstruction.[16]

Like white Republicans, another perceived threat to the southern Democrats in Conway County, the foreign immigrant population, faded away as time wore on. Around 1880 the sudden arrival of hundreds of German Catholic families threatened to overwhelm white Protestant culture in the county seat, Morrilton. The German immigration had virtually ceased by the later 1880s, as most of the railroad land was sold. Cholera, malaria, and other assorted fevers took their toll on the newcomers unaccustomed to the subtropical climate.[17] Still, in 1890 only five of the seventy-five Arkansas counties had a larger foreign-born population than Conway County. While the native white population of the county continued to increase in the 1890s, the numbers of foreign-born citizens actually declined in the decade, from 578 to 383. With social life revolving around their church and school, they remained a community within a community.[18] The "ethnics" who had become involved in local GOP ranks, such as the Volga German Charles Wahl and German American Harry Coblentz, had left the county fearing for their lives. The German Catholics who remained turned out to be no threat after all. By 1890 the German Brass Band performed at Democratic rallies. Catholic residents gave the Democrats their unswerving loyalty by the turn of the century, when the courthouse gang opposed prohibition and kept the county wet while all the contiguous counties went dry.

The Holy Ghost Fathers reluctantly gave up their dreams for a thriving Catholic mission administered from Morrilton. The seminary and novitiate were transferred from Marienstatt monastery to suburban Pittsburgh in 1884, and the Fathers leased and sold most of their lands to local farmers. Marienstatt died as a monastic community in the spring of 1892 when a tornado completely destroyed the church and farm buildings, leaving only the wooden residence standing, but blown off its foundation and leaning precariously against a tree. The community moved into town, joining with the new parish Church of the Sacred Heart, being built to replace the sisters' chapel.[19]

The Catholic efforts to evangelize and educate the local black population also ended in the Jim Crow era. The bishop of Arkansas, Edward Fitzgerald, reported in 1891 that racial prejudice had become so intense that black families were fleeing Morrilton and neighboring Conway. These migrating families, going to Liberia and elsewhere, the bishop explained, had been the mainstay of the Catholic black schools in the two towns.[20] Prejudice against blacks and Catholics eventually intensified to the point that Fitzgerald advised the Holy Ghost Fathers and Cluny Sisters to stop educating African Americans until a later time when anti-Catholic agitation had diminished. The Catholic school for black children closed its doors in Morrilton in 1898.[21]

Of all the groups in Conway County's power struggle, African Americans lost the most. In their election engineering, Conway County Democrats concentrated their attack on what they perceived as the weakest link in the coalition of the rural poor, the two thousand blacks of Howard township. The lynching of Flannagan Thornton in 1893 illustrates well how the color line hardened in Conway County after Democrats solidified their hold on county offices in the 1890s. By the early 1900s, Democrats in the county, as elsewhere in the South, no longer pretended that their party was color-blind. When Carroll Armstrong gave notice by newspaper of the Democratic primary in 1904, he announced that only white Democrats were eligible to vote.[22]

Shut out from politics, African Americans were increasingly excluded from social intercourse with white citizens. Without romanticizing an earlier era, the evidence available suggests that a harsher, more inflexible culture of white racism had set in with the political struggles of the 1880s and 1890s. One sign of this was the decline in black-white cohabitation in the county between 1880 and 1900. The number of blacks living in a subservient position with a white head of household (as servant, cook, laborer, etc.) remained stable between 1880 and 1900. However, census returns show a substantial decline in the number of black households that contained whites as boarders. In 1880 a surprising fourteen households headed by African Americans contained whites as boarders or laborers. In 1900, despite the fact that the white and black population had increased substantially (by 55 percent in the two decades), only one black household included whites. One lone black man had living with him two white children, presumably orphans. Similarly, the 1880 census records four interracial male-female couples living together in Conway County. But twenty years later, no interracial romantic unions were publicly displayed. Interracial cohabitation in Conway County had brought Klan terror in 1868 when the KKK attacked the two black men who lived with white women. Again in 1871 whites terrorized a black family that had adopted an orphaned white girl. But the proscription against blacks and whites living under the same roof obviously did not become ironclad until later.[23]

Unfortunately, it is impossible to determine if this shift in habitation patterns occurred before or after the Jim Crow laws because the manuscript returns for the 1890 census were destroyed by fire. Anecdotal evidence, however, suggests a sharp increase in white racism in Arkansas during the late 1880s and early 1890s. Frederick Douglass visited Arkansas for the first time in February 1889 to lecture in Little Rock and Pine Bluff about the "self-made man." He arrived just when the state was reeling from news of the Clayton assassination. A Little Rock restaurant refused him admission, and Douglass claimed it was the first time in his life that he had been turned away because of his color. Just a few months later, when a Mr. Wooten, a white landowner who lived south of Morrilton, sold some of his land and a cotton gin to several black men, a band of young white men burned down the gin house and forced Wooten to flee the area. Economic self-sufficiency was not to be allowed for African Americans.[24]

The testimony of local residents in Conway County revealed that as late as 1888, blacks and whites drank whiskey together in the same saloon and gambled together at dice games in Plumerville. On the night of Clayton's assassination, both whites and blacks had gathered at a barbershop in Plumerville to watch some black men dance and play the fiddle and banjo. Charles Wahl, the white Republican, before the attempt on his life in December 1888, had made arrangements to sleep in the boardinghouse run by a black woman, Eliza Mason. However, by 1890 the *Arkansas Gazette* noted the opening of a new, specifically black tavern in Morrilton, which blacks called the U.S. Court Saloon. Probably quoting the Morrilton *Headlight*, the *Gazette* concluded that the new bar, "where old 'topes' and coons enjoy themselves," would cast a gloom over the city. As if this constituted a new development, the paper noted that several more taverns were to be put "in negro dives."[25]

Changes in language also reflected a more stridently racist attitude. Previously articles in the *Gazette* had customarily referred to African Americans as Negroes, coloreds, or darkies. But by 1889 terms such as *nigger* and *coon* began to appear with frequency. Typical of the more shrill and hostile tone, the Morrilton *Pilot* in the 1892 campaign railed against the black candidate for representative, W. M. D. Jones, saying, "If the people want the blackest 'nigger' in Arkansas to represent them in Little Rock, they should at once set their wits at work to elect Jones." The paper's editor, Robert Leigh, complained the next year when McKendree College, a white school in Illinois, planned to admit a black girl named May Turner. Notwithstanding the student's many accomplishments, Leigh said, "It's dollars to doughnuts that with all her musk and other refinements, she smells to heaven on a warm day just the same as any other nigger."[26]

By the later 1890s, the idea of African Americans participating in politics had become merely an amusement among Conway County Democrats. At a picnic and campaign rally on a sultry Fourth of July in the 1890s, Charles Jacobsen, Conway County's young Democrat on the way up, introduced candidates from both political parties for the standard speeches. One Republican candidate for tax assessor was a black schoolteacher from Plumerville. Jacobsen remembered the man sweating profusely as he stood in the hot sun to speak, wearing a black Prince Albert coat that hung down to his knees. "Fellow citizens," the candidate said, "I appears before you today as a perspirant for de office of tax possessor." Jacobsen said the black man could not understand why he was so wildly cheered.[27]

African Americans in Conway County had more to worry about than mere ridicule, however. In 1895 a black man was accused of the attempted rape of a white girl in Morrilton. Promptly tried and found guilty, he applied to the governor for a new trial and was denied. He was hung on the evening of June 7, 1895. Just a week later, however, the situation was reversed when a Morrilton white man attempted to rape a black girl. As she struggled with the brute, the girl's father heard her cries and ran to her relief. The father used a club to free his daughter, and a posse of black men caught the fleeing offender. Whereas the black man accused of attempted rape had been hung the week before, this time the county court fined the white attacker fifty dollars. But the court also fined the black girl's father fourteen dollars for using force to rescue his daughter from the would-be white rapist.[28]

Ironically, the largest number of Conway County's black residents had come in the early 1880s from Edgefield and neighboring counties in South Carolina to escape racial terror and the flagrant denial of their most basic rights. Conway County, Arkansas, was supposed to be their promised land. But by the early 1890s, the desperation and hysteria of the back-to-Africa movement shows just how dreadful conditions really were for African Americans in Conway County. Besides the Africa migration, hundreds more fled to Oklahoma and later to points north. Following two decades of phenomenal growth in the black population, the number of African Americans in the county actually declined in the 1890s. The black proportion of the county's population had gone down continually ever since. One hundred years later, in 1990, Conway County had almost exactly the same population it did in 1890, but less than half as many black citizens.

Conway County's experience sheds light on the relationship between violence and racism. Before Arkansas's Jim Crow laws, white violence toward blacks had clear political motivations. Democrats did not want to lose power to anyone, white or black. Poor whites in the northern hills of the county and African Americans had collectively opposed Democratic elites since Reconstruction days when the black and white Republican militia battled the Ku Klux Klan. By the 1880s, white Republicans and Wheelers were the smaller parts of the coalition opposing the Democratic Party. Blacks, however, numbered almost 40 percent of the voting population. More than anyone, the black voter threatened Democratic control. When violence and disfranchisement removed most black voters, the remaining opposition was an insignificant minority.

As an organized, politically conscious, and mobilized group that wielded power through the ballot box, African Americans were much less a victim than a foe before 1890. White Democrats in Conway County continually expressed their fears of the black community. Throughout the period, rumors circulated in the white community of black plans to mob Lewisburg and Morrilton, to burn buildings, and to take white property, even the daughters of white residents. Democratic violence aimed to destroy not blacks but white fears. No evidence suggests, however, that blacks in the county ever organized violently except for self-protection—after the disarming of blacks and Klan terror in 1868, in response to night riding in 1885, and in 1890 when blacks joined with armed white Republicans to police the Plumerville polls. Nonetheless, these fears reveal white perceptions of blacks. Whites spoke not of blacks voting, exercising their rights as citizens, but of mob violence, as if blacks were incapable of anything else.

The racial violence in Conway County before 1892, despicable though it might be, had a political purpose. After electoral fraud, terror, and finally the Jim Crow laws removed the African American as a political threat, the terror continued.[29] As the Thornton lynching of 1893 illustrates, the violence became less political and more purely racial. This New South violence may have been then more insidious, for it was perpetrated against an already vanquished foe.

The murder of John Clayton established the precedent that politically motivated crimes committed by the white Democratic establishment would go unpunished in Conway County. But Clayton's murder was just the climax of three decades of political violence. This account began with a war and ended with a lynching, demonstrating how violence was used consistently to attain political goals from 1861 to 1893. War is by definition an act of political violence. The Civil War had divided Conway County into rival groups, subsistence farmers and planters and their allies, each willing to kill each other to achieve their differing political objectives. James McPherson, the eminent Civil War historian, has shown us recently how highly politicized common folk and soldiers became during the war. Both Union and Confederate troops, he argues, really believed in the political cause for which they were fighting.[30] In Conway County, these soldiers and their kin at the war's end had to live together in the same community. It is no wonder that a state of virtual warfare existed in the county for the next thirty years, until one side finally won.

Both political sides had used violence. Union soldiers and guerrillas had been ruthless to local rebel families during the Civil War. Black and white Republicans organized into paramilitary bands in 1868 to protect the civil rights of freedmen and to combat the terror of the Ku Klux Klan. They had again responded with a show of arms in the 1890 election in an attempt to ensure a fair vote. But it was Democratic elites who relied most on the use of violence as a political weapon and who used it most effectively. From marauding attacks on freedmen in 1867 to Klan terrorism in 1868 and 1885, to the long list of victims in the late 1880s and early 1890s, Democrats established a pattern of physical violence used to intimidate their political opposition. When intimidation was insufficient, the violence spilled into the polling place with theft of ballots at gunpoint and ultimately murder. Through such measures, Democrats in Conway County beat back the challenge in the 1880s by a 40 percent black minority, a smaller but significant number of white Republicans from the northern hills, and the mainly white agrarian populists mobilized by the Agricultural Wheel.

These tactics brought Democrats back to power in Conway County. The Arkansas General Assembly, elected through such measures, would keep them there with the Jim Crow and restrictive voting laws of the 1890s. This is the sad conclusion to the story of Conway County: political violence and electoral fraud worked. The men who conspired to murder John Clayton paid no earthly price for their crimes. Instead, as model politicians of the New South, they ran the county and helped govern the state and nation for the next generation.

Appendix A

Testimony of E. H. Womack and W. D. Allnutt to the U.S. House of Representatives Committee on Elections, Little Rock, May 6, 1890

E. H. Wamuck [*sic*] called, sworn, examined and testified.
Direct ex.:

Q. Where do you reside?
A. I live out here in Benton, Saline County.
Q. Were you in Plummerville on the 29th of January, 1889?
A. Yes, sir. . . .
Q. What time in the night did you get to Mrs. McCraven's house?
A. I think it was about 7 o'clock, or a little after 7. I know it was pretty late when the train got up there.
Q. Did you get supper then?
A. No, sir.
Q. Where did you get your supper then?
A. I got it from Mrs. McCraven.
Q. How long after you got there until you got supper?
A. Just a few minutes. She told me she would fix me supper. They had all been to supper.
Q. She did fix you some supper?
A. Yes, sir.
Q. After you got your supper where did you go?
A. I went into the room where Allnutt and Mr. Clayton was.
Q. Had you been in the room in the early part of the evening?
A. No, sir.
Q. Your first appearance there was after supper?
A. Yes, sir.
Q. Were you acquainted with either of these people?
A. No, sir.
Q. Were you introduced to either of them?
A. Well, not in there; there—they was busy talking. Mrs. McCraven said she would introduce me to them, but they was busy talking, and I just sat down; I didn't have anything to say.

From *Digest of Contested Election Cases*, 739–47.

Q. Did you know either of them at that time?

A. No, sir.

Q. They were both strangers?

A. Yes, sir; but I had learned their names; Mrs. McCraven had told me at supper that Mr. Clayton and Mr. Allnutt were there; she told me she would go in there and introduce them, but they was busy.

Q. What were they doing?

A. I believe then — I don't think they was doing anything but just sitting talking. They was very busy at their books, maybe, and was sitting down. I was sitting down near the table and Mr. Allnutt and Mr. Clayton was close to me, and they were talking.

Q. How long did they remain in that position?

A. I don't remember, but I think Mr. Clayton got up and Mr. Allnutt picked up a paper and was reading a paper.

Q. Sitting near the window?

A. Sitting near the table where the lamp was, right close the window.

Q. How long did they remain there at the table?

A. Well, I don't know exactly; within some 20 or 30 minutes, maybe longer; I couldn't tell exactly.

Q. What was Clayton doing during that interval?

A. Well, now I think I know he was walking the floor for some time.

Q. Was he talking to anybody?

A. Yes, sir; he was talking to Mr. Allnutt as he walked.

Q. Was any portion of their conversation addressed to you?

A. No, sir.

Q. What did he appear to be talking to Allnutt about?

A. Well, he was talking about the election, in the conversation, one thing and another in Conway County. Well, Allnutt was telling him how they had conducted the election.

Q. In that tp. [township] or some other?

A. In that tp. I don't know of any other, but I think may be somebody spoke about Woodruff; I paid no attention.

Q. Where did you say Allnutt was sitting?

A. By the table near the window.

Q. About how late in the evening was Allnutt sitting reading the paper?

A. Well, I expect it was something like half after 7 maybe. Of course it may not be just correct, but something a little after or half after 7 when I went in there, and I sat down there and they sat and talked some, and

Clayton got up and Allnutt got the paper and sat down and was reading. He was sitting down there reading a newspaper.

Q. Well, what then?

A. Well, I, after I sat a while I said I had some writing to do, had some figuring to do. My business was stoneware business, and I had delivered some of my wares at Russell, and was shipping some back from Plummerville to Russell and had to go back there to collect, and get down next day to Little Rock. I had some figuring to do, and when he got up I sat down and was figuring some 20 or 30 minutes, and was writing. It was about 9 o'clock and I was tired and I concluded to go to bed. During that time I was there, almost all the time, Mr. Clayton was walking to the door, and then to the bed and then back to the door, so he walked and turned around back and forth. When I got up out of the chair, he come and didn't get more than halfway down in the chair until the gun was fired, and I said to Mr. Allnutt the lamp had exploded, and he said no it was somebody had killed Clayton. And I said let's pick him up, maybe he ain't dead, and he said somebody shot him through the window. He said "That is just as I expected." He said he was looking for something like that. I said "Is that so?" to Mr. Allnutt, and he said "of course, don't you hear the blood running there. The blood is running just like water out of a jug," and I noticed it after he called my attention to it; at the time I didn't know. The concussion had blowed the lamp out and there was just a little fire in the fire-place. We could just see the body of the man to see he was lying there. We just walked into the other room where Mrs. McCraven was and she asked what was the matter, and we said somebody had shot Clayton. And just about that time there was three persons came in, she said they were her boarders, and we got a lamp and walked back, and we found he had fallen right back with his feet hanging over his chair; I don't think he ever moved at all. . . .

W. D. Allnutt, called, sworn, examined, and testified.

Direct ex.:

Q. Where do you reside?

A. Clarksville, Johnson County.

Q. Where were you on the night of January 29th, 1890?

A. Plummerville.

Q. Where had you been in business and how was you engaged prior to that day?
A. I had been down there taking depositions between Clayton and Breckinridge.
Mr. Cooper. Were they being taken before you or were you acting as attorney?
A. I was notary public; they were being taken before me.
Mr. McClure. About what time in the evening did you and Mr. Clayton get your supper?
A. I suppose somewhere about 7 o'clock.
Q. About how long was you getting your supper?
A. I couldn't tell you about that; I didn't pay any particular attention to the time; I suppose we were at the table about as long as it usually takes a man to eat a meal.
Q. 15 or 20 minutes?
A. Yes, sir.
Q. Did you take supper at Mrs. McCraven's house?
A. Yes, sir.
Q. After you got your supper where did you go next?
A. We remained there all night.
Q. All the balance of the evening?
A. Yes, sir, excepting a few minutes when I went out of the room after he was shot and sent somebody down after a doctor.
Q. Do you know a man named Wamuck [*sic*]?
A. Yes, sir.
Q. Was he in the room the time Clayton was shot?
A. Yes, sir.
Q. How long had he been in the room prior to the shot?
A. He had been there ever since supper; he went in about the time we did, I think.
Mr. Cooper. Is that a sort of a sitting-room for the house as well as a bed-room?
A. Yes, sir.
Q. That is the reason the other folks were in there as well as him?
A. Yes sir. I will not say Wamuck came in with us; it is possible he didn't come until after we had been to supper, but I am under the impression he was there before that.
Mr. McClure. Tell how you spent the early part of the evening; what were you doing after supper?

A. We were in the room talking.

Q. Were you engaged at work there in the preparation of any papers?

A. I was not.

Q. Was he?

A. I don't remember that he was now.

Q. You were just holding a casual conversation?

A. When we first went into the room after supper I sat down and commenced reading a paper, and I think I read there probably 15 or 20 minutes, and I got up from there and went across on the opposite side of the fire-place, and Mr. Wamuck sat down in the chair and he had a little memorandum book he was figuring in.

Q. How long would you think Wamuck was there?

Mr. Cooper. There is a diagram Mr. Wamuck made this morning which is in use; it shows the house and the surroundings.

Mr. McClure. Is this paper now shown you approximately a correct diagram of the house of Mrs. McCraven?

A. Yes, sir; the shape of the house.

Q. And the surrounding grounds?

A. Yes, sir.

Q. Mark the sitting-room, dining-room, and Mrs. Craven's room, etc., mark them 1, 2, 3, 4, 5, 6, and so they can be identified. (Witness does so.)

Q. Now, about what time in the evening was it that Mr. Clayton was shot?

A. Well, sir, as near as I can get at it it was about 10 minutes before 8 o'clock.

Q. Before 8?

A. Yes, sir.

Q. How do you fix the time?

A. I started to tell awhile ago.

Q. Well, go on.

A. When we first came out from supper I sat down to the table, took a newspaper, and read there probably 10 or 15 minutes, or maybe a little longer; then I got up and went over on the other side of the fire-place and Wamuck sat down and figured a little while, probably as much longer; then when he got up to walk across to the fire-place where I was sitting in the chair I got up and invited him to take a seat, and I went over on the other side, and just as I got up to go Mr. Clayton was shot, and I am satisfied it was in about that time. I gather it from that, and when the doctor came up there the first thing was to take out Clayton's watch and look at it.

Q. Was the watch going?

A. Yes, sir.

Q. What time of day was it by the watch?

A. 5 minutes after 8, and he had been dead then, I suppose, 10 or 15 minutes.

Q. Who was in the house when he was shot; was there any other man?

A. There was no man in the house except Mr. Wamuck and myself; Mrs. McCraven's grandson had gone down town; Wamuck was a stranger; I didn't feel like going down there.

Mr. Cooper. You had no watch?

A. No, sir.

Mr. McClure. Wamuck had no watch?

A. I don't know about that. I went into Mrs. McCraven's room and took a lamp and went back into the room where he was, and about the time we got back in these young men came in, and so we sent them down town after the doctor, and by the time they got down there and back they told anybody else they saw that Mr. Clayton had been killed; they went down there and got Dr. Allgood, and when he got up there Mr. Clayton had been dead, I suppose, 10 or 15 minutes.

Q. What examination, if any, was made that night, if any?

A. Out of doors, do you mean?

Q. Oh, no; but in the house, of the body.

A. They examined the body, and took what he had on his person, his watch and money and papers and letters. Dr. Allgood took them off and turned them over to me; we raised him up from where he was lying in the blood and laid him over a little closer to the wall, and put a pillow or something under his head and put a sheet over him and let him lie there all night. Some of them suggested that we take him up and put him on the bed, but I suggested we had better let him stay where he was until the inquest was held. I told them I thought probably it would be better to let him stay there where he was until the coroner's jury viewed the remains or until somebody would come and take charge of it.

Mr. Maish. If I understand you correctly you say you removed the remains of Mr. Clayton?

A. Yes, sir; we just picked him up out of the blood and laid him over a little nearer to the wall.

Q. Did you take him off of the chair where he was lying?

A. Yes, sir; we took his feet down off there and straightened him out, took his shoes off, and put a sheet over him. . . .

Q. What took place the next morning now, so far as making examinations as to tracks was concerned?

A. The first thing next morning when I got up, about sunrise or a little before, it is my impression Mr. Wamuck went with me, and I went out to look for tracks. I first called Mr. Armstrong and woke him, and said we would go out and see if we could see any of these tracks, and after he had dressed he made the remark he would go down to the telegraph office and see if any telegrams had come for him, and for me to go out and look for tracks, and I think Mr. Wamuck went with me, and part way anyhow. He was out to that gate and went in through the gate. I don't remember now, but think he went back to the house, and I went out there to that hole where they come through, and there I turned around and came back.

Q. What did you see in the way of tracks?

A. I saw some tracks of two men coming in and two men going out.

Q. So they returned by the same path they came in?

A. Yes, sir; they went right back the same way, but they didn't strike the same place in the fence. One of them ran right against the fence and knocked off a picket or two from the looks of the hole; he had run over something and fell through the hole. . . .

Mr. Cooper. Do you know how heavy that load was; was it a shotgun and shot?

A. It was loaded with powder and buck-shot. I don't know what the gun was.

Q. Whereabouts did it hit him?

A. Right under the ear; right there [indicating].

Q. Do you know how many buck-shot entered his neck there?

A. No, sir; I don't know how many there were and I did hear Mr. Cook, the undertaker, say too [*sic*]. I don't think he found the whole lot. I think some buck-shot was in his body when he was taken away; it nearly shot his ear off, it was hanging by the skin.

Q. Did Wamuck state that his first impression was the lamp had exploded?

A. Yes, sir; he said, My God, that lamp has exploded and killed Mr. Clayton. And I said to him, some fellow had shot him through the window. I used a very ugly word.

Q. He said you used the word, "as I expected." Did you say that?

A. I don't remember about that, but it's very probable I did say it.

Q. Did you have any reason to expect or to suspect he would be shot?

A. No, sir; but I felt just all the time I was down there that it was a dangerous piece of business; I can't tell why, but I felt that way. . . .

Q. Were you engaged after the coroner's jury had rendered its verdict to put matters in shape and kept you longer than you would have been?

A. It seems to me that I wrote some after that. I picked up a pencil and wrote some for the coroner, but I do not remember what.

Q. Who was on that jury?

A. I couldn't name a man that was on it. I knew several of the men, but I can't tell now.

Q. See if you can't call some of them; who summoned the jury?

A. I think Mr. Bently [*sic*] summoned the jury. Yes, sir; I remember one man was on there is man named Patterson was on the jury, and a man named Pate, Robert Pate, and probably a man named Sagg was on it. I am not sure about him, but I rather think he was.

Appendix B

Judge George S. Cunningham's Charge to the Conway County Grand Jury, March 4, 1889

I come here to plead for law and asked them what it was that protected their wives, their children, and their homes in their absence on business or pleasure; what it was that protected their lives from murderers, their property from theft, and their homes from arson — and reminded them that it was the law, I told them that the people who lived in the towns could easily summon aid when needed, by beck or call, but that those who lived in the country had no Sheriff, no Marshal, no Constable, no near neighbors convenient to aid them in trouble, but that their sole reliance was on the law. Law is a rule of conduct not for the poor, the weak, or the humble alone, but it is also a rule of conduct for the rich, the strong, and the powerful; that it is universal in its application and should be enforced against all alike. An accessory is one who stands by and aids or abets the commission of an offense or not being present aiding or abetting the commission of an offense, has indorsed [*sic*] or encouraged it and is just as guilty in morals as he is in law as the principal offender. And as a general rule is punished the same. Bear in mind this law and you will have plenty of work to do in this county. You will have to investigate the Clayton assassination and whoever aided or abeted [*sic*] by word or deed in that cowardly butchery should be dragged by the throat to justice. They should not be exempt from punishment because of any standing or influence in the community. I do not know who they are. I wish to Heaven I did. I would tell you, but mind you, political assassinations do not originate in the minds of men in the humble walks of life. Men who earn their living by the sweat of their brows, whose lives are poems of honor of industry, do not find it in their minds and hearts to conceive assassinations; but it is conceived and planned by more influential, fine-haired gentlemen who pretend to be respectable. While the cowardly villain who fired the gun that killed Clayton should be caught and hung, the main object of our search should be the dastardly conspirators who instigated it. Some men seemingly want to apologize for or extenuate the horror of this murder on the ground of politics. They remind me of the doctor who

From *Arkansas Gazette*, 10 March 1889.

was a dead shot on fits and every patient he had he had to throw him into fits. They want to throw it into politics. I tell you there is no Democracy or Republicanism in murder. I had as soon punish a Democratic murder as a Republican murder; and I want to appeal to you as Democrats to punish crime, whether the criminal is a Democrat or a Republican; and if the Democracy does this, it will rule the country and rule it forever.

This great Government of ours is sending a fleet and about to engage in war with one of the most powerful nations of Europe because the rights of American citizenship have been ignored and violated in the rocky island of Samoa, 1,000 miles in the South Pacific. It is said our flag fails to protect our citizens there whom it purports and ought to protect. Now I would be willing to sink every dollar's worth of property in this country to show that flag is not an unnecessary symbol or hollow sham, but to convince the world that in truth it does protect American citizenship everywhere. They are entitled to its protection. What do you think of a man who would be found running around and inquiring about a man's politics who had been outraged in Samoa: whether he was a Democrat or Republican? a black man or a white man? The question would not be, "Is he a Democrat or a Republican? a white man or black man?" but "Is he an American citizen?" And the same jealous care ought to be exerted by the courts to protect their rights at home as is used to protect them abroad.

Now, gentlemen, something occurred right here in this town, and the parties who participated in the disgraceful affair ought to be indicted. An American citizen was met at the depot and kicked and cuffed from the depot to the hotel. His hair was pulled, and he was shot with a bullet from a bean-shooter. I say this was a violation of the rights of American citizenship. Mr. Benjamin did not come here to bull-doze anybody—one man could not have done that—but confessedly to see that there was a fair election. If that was his object, it would not have hurt you at all if you had an honest and fair election. It would have been a compliment to you to have had a political enemy present to witness and testify to that fact. This Jury decides questions according to the facts and law, and that is government. This country decides questions by the ballot, and that is government, and every person who opposes a fare [*sic*] and free ballot is a revolutionist, and an enemy to his country.

For the love of justice don't go out and indict some poor fellow for not working the roads when perhaps his family need his services, or some poor, ragged mountaineer for killing a deer on Sunday to satisfy his hunger, and then march into court with measured tread and pharisaical look and say you find nothing against these other men. Don't fool away your time after minnows when there are whales in sight. If you must make a discrimination get after these prominent men and let the others go.

There is no man with three ideas above an oyster who does not know that murder and assassination are the results of the political methods that have been employed in this county to carry the last election, and the meanest man in the country is the professed politician who advocates or indorses [*sic*] such methods. You must stop this ballot-box stealing, farce and fraud, or the title to your property will not be worth the paper it is written on.

What does the law say? The organic law and life of this great Nation says these colored people have a right to vote, and if they have no right to vote, where did you get your right? If they have no right to be Republicans, how did you get your rights to be Democrats? I would urge on you as Democrats that the rights of citizenship must be protected: and at every little precinct in this country there should be a free ballot and a fair count.

Politicians try to scare you with the myth and bugaboo of negro domination. Where have they dominated? No, sirs; it is merely an excuse for committing outrages on their rights, which no sensible man should consider.

Democracy means that the people shall rule, and we are told that it is undemocratic to denounce bulldozery, ballot stealing and assassination. If this be true then I am no Democrat. If apology for bulldozery, ballot-box stealing and assassination constitute Democracy, then may the angels and ministers of God protect me from such Democracy.

Draw a picture of Conway County before the last election, with its beautiful farms, schools and churches, rich and prosperous. What a desirable place to live in; what an inducement to immigration; what a beautiful picture to send to the down-trodden and oppressed people of the earth to induce them to come to this "land of the free and home of the brave." How gladly would they come. But draw in one corner of that picture a mob mistreating Benjamin, and in the other the corpse of Clayton in the cold arms of death and presented to his six motherless children next day as a present. Oh! What a picture! Surely no one would come; they had rather endure all the hardships and oppression of the most despotic Governments than come here. Let us not invite them here until we can protect them in their lives and liberty.

Now, gentlemen, I don't say that the people of Conway County are responsible for these crimes, as a people; but I do say the consequences are just the same. The world will hold you responsible. All the people of England are not responsible for mistreatment of Ireland, nor are the people of Russia for the oppression of Poland; but in the eyes of the world they are responsible.

G. S. Cunningham

Appendix C

Joe Smith's Letter to Detective Wood

Plummerville, Arkansas
March 30.

Mr. ——
Little Rock, Arkansas

Dear Sir—This is to inform you that —— has this day agreed to tell me the facts about what —— told him. He refers to him as the d—— son of a b—— that killed John M. Clayton. He told —— that he was afraid to talk what he did know about it. —— says he will swear to many other things that will be good for the Government. He will also swear that —— was at Plummerville on the 6th night of November, and many others who were there from Morrilton. You will also do a good piece of work by having —— come down where you are. He knows all about the killing of Clayton. You must have —— and the two other men who live at Menifee. They are good witnesses. I will point them out to you in different places when we all get down to the Rock [Little Rock]. I can find out many more things in regard to the Clayton matter. I was up to Morrillton to-day. The boys who were with —— on the night of the killing have all been sent off. I am trying to find out where they are. One of them saw the shooting. I wish it was so that I could see you about this time. One man who is now watching two white men heard one of them telling the other, —— had a hand in the killing. Two of these men are relatives. I am now at work trying to find out more about them. You may look out for another letter from me to-morow. I remain yours as ever,

Signed,
J. P. Smith.

From St. Louis *Globe-Democrat*, 1 April 1889. Words were blanked out presumably by the newspaper or the Pinkerton Detective.

Appendix D

Letter of N. M. Rogers of Liberia to His Family in Morrilton, Arkansas

Johnsonville, Liberia
September 20, 1895

Mr. Green Rogers, Morrilton, Ark., USA

Dear Father,
Yours of the past month came to hand, found all well, and hope when these few lines come to hand will find you all the same. I was glad to hear from you.

You was asking me about the times. The times are very hard with new people, but I would not exchange homes if some one would give me a place there and stock to work it. A man can live here when he has one or two years experience of the country and you won't have to work half as hard as you do over there.

We don't have everything here as plentiful as there, but in a few years when we begin to raise our coffee we will have what we want. You may hear that you can't raise corn and hogs, but I raise my corn and hogs and have my own bread. There are some people who come out here and as soon as they get sick, or before they know anything about the country, they will go back and tell that they can't live here, but it is a mistake, any man can live here if he works. We have to work anywhere we go. One thing I like, there are no white men to give orders; and when you go in your house, there is no one to stand out, and call you to the door and shoot you when you come out. We have no foreman over us; we are our own boss. We work when we want to, and sit down when we choose, and eat when we get ready.

I'a, you had better make up your mind and come over here. You will not suffer, and if you will, let me know in your next letter. Write as soon as you get this.

A few words to Clara
Dearest Sister, I am glad to hear that you have professed a hope in

From *The Voice of Missions* (an African Methodist Episcopal Church mission magazine), February 1896.

Christ, but it is not anything to profess, but the thing is to live a Christian and to know that you are truly converted and born of God, and live according. I trust we will meet again. Tell John Polk [the brother-in-law] I want him to come out here before he gets too old, where your children will be free, and what you make will be yours.

A few words to Mary
[unclear] to drop you a few words. Mary, I have not got those pictures, but I am going to try and get them. You and your husband must make up your mind to come out here. This is the colored man's home, the only place on earth where they have equal rights, and when you once get a start it will last you until death.

You can raise nearly everything here that you can there. We don't have the horse here, where we are, but they are here. We have the cow here, but they don't grow as large here as in the United States.

We raise chickens, geese, turkeys, guinea fowls and other fowls that you raise there; and you can live easier working three days in a week, than you can there working every day in the week and on Sunday too.

We have the same God here that you have there. Tell Aunt Mary, howdy, tell her I want to hear from Thomas Sirait, so I can write to him how times are.

Love to Bro. Toombs, tell him I am still in the faith, that I am an ordained deacon in the Morning Star Church.

Sarah says, write to her. Write soon and let us hear from you.

Yours truly,
N. M. Rogers

Notes

Introduction

1. For theoretical discussions of political violence, see H. L. Nieburg, *Political Violence and the Behavioral Process* (New York: St. Martins, 1969); Richard E. Rubenstein, *Rebels in Eden: Mass Political Violence in the United States* (Boston: Little, Brown, 1970); and Peter Merkl, *Political Violence and Terror: Motifs and Motivations* (Berkeley: University of California Press, 1986). Hofstadter's words can be found in his article "Reflections on Violence in the United States," in *American Violence: A Documentary History*, ed. Richard Hofstadter and Michael Wallace (New York: Knopf, 1970), 6. For a discussion of southern violence, see George C. Rable, *But There Was No Peace: The Role of Violence in the Politics of Reconstruction* (Athens: University of Georgia Press, 1984), 1–3, 13; Bertram Wyatt-Brown, *Honor and Violence in the Old South* (New York: Oxford University Press, 1986); Sheldon Hackney, "Southern Violence," in *Violence and Culture in America: Historical and Comparative Perspectives*, ed. Hugh Davis Graham and Ted Robert Gurr (Washington, D.C.: Government Printing Office, 1969), 387–401; and Dickson D. Bruce Jr., *Violence and Culture in the Antebellum South* (Austin: University of Texas Press, 1979). For a gripping case study of political violence in Civil War North Carolina, see Phillip Shaw Paludan, *Victims: A True Story of the Civil War* (Knoxville: University of Tennessee Press, 1981).
2. For a discussion of Woodward's childhood in Arkansas, see John Herbert Roper, *C. Vann Woodward, Southerner* (Athens: University of Georgia Press, 1987), 6–30.
3. See for example Jonathan M. Wiener, *Social Origins of the New South: Alabama: 1860–1885* (Baton Rouge: Louisiana State University Press, 1978), which examines five black-belt Alabama counties; Randolph B. Campbell, *A Southern Community in Crisis: Harrison County, Texas, 1850–1880* (Austin: Texas State Historical Society, 1983); Michael Wayne, *The Reshaping of Plantation Society: The Natchez District, 1860–1880* (Baton Rouge: Louisiana State University Press, 1983); Robert L. Brandfon, *Cotton Kingdom of the New South: A History of the Yazoo Mississippi Delta from Reconstruction to the Twentieth Century* (Cambridge: Harvard University Press, 1967); Crandall Shifflett, *Patronage and Poverty in the Tobacco South: Louisa County, Virginia, 1860–1900* (Knoxville: University of Tennessee Press, 1982); Steven Hahn, *The Roots of Southern Populism: Yeoman Farmers and the Transformation of the Georgia Upcountry, 1850–1890* (New York: Oxford University Press, 1983). For one of the best regional studies within

the Deep South, see James C. Cobb, *The Most Southern Place on Earth: The Mississippi Delta and the Roots of Regional Identity* (New York: Oxford University Press, 1992).

4. Although some fine work has been done on antebellum, Civil War, and twentieth-century Arkansas, only one analytical scholarly book, John W. Graves's pioneering work on black Arkansans, has looked at the state in the period between Reconstruction and the 1890s. See his *Town and Country: Race Relations in an Urban-Rural Context, Arkansas, 1865–1905* (Fayetteville: University of Arkansas Press, 1990).

5. Still the best work on southern disfranchisement is J. Morgan Kousser, *The Shaping of Southern Politics: Suffrage Restriction and the Establishment of the One-Party South, 1880–1910* (New Haven: Yale University Press, 1974). For some of the best recent work on lynchings, see W. Fitzhugh Brundage, *Lynching in the New South: Georgia and Virginia, 1880–1930* (Urbana: University of Illinois Press, 1993); George C. Wright, *Racial Violence in Kentucky, 1865–1940: Lynchings, Mob Rule, and "Legal Lynchings"* (Baton Rouge: Louisiana State University Press, 1990); and Stewart E. Tolnay and E. M. Beck, *Festival of Violence: An Analysis of Southern Lynchings, 1882–1930* (Urbana: University of Illinois Press, 1995).

1 Local Divisions and Lasting Grudges: Civil War and Reconstruction

1. Population figures from James M. Woods, *Rebellion and Realignment: Arkansas's Road to Secession* (Fayetteville: University of Arkansas Press, 1987), 186, 191; cotton statistics from U.S. Manuscript Census Returns, Seventh Census, 1850, Agriculture Schedule, Conway County, Arkansas; U.S. Manuscript Census Returns, Eighth Census, 1860, Agriculture Schedule, Conway County, Arkansas.

2. Little Rock *Arkansas Gazette*, 18 June 1852, records that Emzy Wilson, who lived near Lewisburg, sold 66 bales raised on his plantation to M. Greenwood and Co. merchants of New Orleans for $2,793.72. Wilson informed readers that plenty of vacant land as good as his remained in the county.

3. *Arkansas Gazette*, 9 February 1855.

4. U.S. Manuscript Census Returns, Eighth Census, 1860, Agriculture Schedule and Slave Schedule, Conway County, Arkansas.

5. U.S. Manuscript Census Returns, Eighth Census, 1860, Agriculture Schedule, Population Schedule, Conway County, Arkansas.

6. *Arkansas Gazette*, 9 February 1855, 9 July 1859, and 6 August 1859. For more information on Lewisburg, see Nina McReynolds, "A Town That

Disappeared: Lewisburg, Arkansas," (M.S.E. thesis, University of Central Arkansas, 1958); *Historical Reminiscences and Biographical Memoirs of Conway County, Arkansas* (Little Rock: Arkansas Historical Publishing Company, 1890), 36–37.

7. Robert Tracy McKenzie, in *One South or Many? Plantation Belt and Upcountry in Civil War–Era Tennessee* (Cambridge: Cambridge University Press, 1994) argues that the differences between upland and lowland cultures have been exaggerated by historians. His research on selected east, middle, and west Tennessee counties shows that lowland farmers were more self-sufficient than previously thought, growing enough food crops to feed themselves while devoting extra land to cotton. On the other hand, upland small farmers in Tennessee, he found, were considerably involved in a market economy through the raising of livestock. See especially his discussion, 32–48.

8. The vote was 267 for Johnson, 202 for Preston (Woods, *Rebellion and Realignment*, 184).

9. *Arkansas Gazette*, 31 May 1856. For a discussion of the national context of these developments, see Tyler Anbinder, *Nativism and Slavery: The Northern Know Nothings and the Politics of the 1850s* (New York: Oxford University Press, 1992); and David M. Potter, *The Impending Crisis, 1848–1861* (New York: Harper and Row, 1976).

10. See Woods's analysis of the vote on a county-by-county basis in *Rebellion and Realignment*, 110–12. The state election tally can be found in the *Arkansas Gazette*, 8 December 1860.

11. Woods, *Rebellion and Realignment*, 116–21. For comparative works that examine the politicization of the upland-lowland split elsewhere in the South during the secession crisis, see James M. McPherson's discussion of the Upper South in *The Battle Cry of Freedom: The Civil War Era* (New York: Oxford University Press, 1988), 276–307; Wayne Durrill, *War of Another Kind: A Southern Community in the Great Rebellion* (New York: Oxford University Press, 1990); Hahn, *The Roots of Southern Populism;* J. William Harris, *Plain Folk and Gentry in a Slave Society: White Liberty and Black Slavery in Augusta's Hinterlands* (Middletown, Conn.: Wesleyan University Press, 1985); Michael P. Johnson, *Toward a Patriarchal Republic: The Secession of Georgia* (Baton Rouge: Louisiana State University Press, 1977); and William L. Barney, *The Secessionist Impulse: Alabama and Mississippi in 1860* (Princeton: Princeton University Press, 1974).

12. *Arkansas Gazette*, 19 January 1861. Of the seven leaders of the meeting named in the *Gazette* article, four owned slaves (Samuel J. Stallings, 6; Thomas T. Henry, 1; Thomas Jefferson Williams, 1; Bryant V. King, 2). U.S. Manuscript Census Returns, Eighth Census, 1860, Slave Schedule, Conway County, Arkansas. According to Carl Degler, most southern

Unionists did not oppose slavery. See his *The Other South: Southern Dissenters in the Nineteenth Century* (New York: Harper and Row, 1974), 184.

13. Little Rock *True Democrat*, 19 January 1861.

14. Supporters of a secession convention won by a statewide vote of 27,412 to 15,826. Woods, *Rebellion and Realignment*, 130.

15. Mary Stallings Wilbourn, interview, 24 February 1994; *Arkansas Gazette*, 23 February 1861.

16. For an analysis of the degree to which this upland-lowland split prevailed in the secession voting, see Woods, *Rebellion and Realignment*, 136–48.

17. S. J. Stallings to Jesse Turner, 19 April 1861, Jesse Turner Papers, Manuscript Department, William R. Perkins Library, Duke University, Durham, N.C.

18. Woods, *Rebellion and Realignment*, 159–60, 196. In addition to Woods's excellent account of the politicking preceding Arkansas's secession, see Elsie Mae Lewis, "From Nationalism to DisUnion: A Study of the Secession Movement in Arkansas, 1860–1861" (Ph.D. diss., University of Chicago, 1946); and Michael B. Dougan, *Confederate Arkansas: The People and Policies of a Frontier State in Wartime* (Tuscaloosa: University of Alabama Press, 1976).

19. *True Democrat*, 2 May, 6 June 1861.

20. *Historical Reminiscences and Biographical Memoirs of Conway County, Arkansas*, 16–17; John Harrell, *Arkansas*, vol. 10 of *Confederate Military History*, 12 vols. (Atlanta: Confederate Publishing Company, 1899), 306.

21. See James M. McPherson, *What They Fought For, 1861–1865* (Baton Rouge: Louisiana State University Press, 1994).

22. For information on the peace societies, see Ted Worley, "The Arkansas Peace Society of 1861: A Study of Mountain Unionism," *Journal of Southern History* 24 (November 1958): 445–56; Ted Worley, "Documents Relating to the Arkansas Peace Society of 1861," *Arkansas Historical Quarterly* 17 (spring 1958): 82–111. Records show that local authorities apprehended members of the peace society in Van Buren, Searcy, Marion, Carroll, Izard, and Fulton Counties. In his account of Arkansas Unionism written in 1863, Albert Webb Bishop says a chapter of the peace society was organized in Conway County; however, no one there was ever taken into custody. See his *Loyalty on the Frontier, or Sketches of Union Men of the South-west* (St. Louis: R. P. Studley, 1863), 133. For a comparative perspective, see Richard B. McCaslin's study of Confederate vengeance against suspected Unionists in Texas in *Tainted Breeze: The Great Hanging at Gainesville, Texas, 1862* (Baton Rouge: Louisiana State University Press, 1994); and Wesley S. Thompson's account of an Alabama county that seceded from the Con-

federacy, *"The Free State of Winston": A History of Winston County, Alabama* (Winfield, Ala.: Pareil Press, 1968).

23. Williams had served on the committee that drew up the antisecessionist resolutions in December 1860. See Kenneth C. Barnes, "The Williams Clan: Mountain Farmers and Union Fighters in North Central Arkansas," *Arkansas Historical Quarterly* 52 (autumn 1993): 286–317.

24. Albert Webb Bishop, *Report of the Adjutant General of the State of Arkansas*, in 39th Congress, 2d Session, Senate Miscellaneous Documents, No. 53, 245; Leroy Williams Pension File, National Archives, Washington, D.C.; *Historical Reminiscences of Conway County*, 15–16. One of Williams's band of resisters was Ananias Stobaugh, who had been arrested six months earlier for his activity with the peace society in Van Buren County. Impressed into service in the rebel army, Stobaugh must have deserted and made his way back to Arkansas sometime in the spring of 1862. When arrested for his membership in the peace society, Stobaugh had in his possession one of the only surviving oaths of the secret organization. The Stobaughs were another Disciples of Christ clergy family and had known the Williams family before the war. See Kie Oldham Collection, Box 2, item 110d, Arkansas History Commission, Little Rock; and Ananias Stobaugh, Pension File, National Archives, Washington, D.C.

25. The *True Democrat*, 30 March 1862, printed a letter from a rebel soldier from the Confederate camp on Devil's Creek in Conway County.

26. Bishop, *Report of the Adjutant General*, 245; James W. Demby, *Mysteries and Miseries of Arkansas, or a Defence of the Loyalty of the State* (St. Louis: privately printed, 1863), 11–12, 44; Morton W. Williams Pension File, National Archives, Washington, D.C. For a comparison of these Conway County Unionists to others in the South, see Richard Current, *Lincoln's Loyalists: Union Soldiers from the Confederacy* (Boston: Northeastern University Press, 1991).

27. Little Rock *National Democrat*, 20 October 1863. General Steele established this paper as his official mouthpiece after his occupation of Little Rock. U.S. War Department, *The War of the Rebellion: A Compilation of the Official Records of the Union and Confederate Armies* (Washington, D.C.: Government Printing Office, 1880–1901), series 1, vol. 22, part 2, 533; Descriptive Book, Third Arkansas Cavalry, National Archives, Washington, D.C.

28. Regimental Order 31, 18 July 1864, in Regimental Letter and Order Book, Third Arkansas Cavalry, National Archives, Washington, D.C. Michael Fellman describes similar conditions in Missouri in his book *Inside War: The Guerrilla Conflict in Missouri during the American Civil War* (New York: Oxford University Press, 1989). For more information about Colo-

nel Witt and his men, see Brian Dirck, "Witt's Cavalry: An Arkansas Guerrilla Unit," *Faulkner Facts and Fiddlings* 36 (1994): 63–76.

29. *War of the Rebellion*, ser. 1, vol. 48, pt. 1, 111, 885; Thomas Jefferson Williams, Widow's Pension Application, National Archives, Washington, D.C.; Arlie Williams, interview, 7 February 1992; Ruth Cupit, interview, 15 February 1992; Emma Sue Beavers, interview, 8 May 1992; Maxine Kelly, interview, 12 April 1992.

30. *War of the Rebellion*, ser. 1, vol. 48, pt. 2, 494–95, 844–45. In the spring of 1865, the Union army formed three militia companies of local Unionists in Conway County. Nathan Williams was commissioned as captain of the first company just two weeks after his father's death. In April another veteran of the Williams company, George M. Galloway, formed a second company, and Anthony Hinkle, a Unionist merchant in Springfield, became captain of a third company. Adjutant General's Office Papers, Box 6: Commissions Box, 50, Arkansas History Commission, Little Rock.

31. A description of wartime Lewisburg appeared in the Morrilton *Arkansas Unit*, 1 August 1929. *National Democrat*, 26 December 1863; "Recollections of Emily Elizabeth Hervey Howard," written down by her grandson, Melbourne Moose, ca. 1926, Morrilton, Arkansas, in Moose-Hervey family papers, private collection of Clarkia Turney, Morrilton.

32. The Kurtz story was contributed by Mary Stallings Wilbourn to *Conway County, Our Land, Our Home, Our People* (Little Rock: Historical Publications of Arkansas, 1989), 459. Estimate on slaves is from Carl Moneyhon, *The Impact of the Civil War and Reconstruction on Arkansas: Persistence in the Midst of Ruin* (Baton Rouge: Louisiana State University Press, 1994), 134. Figures on abandoned plantations came from Randy Finley, "The Freedman's Bureau in Arkansas" (Ph.D. diss., University of Arkansas, 1992), 230.

33. Ted Worley, ed., "The Diary of Lieutenant Orville Gillet, U.S.A., 1864–1865," *Arkansas Historical Quarterly* 17 (1958): 183; "Civil War Letters of John Patterson," *Pulaski County Historical Society Review* 6 (1958): 34; *National Democrat*, 2 April 1864.

34. Frederick Steele to O. O. Washburn, 17 May 1864; Steele to W. S. Rosecrans, 11 September 1864; Steele to E. R. S. Canby, 12 September 1864; in Box 2, General Frederick Steele Collection, Department of Special Collections, Meyer Library, Stanford University. For more information about Confederate and Union military actions in the area, see *Official Records*, ser. 1, vol. 34, pt. 1, 924–28; pt. 3, 635, 670–71, 930–32; vol. 41, pt. 3, 104, 116–17, 223.

35. Charles Royster's *The Destructive War: William Tecumseh Sherman, Stonewall Jackson, and the Americans* (New York: Alfred A. Knopf, 1991) argues persuasively that the Civil War was the first "modern" war in that its

leaders planned awesome destruction aimed explicitly at civilian populations. See also Mark Grimsley, *The Hard Hand of War: Union Military Policy toward Southern Civilians, 1861–1865* (Cambridge: Cambridge University Press, 1995).

36. For a discussion of Reconstruction in Arkansas see Moneyhon, *The Impact of the Civil War and Reconstruction on Arkansas;* and Michael B. Dougan, *Arkansas Odyssey: The Saga of Arkansas from Prehistoric Times to Present* (Little Rock: Rose Publishing, 1994), 235–65. For a dated, but still the most thorough, examination of the politics of Arkansas's Reconstruction, see Thomas S. Staples, *Reconstruction in Arkansas, 1862–1874* (New York: Columbia University Press, 1923). Staples was a student of William A. Dunning, and his interpretation reflects that of his mentor. For a discussion of the pitfalls of Presidential Reconstruction, see Eric Foner, *Reconstruction: America's Unfinished Revolution, 1863–1877* (New York: Harper and Row, 1988), 176–227. A list of legislators and local officials is in *Historical Report of the Secretary of State* (Little Rock: State of Arkansas, 1968).

37. William Morgan to Maj. John Tyler, 29 January 1867; Morgan to Col. Henry Page, 2 February 1867; Morgan to Lt. John Tyler, 1 March 1867; Morgan to Maj. Gen. O. O. Howard, 2 March 1867, Freedmen's Bureau Records: Arkansas, Field Office: Dardanelle/Lewisburg, National Archives, Washington, D.C. (microfilm). See also Randy Finley, "The Freedmen's Bureau in Arkansas" (Ph.D. diss., University of Arkansas, 1992), 370; Randy Finley, *From Slavery to Uncertain Freedom: The Freedmen's Bureau in Arkansas, 1865–1869* (Fayetteville: University of Arkansas Press, 1996), 83, 104; Foner, *Reconstruction*, 164–70; and Dougan, *Arkansas Odyssey*, 238. For a discussion of the disorder and violence throughout the South during Presidential Reconstruction, see Dan T. Carter, *When the War Was Over: The Failure of Self-Reconstruction in the South, 1865–1867* (Baton Rouge: Louisiana State University Press, 1985), 6–23.

38. *Arkansas Gazette*, 5 November 1867; *Historical Reminiscences and Biographical Memoirs of Conway County*, 18–19.

39. For more on Arkansas's most fascinating governor before Bill Clinton, see Powell Clayton's semiautobiographical *The Aftermath of the Civil War in Arkansas* (New York: Neale Publishing, 1915). Until the last generation, Arkansas histories have portrayed Clayton in the most villainous of terms. For more recent and judicious assessments, see William H. Burnside, *The Honorable Powell Clayton* (Conway: University of Central Arkansas Press, 1991); and Richard Nelson Current, *Those Terrible Carpetbaggers* (New York: Oxford University Press, 1988).

40. The conversion of wartime Unionism to Republicanism during Reconstruction took place throughout upland regions of the South. See Foner, *Reconstruction*, 300–307; and Gordon B. McKinney, *Southern Moun-*

tain Republicans: Politics and the Appalachian Community (Chapel Hill: University of North Carolina Press, 1978), 30–61.

41. U.S. Manuscript Census Returns, 1860 and 1870, Population Schedules, Conway County, Arkansas. Most members of this Conway County "elite" would rank as moderately prosperous farmers in more wealthy areas of the South. But despite the modest scale, these landowners constituted the local aristocracy relative to the small subsistence farmers. For Moneyhon's argument, see *The Impact of the Civil War and Reconstruction on Arkansas.* Robert McKenzie's recent comparison of upland and lowland counties in Tennessee demonstrated that the Civil War turmoil did not substantially alter the distribution of wealth in upland or lowland regions. All regions lost wealth because of the war, but prewar inequalities remained. See *One South or Many?* 119–20. See also Dwight B. Billings Jr.'s study of planter persistence, *Planters and the Making of a "New South": Class, Politics, and Development in North Carolina, 1865–1900* (Chapel Hill: University of North Carolina Press, 1979); Joseph P. Reidy, *From Slavery to Agrarian Capitalism in the Cotton Plantation South: Central Georgia, 1800–1880* (Chapel Hill: University of North Carolina Press, 1992); Wiener, *Social Origins of the New South;* and Jay Mandle, *The Roots of Black Poverty: The Southern Plantation after the Civil War* (Durham, N.C.: Duke University Press, 1978).

42. Little Rock *Republican,* 31 August 1868.

43. *Arkansas Gazette,* 1 September 1868. Just a few days earlier, the paper had reported a contrary and more political version of the event. In this account, three black Republicans came during the night to the house of a freedman who supported the Democratic Party. They called him out. As he was dressing, his dog barked, and the Republicans dispatched the dog with a shot. Fearing he would be next, the black man refused to come out of the house, and his assailants finally dispersed. *Arkansas Gazette,* 28 August 1868.

44. *Arkansas Gazette,* 1 September 1868; Little Rock *Republican,* 29 August 1868. To justify disarmament, Eugene Henry wrote in the *Gazette* (15 September 1868) that the Negroes "stood in the streets consulting and wagging their heads in a most disorderly manner."

45. *Arkansas Gazette,* 1 September 1868.

46. *Arkansas Gazette,* 1 September 1868. See the Republican and Democratic accounts of these events in Powell Clayton's *The Aftermath of the Civil War in Arkansas,* 144–51; and John Mortimer Harrell, *The Brooks and Baxter War: A History of the Reconstruction Period in Arkansas* (St. Louis: Slawson Co., 1893), 72–78.

47. *Arkansas Gazette,* 1 September 1868; Little Rock *Republican,* 2 September 1868. George Rable, in *But There Was No Peace,* 71, uses the story of this incident in Conway County as an example of "manufactured tales of

black insurrection," which he said circulated throughout the South during Radical Reconstruction.

48. *Arkansas Gazette*, 29 August 1868, 1 September 1868; *Van Buren Press*, 11 September 1868. Clayton denied that he dispatched the black militia to the scene of the disorder (*The Aftermath of the Civil War in Arkansas*, 149). Otis A. Singletary, in *Negro Militia and Reconstruction* (Austin: University of Texas Press, 1957), argues that the Republican militia, and particularly black militia companies, were more active in Arkansas than any other southern state. Singletary, a southerner writing in 1957, suggested that the Ku Klux Klan was a conservative reaction to militia violence. More recent studies suggest it was the other way around. See Rable, *But There Was No Peace*, 73, 104–5. For a comparative view of political organization of blacks by Republicans, see Michael W. Fitzgerald, *The Union League Movement in the Deep South: Politics and Agricultural Change during Reconstruction* (Baton Rouge: Louisiana State University Press, 1989).

49. Little Rock *Republican*, 2 September 1868; *Arkansas Gazette*, 1 September 1868, 8 September 1868; Harrell, *The Brooks and Baxter War*, 73. The Conway County Court Record Book, July 1868–May 1871, 55–56, 81, Conway County Courthouse, Morrilton, lists the payments to individual members of the posse. Most were veterans of the Williams Union company and their kin.

50. Abstract of letters by A. G. Carroll, Anthony Hinkle, John Matthews, and A. F. Livingston, September–October 1868, in Correspondence Registers, 1868–1871, Powell Clayton's Correspondence, Arkansas History Commission, Little Rock. Commissions for the officers of the militia can be found in Adjutant General's Office Papers, Box 8: Militia Roster, County Organizations, 1868. The Conway County Court Record Book, July 1868–May 1871, 38, records the pay for men serving in the registrar's posse; *Weekly Arkansas Gazette*, 29 September 1868 (refers to report in the St. Louis *Democrat*); see also issue of 17 November 1868. For a discussion of the organization of the Ku Klux Klan and its activity in Arkansas in 1868, see Allen W. Trelease, *White Terror: The Ku Klux Klan Conspiracy and Southern Reconstruction* (New York: Harper and Row, 1971), 149–74. See also Foner's discussion of Klan violence in *Reconstruction*, 425–44.

51. *Journal of the Senate of Arkansas, 1868–1869* (Little Rock: State Printers, 1869), 353; *Arkansas Gazette*, 26 November 1868; John L. Matthews, letters of 4 and 10 November 1868, Powell Clayton's Correspondence.

52. R. H. Perry testimony, 1903–1904, Contested Election: Clayton vs. Breckinridge, Committee on Elections, 51st Congress, 1889–1890, National Archives, Washington, D.C. (four volumes of manuscript testimony, paginated consecutively, hereafter cited as CvB); *New York Times*, 10 December 1868; *Arkansas Gazette*, 10 December 1868. For a discussion of

interracial cohabitation in this era, see Martha Hodes, "Wartime Dialogues on Illicit Sex: White Women and Black Men," in *Divided Houses: Gender and the Civil War*, ed. Catherine Clinton and Nina Silber (New York: Oxford University Press, 1992), 230–42.

53. R. F. Hooper testimony, CvB, 1233; Clayton, *The Aftermath of the Civil War in Arkansas*, 153.

54. *New York Times*, 10 December 1868; *Arkansas Gazette*, 10 December 1868; Harrell, *The Brooks and Baxter War*, 76–78; Thomas J. Reynolds, *The Pope County Militia War* (1908; reprint, Little Rock: Foreman-Payne, 1968), 24; John L. Matthews, letter of 9 December 1868, Powell Clayton's Correspondence.

55. Clayton, *The Aftermath of the Civil War in Arkansas*, 152; Harrell, *The Brooks and Baxter War*, 77; *Arkansas Gazette*, 10 December 1868.

56. Letter of L. B. Umpfleet, 1 December 1868, in "Testimony Taken by the Joint Select Committee to Inquire into the Condition of Affairs in the Late Insurrectionary States," in *42d Congress, 2d Session, Senate Report No. 41, pt. 13*, 326.

57. Harrell, *The Brooks and Baxter War*, 77–78; *Arkansas Gazette*, 20 and 22 December 1868; Clayton, *The Aftermath of the Civil War in Arkansas*, 154–63; Little Rock *Republican*, 30 December 1868.

58. Petitions received, 9 and 21 December 1868, Powell Clayton's Correspondence; *Van Buren Press*, 12 January 1869; *Arkansas Gazette*, 8 January 1869.

59. Although Eric Foner argues that blacks were active participants in Reconstruction, not just passive bystanders, he also emphasizes that a substantial number of southern whites were willing, despite pervasive racism, to link their fortunes with those of blacks. Events in Conway County affirm both of these themes. Foner views Powell Clayton, in comparison to other southern governors, as singularly effective in dealing with Klan violence because of his willingness to suspend the normal legal process and use force. See Foner's *Reconstruction*, xxvi–xxvii, 291–307, 440. George Rable, in *But There Was No Peace*, 105, similarly argued that Clayton's vigorous use of martial law and the Republican militia broke the Klan in Arkansas and served as an example for other southern governors.

60. *Arkansas Gazette*, 28 August 1869; indictment of Henry is found in Conway County Circuit Court Book, 1865–1875, for date 19 April 1870, n.p., Conway County Courthouse, Morrilton; complaint about Hinkle is found in John C. Gregory, letter of 11 May 1869, Powell Clayton's Correspondence; *Journal of the Senate of Arkansas, 1871* (Little Rock: State Printers, 1871), 310–11. After Hinkle was replaced by a carpetbagger from Lewisburg, A. D. Thomas, who was appointed by Governor Powell, Hinkle

went to the courthouse and took back his office at gunpoint. Thomas fled to Little Rock to report to the governor. *Arkansas Gazette*, 31 December 1871.

61. *Arkansas Gazette*, 5 August 1871; Singletary, *Negro Militia during Reconstruction*, 149.

62. *Arkansas Gazette*, 27 October 1871, 8 November 1872; *Historical Reminiscences and Biographical Memoirs of Conway County*, 18–19.

2 Motives for Murder: Democrats and Republicans Compete for Power, 1872–1888

1. Alpha Talley English, ed., *Menifee: Past and Present* (Menifee, Ark.: Women's Civic League, 1976), 6, 8–10.

2. *Arkansas Gazette*, 31 January, 26 and 27 April 1873; Harrell, *The Brooks and Baxter War*, 173–74. When Hinkle lost his bid for county clerk through this trickery, he filed suit against Thomas, and the case was eventually appealed to the Arkansas Supreme Court, which ruled in Thomas's favor. See "Thomas et al. vs. Hinkle," *Arkansas Reports* 35 (1879–1880): 450–58. For more information on the Radical Republicans' deal for the railroads, see Mark W. Summers, *Railroads, Reconstruction, and the Gospel of Prosperity: Aid under the Radical Republicans, 1865–1877* (Princeton: Princeton University Press, 1984), 259. For a close analysis of the politics of Reconstruction in the 1870s, see William Gillette, *Retreat from Reconstruction, 1869–1879* (Baton Rouge: Louisiana State University Press, 1979).

3. *Republican*, 7 August 1872; *Arkansas Gazette*, 8 November 1874, 4 August 1876.

4. *Arkansas Gazette*, 21 May 1874; Harrell, *The Brooks and Baxter War*, 219. For more information about the Brooks-Baxter war, see Earl F. Woodward, "The Brooks and Baxter War in Arkansas, 1872–1874," *Arkansas Historical Quarterly* 30 (winter 1971): 315–36; Dougan, *Arkansas Odyssey*, 258–63; and Gillette, *Retreat from Reconstruction*, 136–44.

5. *Arkansas Gazette*, 25 August 1874, 8 November 1874.

6. *Arkansas Gazette*, 15 February 1875, 25 May 1877; W. G. Gray testimony, CvB, 1213–16; R. F. Hooper testimony, CvB, 1236; E. B. Henry testimony, CvB, 1925. For the story of Henry's encounter with the black militia and Matthew's murder, see Little Rock *Arkansas Democrat*, 26 July 1881.

7. Conway County Circuit Court Record Book, April 1876–September 1879. See also cases that were appealed to the Arkansas Supreme Court, "Kearney v. Moose," *Arkansas Reports* 37 (1881): 37–39; "Gill v. State," and "Jamison v. State," *Arkansas Reports* 38 (1882): 445, 524–27. The ninth military district of the state comprised Conway, Pope, Yell, Perry, Faulkner,

and Van Buren Counties. For commissions of the militia officers, representing local Democratic families, Hervey, Armstrong, Reid, etc., see Adjutant General's Office Papers, Boxes 9–11. For a discussion of the waning national concern over southern politics, see Gillette, *Retreat from Reconstruction*, 363–80.

8. *Arkansas Gazette*, 20 February 1879; U.S. Bureau of the Census, *Ninth Census of the United States*, through *Eleventh Census of the United States* (Washington, D.C.: Government Printing Office, 1872–1895). For the context of this black migration to Conway County, see John William Graves, *Town and Country: Race Relations in an Urban-Rural Context, Arkansas, 1865–1905*, 59–61, 91–96; Robert B. Walz, "Migration into Arkansas, 1834–1880" (Ph.D. diss., University of Texas, 1958); Fon Louise Gordon, *Caste and Class: The Black Experience in Arkansas, 1880–1920* (Athens: University of Georgia Press, 1995), 8–22; William Cohen, *At Freedom's Edge: Black Mobility and the Southern White Quest for Racial Control, 1861–1915* (Baton Rouge: Louisiana State University Press, 1991); and Nell I. Painter, *The Exodusters: Black Migration to Kansas after Reconstruction* (New York: Knopf, 1977).

9. *Arkansas Gazette*, 12 December 1878; Gordon, *Caste and Class*, 1–22. Gordon entitles her chapter about the 1880s "Paradise Lost."

10. This estimation comes from Orville Vernon Burton, *In My Father's House Are Many Mansions: Family and Community in Edgefield, South Carolina* (Chapel Hill: University of North Carolina Press, 1985), 238.

11. Cohen, *At Freedom's Edge*, 154.

12. See Orville Vernon Burton, "Race and Reconstruction: Edgefield County, South Carolina," *Journal of Social History* 12 (fall 1978): 40–45. Edgefield County nurtured some of the most infamous racial conservatives in South Carolina's history, ranging from the notorious racist governor Ben Tillman to Strom Thurmond.

13. Quoted in Cohen, *At Freedom's Edge*, 155.

14. For a discussion of the Liberian migration movement in South Carolina during the 1870s, see Cohen, *At Freedom's Edge*, 154–60. On the movement in South Carolina in 1877–1878, see Orville Vernon Burton, "Ungrateful Servants? Edgefield's Black Reconstruction: Part 1 of the Total History of Edgefield County, South Carolina" (Ph.D. diss., Princeton University, 1975), 157–66; and George Brown Tindall, *South Carolina Negroes, 1877–1900*, 153–68.

15. For a discussion of these changes in the election laws, see Tindall, *South Carolina Negroes*, 68–71.

16. Charleston *News and Courier*, 28 December 1881, 2 and 6 January 1882; *New York Times*, 12 January 1882.

17. *News and Courier*, 28 December 1881, 2 January 1882. In contrast to

the Charleston paper, which called the settlers prosperous, the *Arkansas Gazette*, 27 December 1881, reported that most of the 150 blacks who arrived in Morrilton from South Carolina "are said to be almost destitute."

18. *News and Courier*, 2 January 1882. One black family who migrated to Conway County from South Carolina still recalls more than a hundred years later how the family sang spirituals, "Oh, Ain't That Good News!", "Oh, What a Morning!", "Steal Away," and others as they made their way. "Happy Bend Community Historical Project Souvenir Booklet," prepared for the Homecoming Celebration of the Pilgrim Rest No. 2 Missionary Baptist Church, Kenwood, Arkansas, 6–7 July 1991, courtesy of Loretha Hendrix.

19. *News and Courier*, 2 January 1882; Augusta, Georgia, *Chronicle and Constitutionalist*, 7 January 1882. Tindall, in *South Carolina Negroes*, 174, says the emigrant train rate from upland South Carolina to Little Rock was $22.50.

20. *News and Courier*, 30 December 1881, 2 January 1882; *Edgefield Chronicle*, 4 January 1882. The *New York Times* reported 12 January 1882 that 10,000 South Carolina blacks in all had recently migrated.

21. *News and Courier*, 24 January 1882; *Edgefield Chronicle*, 25 January 1882.

22. For a discussion of how violence and intimidation shut down black voting in many areas of the Deep South in the mid-1870s, see Michael Perman, "Counter Reconstruction: The Role of Violence in Southern Redemption," in *The Facts of Reconstruction: Essays in Honor of John Hope Franklin*, ed. Eric Anderson and Alfred A. Moss Jr. (Baton Rouge: Louisiana State University Press, 1991), 121–40.

23. See Foner, *Reconstruction*, 590; and Gordon, *Caste and Class*, 13.

24. For the story of the German migration to the Arkansas River Valley, see Jonathan James Wolfe, "Background of German Immigration," *Arkansas Historical Quarterly* 25 (1966): 151–82, 248–78, and 354–85. The history of Holy Ghost mission colony to Arkansas is told convincingly by Henry J. Koren, who based his account on Father Strub's reports to the American headquarters of the Holy Ghost order in Pittsburgh. See Koren, *The Serpent and the Dove: A History of the Congregation of the Holy Ghost in the United States, 1745–1984* (Pittsburgh: Spiritus Press, 1985), 105–24.

25. Koren, *The Serpent and the Dove*, 110–14. The *Arkansas Gazette*, 1 April 1880, described the ceremony, splendid dinner, and entertainments of the day.

26. Wolfe, "Background of German Immigration," 177–78.

27. Ibid., 362; *Arkansas Gazette*, 24 April 1880.

28. Wolfe, "Background of German Immigration," 110–11.

29. Ibid., 120–24. See also the description of the Morrilton white and

colored schools in *Handbook of the Arkansas River Valley among the "Valley Route" between Van Buren and Little Rock* (Chicago: C. S. Burch, 1887), 39–40.

30. *Arkansas Gazette*, 19 September 1880, 5 and 6 September 1882. The Conway County correspondent obviously exaggerated his report, for there were only 377 foreign-born residents in the county when the 1880 census was taken. *Compendium of the Eleventh Census: 1890*, 476. For an examination of the ephemeral Greenback Party in Arkansas, see Judith Barjenbruch, "The Greenbacker Political Movement: An Arkansas View," *Arkansas Historical Quarterly* 36 (summer 1977): 107–22. For comparative views, see also Roger L. Hart, *Redeemers, Bourbons, and Populists: Tennessee, 1870–1896* (Baton Rouge: Louisiana State University Press, 1975); and Michael R. Hyman, *The Anti-Redeemers: Hill-Country Political Dissenters in the Lower South from Redemption to Populism* (Baton Rouge: Louisiana State University Press, 1990), 54–74. Hyman discusses opposition in the 1870s and early 1880s to the Democratic Party on the local level by small farmers. See also Edward L. Ayers's discussion of Greenbackism in *The Promise of the New South: Life after Reconstruction* (New York: Oxford University Press, 1992), 45–46.

31. *Arkansas Democrat*, 19 August 1881; *Arkansas Gazette*, 20 and 24 August 1884.

32. Constitutionally the county judge should not have such powers. *Arkansas Gazette*, 24 March 1882, 5 April 1884; Conway County Court Record Book, October 1882–April 1885, 437.

33. Fred W. Allsopp, *History of the Arkansas Press for a Hundred Years or More* (Little Rock: Parke-Harper, 1922), 114–15.

34. See F. Clark Elkins, "Arkansas Farmers Organize for Action, 1882–1884," *Arkansas Historical Quarterly* 13 (autumn 1954): 231–48; F. Clark Elkins, "The Agricultural Wheel: County Politics and Consolidation, 1884–1885," *Arkansas Historical Quarterly* (summer 1970): 152–75; Randy Henningson, "Upland Farmers and Agrarian Protest: Northwest Arkansas and the Brothers of Freedom" (M.A. thesis, University of Arkansas, 1973); W. Scott Morgan, *History of the Wheel and Alliance and the Impending Revolution* (1891; reprint, New York: Burt Franklin, 1968); and Theodore Saloutos, *Farmer Movements in the South, 1865–1933* (Lincoln: University of Nebraska Press, 1964), 60–68.

35. See the descriptions of Morrilton in the *Arkansas Gazette*, 21 July 1887; and *Historical Reminiscences and Biographical Memoirs of Conway County*, 34–35. Morrilton population figures come from *Compendium of the Eleventh Census: 1890*, Part I (Washington, D.C.: Government Printing Office, 1892), 60. For a discussion of town growth in the late-nineteenth-century South, see Ayers, *The Promise of the New South*, 55–80.

36. *Handbook of the Arkansas River Valley*, 42; R. H. Loughridge, "Report on Cotton Production in Arkansas," in *Tenth Census of the United States, 1880*, vol. 5 (Washington, D.C.: Government Printing Office, 1884), 81–82; Henningson, "Upland Farmers and Agrarian Protest," 21.

37. Howard N. Rabinowitz, *The First New South, 1865–1920* (Arlington Heights, Ill.: Harlan Davidson, 1992), 7. For a discussion of the experience of two Georgia counties with the arrival of the commercial economy, see Hahn, *The Roots of Southern Populism*, 170–203. See also Harold D. Woodman, "Sequel to Slavery: The New History Views the Post-Bellum South," *Journal of Southern History* 43 (November 1977): 523–54.

38. See the discussion of agrarian conditions in Arkansas in Graves, *Town and Country*, 61–62, 135.

39. Henningson, "Upland Farmers and Agrarian Protest," 49; Stout's answers to the census questionnaire are recorded in Loughridge, "Cotton Production in Arkansas," 101–8. For further information on agriculture, land tenure, and the crop lien system in this period, see Gavin Wright, *The Political Economy of the Cotton South: Households, Markets, and Wealth in the Nineteenth Century* (New York: W. W. Norton, 1978); Michael Schwartz, *Radical Protest and Social Structure: The Southern Farmers' Alliance and Cotton Tenancy, 1880–1890* (New York: Academic Press, 1976); Reidy, *From Slavery to Agrarian Capitalism in the Cotton Plantation South*, 215–41; and Roger L. Ransom and Richard Sutch, *One Kind of Freedom: The Economic Consequences of Emancipation* (Cambridge: Cambridge University Press, 1977).

40. Henningson, "Upland Farmers and Agrarian Protest," 61–62, 75. See Wayman Hogue's reminiscences of youth in northern Arkansas, *Back Yonder: An Ozark Chronicle* (New York: Minton, Balch, and Co., 1932), 194–97. For more on the rural antipathy toward town dwellers and the role of local merchants, see Ayers, *The Promise of the New South*, 57–58, 81–103. E. P. Thompson, in his classic work *The Making of the English Working Class* (Harmondsworth, England: Penguin Books, 1963), 9–10, describes class as happening "when some men as a result of common experiences (inherited or shared), feel and articulate the identity of their experiences as being between themselves, and as against other men whose interests are different from (and usually opposed to) theirs." The Arkansas agrarian movement obviously shows all these signs of class conflict. See also Leon Fink, *Workingmen's Democracy: The Knights of Labor and American Politics* (Urbana: University of Illinois Press, 1983), for a discussion of the political culture of another working-class radical group in the 1880s.

41. By 1884 the *Arkansas Mansion*, the black newspaper published in Little Rock, was encouraging its readers to grow food crops instead of just cotton. The *Mansion* reminded African Americans that with the common pattern

of advances, debts, and mortgaged land in central Arkansas, a cotton bale's selling price was less than the cost to produce it. See article: "Raise Something to Eat," *Arkansas Mansion*, 23 February 1884.

42. Henningson, "Upland Farmers and Agrarian Protest," 80, 99–104, 123.

43. Elkins, "The Agricultural Wheel," 160–65; *Arkansas Gazette*, 3, 4, and 6 September 1884, 6 November 1884; *Biennial Report of the Secretary of the State of Arkansas* (Little Rock: 1884), 16–17.

44. *Conway County, Our Land, Our People*, 454; *Historical Reminiscences of and Biographical Memoirs of Conway County*, 55; *Arkansas Gazette*, 21 July 1887.

45. Morrilton *Headlight* report described in *Fort Smith Elevator*, 17 October 1884.

46. *New York Times*, 25 February 1885; *Arkansas Gazette*, 24 February 1885.

47. *Arkansas Gazette*, 13 and 17 March, 2 and 18 April 1885.

48. *Arkansas Gazette*, 2 and 22 April, 22 August 1885; *Fort Smith Elevator*, 25 July 1885.

49. *Arkansas Gazette*, 30 October 1985.

50. For a discussion of how the Reconstruction experience was fashioned after Redemption into radical racism, see Joel Williamson, *The Crucible of Race: Black-White Relations in the American South since Emancipation* (New York: Oxford University Press, 1984), 79–85.

51. Delegates of the Agricultural Wheel came to the Springfield meeting from Faulkner, White, Lonoke, Woodruff, and Van Buren Counties, and the Brothers of Freedom was represented by agrarians from Pope, Van Buren, and Conway Counties. The meeting was described in the *Lead Hill Bugle*, 20 December 1884. For a description of Springfield, Conway County's agrarian stronghold, see *Arkansas Gazette*, 21 December 1886. John Wheeler, in his study of agrarian populism in Arkansas in the 1890s, found that the strongest and most persistent populist movements succeeded not in the deep delta or mountain regions of the state but in the transitional terrain in between, the lowland hills of north-central and southwestern Arkansas. In these zones, farmers devoted considerable acreage to cotton but, with poorer soil and more difficult terrain, received much lower yields than in the east Arkansas delta. Therefore, with plummeting cotton prices, these farmers found themselves more hard-pressed than mountain farmers, who grew little cotton, or the delta farmers, whose productivity was so much higher. Conway County fits this pattern well. See Wheeler, "The People's Party in Arkansas, 1891–1896" (Ph.D. diss., Tulane University, 1975), 13, 291–92.

52. For these figures, see *Eleventh Census of the United States*, Statistics on

Agriculture (Washington, D.C.: Government Printing Office, 1895), 357, 393; Report on Real Estate Mortgages (Washington, D.C.: Government Printing Office, 1895), 134; Farms and Homes: Proprietorship and Indebtedness (Washington, D.C.: Government Printing Office, 1896), 288. For the number of all mortgages (not just real estate) in 1885, see *Arkansas Gazette*, 25 July 1885.

53. *Fort Smith Elevator*, 13 November 1885; Conway County Court Record Book, July 1885–December 1887. Only one known copy of the *Morrilton Star* has survived, the issue of 10 June 1886. It is preserved in the Morrilton Museum.

54. *Arkansas Gazette*, 16 May 1886, 11 July 1886.

55. *Fort Smith Elevator*, 3 September 1886; *Arkansas Gazette*, 27 August 1886.

56. Returns for the September 1886 election in Conway County by precinct are in CvB, 970.

57. G. H. Taylor testimony, CvB, 1284–87; United States House of Representatives, *Digest of Contested Election Cases in the Fifty-First Congress Compiled under Resolution of the House, by Chester H. Rowell, Clerk to the Committee on Elections* (Washington, D.C.: Government Printing Office, 1891), 682. Hereafter cited as *Digest of Contested Election Cases.*

58. *Fort Smith Elevator*, 24 September 1886, from reports in the *Headlight.* A young prominent black leader with connections throughout the state, Trower served as a trustee for Shorter College, the African Methodist Episcopal college in North Little Rock; see Charles Spencer Smith, *A History of the African Methodist Episcopal Church* (Philadelphia: AME Church, 1922), 362.

59. John Mason to Arkansas History Commissioner Dallas T. Herndon, 2 April 1941, Individual File: John Madison [*sic*] Clayton, Arkansas History Commission, Little Rock; John Mason, audiotaped interview by Polly Church, 29 April 1978. John Mason is a particularly credible oral source. Born in Plumerville in 1899, his grandfather, Cyrus McCullough, was a witness and participant in the events described in this study. As a high school history teacher and school superintendent for many years, with a master's degree in history, Mr. Mason paid special attention to these stories he heard as a young man. This is evidenced by his attempt to preserve these accounts through his communication with Arkansas History Commissioner Herndon as early as 1941. Trower's move from Morrilton to Batesville is documented by his attendance at the annual conference of the AME Church. See Minutes of the 21st Session of the Arkansas Annual Conference of the African Methodist Episcopal Church, Batesville, 14–20 November 1888, Arkansas History Commission, Little Rock.

60. "Recollections of Emily Elizabeth Hervey Howard," Turney Papers.

3 Murder and Fraud: How Democrats Reclaimed Conway County, 1888–1889

1. For biographical information about John Clayton, see James W. Leslie, *Pine Bluff and Jefferson County: A Pictorial History* (Virginia Beach, Va.: Donning, 1981), 84; and *The Goodspeed Biographical and Historical Memoirs of Central Arkansas* (Chicago: Goodspeed Co., 1889), 163.
2. Curtis Barnes, "History of the Hopewell Community" (M.S.E. thesis, University of Central Arkansas, 1956), 1–2. One of Barnes's informants was W. B. McFarlin, who at age twelve was one of the original settlers from Georgia.
3. See Clifton Paisley, "The Political Wheelers and Arkansas' Election of 1888," *Arkansas Historical Quarterly* 25 (spring 1966): 3–21. In neighboring Faulkner County, which had been formed largely from Conway County in the division of 1873, Republicans at their party caucus in July demanded three positions on the fusion ticket for county offices as their price for allying with the Wheel. The Wheel was to meet on August 4 to fill out the ticket. Local Democrats urged Wheelers not to degenerate to such low-down behavior as the Republicans. While denouncing Republicans, the Democrats appealed in polite terms for the support of "democrats in the Agricultural Wheel, who have for any reason temporarily left the democratic party." Conway *Log Cabin Democrat*, 21 July 1888. For more on the organization of the national Union Labor Party, see Fink, *Workingmen's Democracy*, 27.
4. *Arkansas Gazette*, 31 July 1888, 25 and 26 August 1888, 2 September 1888.
5. Gov. Simon P. Hughes to W. J. Stowers, 27 August 1888, Simon P. Hughes Papers, Outgoing Letterbook, RG-11, SG-2, Ser. D, Arkansas History Commission; Gov. James P. Eagle testimony, CvB, 820–22; S. R. Allen testimony, CvB, 1220. The governor apparently sent arms to several other politically volatile areas of the state, such as Forrest City and Woodruff County, shortly before the election. See St. Louis *Globe-Democrat* report of 3 September 1888. *The Globe-Democrat* sent a reporter to Arkansas to cover the election.
6. See the account in the St. Louis *Globe-Democrat*, 3 September 1888. Republican sheriff Coblentz had visited Little Rock and shared his description of the state of affairs in Conway County with state Republican leaders.
7. W. J. Stowers testimony, CvB, 2080–86; St. Louis *Globe-Democrat*, 4 September 1888; *Washington Post*, 4 February 1889; *Arkansas Gazette*, 6 September 1888. See also Mrs. Eleanor Wood Moose's account in *Bits of Conway County Heritage* (Morrilton: Daughters of the American Revolution, 1976), 43.

8. Enoch Armstead testimony, CvB, 537–41; Judge G. H. Taylor testimony, CvB, 1288; returns for September 1886 and 1888 elections are in CvB, 970–72. The St. Louis *Globe-Democrat* report of 4 September 1888 under the headline "Law and Order Trampled Under Foot in Conway County," suggested that Republican election judges were forcibly replaced by Democrats in Springfield as well as in Morrilton and Plumerville.

9. *Digest of Contested Election Cases*, 682, 767; Paisley, "The Political Wheelers and Arkansas' Election of 1888," 18.

10. St. Louis *Globe-Democrat*, 6 September 1888; *Arkansas Gazette*, 5 and 6 September 1888.

11. *Digest of Contested Election Cases*, 681; *Arkansas Gazette*, 13, 20, and 31 October 1888, 2 and 3 November 1888.

12. G. H. Taylor testimony, CvB, 1282; Stowers admitted to telling the story, W. J. Stowers testimony, CvB, 2088.

13. Harry Miller testimony, CvB, 684–90; James Pope testimony, CvB, 693–94.

14. *Digest of Contested Election Cases*, 684, 717, 767; M.D. Shelby testimony, CvB, 2049; Morrilton *Headlight* article of 8 November 1888, copied in CvB, 2126; *Arkansas Gazette*, 6 and 7 November 1888.

15. Enoch Armstead testimony, CvB, 537–40; Charles Reid testimony, CvB, 815; *Digest of Contested Election Cases*, 681–83; *United States v. Thomas C. Hervey, William T. Hobbs, and William Palmer*, Eastern District of Arkansas, Federal Court Case File CCR986, National Archives, Southwest Region, Fort Worth, Texas.

16. Enoch Armstead testimony, CvB, 541–45; *Digest of Contested Election Cases*, 683; *Arkansas Gazette*, 19 and 28 April 1889; *United States v. Charles C. Reed, James Lucas, and John O. Blakeney*, Eastern District of Arkansas, Federal Court Case File CCR989, National Archives, Southwest Region, Fort Worth, Texas. Charles Reid Sr., the father of the young Charles, had a checkered past. In 1874 he exchanged hot words with another lawyer, Samuel Hill, in a Lewisburg courtroom until the court had to intervene to stop the two men. Afterward they resumed their quarrel in a store where Hill threw a couple of two-pound weights at Reid. Reid pulled out a pistol and shot Hill, killing him almost instantly. A coroner's inquest ruled it justifiable homicide. Reid died a few years later, bankrupt, owing Conway County several thousand dollars of tax money he had collected on behalf of the county from the Little Rock–Fort Smith Railroad Company. See *Arkansas Gazette*, 20 March 1874; and "Conway County et al. v. Little Rock and Fort Smith Railway Company," in *Reports of Cases at Law and in Equity Argued and Determined in the Supreme Court of the State of Arkansas*, May Term, 1882, 39 (Fort Smith: F. S. Calver-McBride, reprint edition, 1920), 50–54.

17. *Digest of Contested Election Cases*, 683; Charles Wahl testimony, CvB, 882–83; W. T. Hobbs testimony, CvB, 1814–16. See also Hervey's testimony before federal court, reported in *Arkansas Gazette*, 27 February 1889 and 3 May 1889.
18. Warren Taylor testimony, CvB, 882–83; New York *Press*, 22 May 1890; Charles Reid testimony, CvB, 775–86; see also the testimony of Warren Taylor, Charles Reid, George Washington, and others reported in *Arkansas Gazette*, 23, 26, and 27 April 1889, and 24 November 1889.
19. *Arkansas Gazette*, 27 February 1889; Benjamin G. White testimony, CvB, 1928.
20. See the discussion in Clifton Paisley, "The Political Wheelers and Arkansas' Election of 1888," *Arkansas Historical Quarterly* 25 (1966): 3–21.
21. *Digest of Contested Election Cases*, 681, 768; *Arkansas Gazette*, 15 November 1888, 27 December 1888; New York *World*, 6 July 1889.
22. Warren Taylor testimony, CvB, 943–44, 952; *Arkansas Gazette*, 6 and 13 January 1889; *Digest of Contested Election Cases*, 684. In a plea on the floor of the U.S. House of Representatives, Congressman Breckinridge repeated the ludicrous story that Republicans had stolen the ballot box. New York *Press*, 6 September 1890.
23. Interview with Oliver Bentley's grandson, Robert Cruce, 14 December 1992. Charles Wahl testimony, CvB, 882–83; W. T. Hobbs testimony, CvB, 1814–16.
24. Warren Taylor testimony, CvB, 928; *Digest of Contested Election Cases*, 685–86; *Fort Smith Elevator*, 7 December 1888; *New York Press*, 22 May 1890; Gordon Earl Bentley, interview of 7 October 1992. Eleanor Wood Moose's account in *Bits of Conway County Heritage*, 44, also suggests Bentley was shot five times.
25. S. N. Landers testimony, CvB, 1957–60; B. G. White testimony, CvB, 1928–31; Charles Wahl testimony, CvB, 885–900; Eliza Mason testimony, CvB, 901; *Digest of Contested Election Cases*, 768; *Arkansas Gazette*, 22 November 1889, 2 May 1890. One might note that the *Gazette* did not report either the killing of Bentley or the attempted assassination of Wahl as news items.
26. *Digest of Contested Election Cases*, 768; *United States v. Benjamin G. White, Cyrus H. McCullough, Russell Watson, William Durham, and William Palmer*; Eastern District of Arkansas, Federal Court Case File CCR1022, National Archives, Southwest Region, Fort Worth, Texas; Conway County Circuit Court, Criminal Record Book, March 1889–October 1899, 138–39, 383; *Arkansas Gazette*, 27 February 1889.
27. New York *World*, 6 July 1889, reported Hervey's remarks; G. H. Taylor testimony, CvB, 1279; statement of John McClure, CvB, supporting documents, 16x.

28. Poindexter Fiser of Morrilton, interview of 2 December 1992, says even the choice of Clayton's room had been prearranged by his assassins; John Simms testimony, CvB, 1747–48; A. W. Middlebrook testimony, CvB, 1261–63; Carroll Armstrong testimony, CvB, 2013–14.
29. A. W. Middlebrook testimony, CvB, 1261–63; *Digest of Contested Election Cases*, 684–85; *Arkansas Gazette*, 9 May 1890.
30. Oliver T. Bentley testimony, CvB, 762–64; C. C. Reid testimony, CvB, 790–92; statement by John McClure, CvB, supporting documents, 18x; *Digest of Contested Election Cases*, 684; *Arkansas Gazette*, 17 February 1889, 1 May 1890.
31. John Mason to Ernie Dean, 26 February 1980, Small Manuscripts Collection, Box LXXII, No. 17, Arkansas History Commission. John Mason interview. Mrs. Clarkia Turney of Morrilton also tells the same basic story. In her version, the group of conspirators was smaller, numbering around eight, and no one supposedly knew who drew the short straw. Clarkia Turney interview, 6 January 1993. In the version told by James Malone, the grandson of store owner A. D. Malone, the men drew marbles to see who would kill Clayton. The killer drew the black ball. James Malone Sr. interview, 25 February 1994. In Willie Belle Reddig's version, money exchanged hands at the meeting, Reddig interview, 28 February 1994. See also Eleanor Wood Moose's account of the meeting in *Bits of Conway County Heritage*, 44.
32. *Digest of Contested Election Cases*, 685; W. H. Clayton testimony, CvB, 1030; John Mason to Ernie Deane.
33. The genealogical connection between Bob Pate and the Pate family of Van Buren County cannot be precisely traced. Wills, tax assessments, and family testimony suggest that the families were connected. John Mason says he discussed Clayton's murder in the early 1930s with members of the Pate family in Clinton and that they "just laughed about it." John Mason interview; Emma Sue Beavers interview, 8 May 1992. The sighting of Pate at the murder scene by the black men and Pate's account of Reconstruction is reported in the New York *World*, 6 July 1889.
34. John Mason interview; M. D. Shelby testimony, CvB, 2048; *Arkansas Gazette*, 21 November 1889, 3 May 1890.
35. *Arkansas Gazette*, 31 January 1889; Pine Bluff *Commercial*, 3 February 1889; Russellville *Democrat*, 7 February 1889; see Allnutt's testimony, recorded in *Digest of Contested Election Cases*, 739–46. J. M. Johnston, who was present at the coroner's hearing in 1889, remarked sixty years later to Neil Hobbs Horton, owner of the All-in-One Store in Plumerville, that "any one of a number of men including some of those on the coroner's jury could have committed the crime." Horton was interviewed by James W. Leslie for an article he wrote on the Clayton assassination in the *Arkansas Gazette*, 17 June 1973.

36. St. Louis *Globe-Democrat*, 31 January 1889; New York *World*, 6 July 1889.

37. Fiftieth Congress, Second Session, House of Representatives, *Miscellaneous Document, No. 115, Clayton vs. Breckinridge;* the Kansas resolution was mentioned by Arkansas representative John H. Rogers in a speech delivered to the House floor on 23 April 1890, and a copy of the speech is in File 6, John H. Rogers Family Collection, University of Arkansas at Little Rock Archives. *North American Review* 148 (March 1889): 287–93.

38. *Digest of Contested Election Cases*, 686, 773–78; New York *World*, 6 July 1889.

39. The first letter, received 4 March 1889, read: "I am the man who killed J. M. Clayton. I went to Plumerville to kill Powell Clayton. Powell Clayton had my father and brother killed when I was a child. I have been west for 19 years, and returned to Fort Smith just after the election expecting to meet Powell Clayton at Plumerville, but did not, but will get him yet before I die—the son of a bitch killed my father and brother. Don't blame any one in a [illegible] and I am a Republican." CvB, 1352. The second letter, postmarked from New Hampshire in June 1889, can be found in CvB, supporting documents. Bentley's profession of ignorance of the relationship between Powell and John Clayton can be found in the New York *World*, 8 July 1889.

40. Warren Taylor testimony, CvB, 930; *Arkansas Gazette*, 31 January 1889, 1, 5, 6, 10, and 26 February 1889, 10 March 1889; New York *World*, 20 July 1889.

41. Information on Cunningham is found in his obituary in Center Ridge *Conway County Banner*, 24 March 1904. Discussion of Cunningham's lecture is in *Arkansas Gazette*, 10 and 13 March 1889. Arkansas author Alice French said a member of the grand jury had told her the story that the criminals had fled the state. See her account under the nom de plume Octave Thanet in "Town Life in Arkansas," *Atlantic Monthly* 68 (September 1891): 336.

42. *Digest of Contested Election Cases*, 771; G. F. Christenberry testimony, CvB, 1942; Robert L. Pate testimony, CvB, 730–31. The New York *World*, 6 July 1889, reported that Pate had told John McClure in an unguarded moment that he had conversed with Bentley for a short time, meeting him by the depot in Plumerville earlier on the day of Clayton's murder. Albert Wood's report on his investigation unfortunately has disappeared. However, the Clayton brothers gave copies of the report to their lawyer, John McClure, and to members of the congressional subcommittee who in 1890 investigated the Clayton murder and the stolen election. The partial contents of the report can be established only by the questions posed by the examiners.

43. W. J. Stowers testimony, CvB, 2094; W. M. Scarborough testimony, CvB, 1901–2; John Hinkle testimony, CvB, 1885. Hinkle was the lawyer whom Bentley visited on 29 January 1889.

44. *Arkansas Gazette*, 2, 7, and 30 April 1890, 2 May 1890; *Digest of Contested Election Cases*, 685; the St. Louis *Globe-Democrat*, 1 April 1889, carried a front page sensationalized headline about the murder ("Killed at Plumerville—Murder of a Negro Who Knew Too Much about the Clayton Affair—An Arkansas Town That Is Writing Its History in Blood") and printed a copy of Smith's letter to Detective Wood.

45. *Arkansas Gazette*, 7, 14, and 18 April 1889. The *Gazette* account is probably based on news forwarded by the Morrilton *Headlight*. Editor J. O. Blakeney interviewed Richmond in his jail cell. J. O. Blakeney testimony, CvB, 2067–68; *Fort Smith Elevator*, 5 April 1889. Breckinridge's speech is discussed in the *Arkansas Gazette*, 11 March 1890.

46. R. H. Gray testimony, CvB, 1306; *Arkansas Gazette*, 3 April 1889; Conway County Indictments Record Book, 1887–October 1890, 401–2. This entire incident illustrates the old southern police saying quoted by Edward Ayers in his study of southern violence, *Vengeance and Justice*, 231: "If a nigger kills a white man, that's murder. If a white man kills a nigger, that's justifiable homicide. If a nigger kills another nigger, that's one less nigger."

47. New York *World*, 6 July 1889. The *World*'s reporter, John C. Klein, interviewed W. H. and Powell Clayton in Fort Smith; Governor James P. Eagle, Congressman Breckinridge, and John McClure in Little Rock; Sheriff Shelby, W. J. Stowers, and Oliver Bentley in Morrilton; and several Plumerville residents including John Simms, Bert Walley, Mrs. McCravens, Bill Palmer, and others.

48. *Arkansas Gazette*, 27 February 1889, 1 March 1889; *New York Times*, 1 March 1889.

49. *United States v. Thomas C. Hervey, William T. Hobbs, William Palmer*; *New York Times*, 22 April 1889.

50. *Arkansas Gazette*, 28 April 1889, 7 May 1889; *New York Times*, 28 April 1889. For information on Reid, see *Historical Reminiscences and Biographical Memoirs of Conway County*, 100–101. Judge Caldwell had come to Arkansas in 1864 with an Iowa regiment of the Union army and stayed to open the first session of federal court in Little Rock after the war. John Hallum, *Biographical and Pictorial History of Arkansas* (Albany: Weed, Pursons, and Company, 1887), 482.

51. *Arkansas Gazette*, 23 April 1889; Warren Taylor testimony, CvB, 933–34, 948.

52. Charles Reid testimony, CvB, 808; *United States v. Charles Reid, et al.*; *Arkansas Gazette*, 23, 26, and 27 April 1889.

53. *Arkansas Gazette*, 7, 9, and 10 May 1889.
54. *Arkansas Gazette*, 7 May 1889, 19 November 1889.
55. *Arkansas Gazette*, 25 July 1889, 1–2 August 1889. Warren Taylor had suggested in his testimony in Washington, D.C., in 1890 that threats on Cunningham's life had motivated his move to Oklahoma. Taylor was also living in Guthrie, Oklahoma, at the time of his trip to Washington. *Arkansas Gazette*, 30 May 1890. The New York *World*, 6 July 1889, originally published the charge that Cunningham had fled fearing for his life. The *World* made the charge after sending a reporter to Conway County to investigate. Cunningham eventually moved back to Dardanelle, where he died in 1904 as the result of an accidental discharge of a gun. His obituary appeared in the Center Ridge *Conway County Banner*, 24 March 1904.
56. *Arkansas Gazette*, 19 November 1889. Thomas L. Cox, the former Morrilton schoolmaster, by the early 1900s worked as the railroad industry's point man with the state legislature. In 1908 he admitted he had bribed legislators to secure favorable legislation for the railroads. Several of the legislators were convicted for taking his bribes, but a statute of limitations protected Cox from prosecution. See Richard L. Niswonger, *Arkansas Democratic Politics, 1896–1920* (Fayetteville: University of Arkansas Press, 1990), 111.
57. *Arkansas Gazette*, 21, 22, 23, 24, and 26 November 1889.
58. *Digest of Contested Election Cases*, 778–79; *Arkansas Gazette*, 4 and 13 May 1889; *Fort Smith Elevator*, 9 and 16 May 1889.
59. New York *Press*, 22 May 1890, 4 September 1890; *Fort Smith Elevator*, 30 May 1890; *Digest of Contested Election Cases*, 679.

4 Consequences of Murder: Things Fall Apart, 1890–1893

1. W. D. Leslie to William Coppinger, 18 August 1890, Reel 134; B. T. Willis to Coppinger, 14 October 1890, Reel 135, American Colonization Society Records, Library of Congress, Washington D.C.
2. Gordon, *Caste and Class*, 2, 31–32. For a discussion of the Republican Party organization in Arkansas, see Marvin Frank Russell, "The Republican Party in Arkansas, 1874–1913" (Ph.D. diss., University of Arkansas, 1985); and Charles Rector, "Lily-White Republicanism: The Arkansas Experience, 1877–1928," *Ozark Historical Review* 22 (spring 1993): 49–68. For more on the political context of the early 1890s, see Nell Irvin Painter, *Standing at Armageddon: The United States, 1877–1919* (New York: W. W. Norton, 1987), 60–114.
3. *Arkansas Gazette*, 5, 26, and 30 August 1890.

4. *Arkansas Gazette*, 24 July 1890, 5, 13, and 19 August 1890. For a discussion of the problems inherent in any alliance of poor whites and blacks, see W. E. B. DuBois's monumental work, *Black Reconstruction in America* (New York: Russell and Russell, 1935).

5. *Historical Reminiscences and Biographical Memoirs of Conway County*, 33; *Arkansas Gazette*, 29 August 1890, 2 September 1890. Gratten owned 180 acres of land in Howard township in 1880 (1880 Census, Agriculture Schedule, manuscript returns). He was a delegate for Conway County in 1883 to the state colored convention in Little Rock and in 1884 served as an officer of the state Republican committee. Little Rock *Arkansas Mansion*, 1 September 1883, 12 April 1884.

6. St. Louis *Globe-Democrat*, 31 August 1890. The article also appeared on the first page of the New York *World*, 1 September 1890. The *Arkansas Gazette* did not report the incident as news. Articles appeared on 2 September and 13 September only to deny the accuracy of reports appearing in northern newspapers such as the *Globe-Democrat* and New York *Tribune*. Chairman Lacey of the Committee on Elections read the *Tribune* account of Small's beating to the House of Representatives just before the congressmen voted to unseat Clifton Breckinridge.

7. *Arkansas Gazette*, 4 and 10 September 1890; Conway County Court Record Book, April 1890–April 1892, 140; St. Louis *Globe-Democrat*, 31 August 1890.

8. *Arkansas Gazette*, 9, 11, 12, and 15 October 1890; Morrilton *Pilot*, 21 November 1890; Conway County Circuit Court, Criminal Record Book, March 1889–October 1899, 138–39; Conway County Indictment Book, October 1890, 431.

9. *Arkansas Gazette*, 9 and 22 November 1890.

10. For a discussion of the separate-coach law of 1891, see Graves, *Town and Country*, 150–63. The *New York Times*, 27 March 1891 reported that Miss Jennie Delaney of Little Rock painted the life-size portrait of Davis in only twenty days and that it was received in the senate chambers with cheers.

11. See the excellent discussion of electoral change in Graves, *Town and Country*, 164–73; and Kousser, *The Shaping of Southern Politics*, 123–30.

12. Originally published in the *Arkansas Gazette*, 2 September 1892, quoted in Graves, *Town and Country*, 176.

13. Morrilton *Pilot*, 21 November 1890, 5 August 1892.

14. Any organization of black Alliance lodges must have come through the separate Colored Farmers' Alliance, which by 1890 claimed 20,000 members in Arkansas. Arkansas's Agricultural Wheel had been open to black membership in separate local lodges. But with the merger in December 1888 with the Farmers' Alliance, the organization became limited to whites only. See Graves, *Town and Country*, 202–5. Lawrence Goodwyn, the pre-

eminent historian of America's agrarian populist movement, suggests that Arkansas's populists showed the most liberal record in matters of race of any of the southern groups. See his *Democratic Promise: The Populist Movement in America* (New York: Oxford University Press, 1976), 298. For a detailed examination of blacks and the populist movement, see Gerald H. Gaither, *Blacks and the Populist Revolt: Ballots and Bigotry in the "New South"* (Tuscaloosa: University of Alabama Press, 1977).

15. *Arkansas Gazette*, 5 July 1891, 13 August 1891; Morrilton *Pilot*, 28 August 1891. For a discussion of the subtreasury plan, see Lawrence Goodwyn, *The Populist Movement: A Short History of the Agrarian Revolt in America* (New York: Oxford University Press, 1978), 90–93, 301–7.

16. Morrilton *Pilot*, 13 February 1891, 5 July 1891, 22 July 1892; *Historical Reminiscences and Biographical Memoirs of Conway County*, 18–19, 33.

17. Morrilton *Pilot*, 22 July 1892.

18. See sketch of Jacobson in Fay Williams, *Arkansans of the Years* (Little Rock: C. C. Allard, 1953), 3:165; Morrilton *Pilot*, 22 July 1892, 12 August 1892, 16 September 1892.

19. Kousser, *The Shaping of Southern Politics*, 127–29; Graves, *Town and Country*, 166. See also the discussion of the effects of disfranchisement in Raymond Arsenault, *The Wild Ass of the Ozarks: Jeff Davis and the Social Bases of Southern Politics* (Knoxville: University of Tennessee Press, 1988), 41–46.

20. *Digest of Contested Election Cases*, 708–9; Morrilton *Pilot*, 19 August 1892, 16 September 1892, 18 November 1892; *Arkansas Gazette*, 22 November 1890.

21. Morrilton *Pilot*, 2 and 16 September 1892; *Arkansas Gazette*, 7 September 1894; quote comes from *Arkansas Gazette*, 4 September 1894.

22. Abner Downs to William Coppinger, 6 April 1889; Anthony Lipscomb to Coppinger, 20 August 1889, 30 October 1889, 7 January 1890, and 7 June 1890; Microfilm Reel 132, American Colonization Society Records, Library of Congress, Washington, D.C. (hereafter cited as ACS).

23. For a discussion of the background of the Liberia migration of the 1890s, see Edwin S. Redkey, *Black Exodus: Black Nationalist and Back-to-Africa Movements, 1890–1910* (New Haven: Yale University Press, 1969), 1–23.

24. W. D. Leslie to Coppinger, 18 August 1890, Reel 134, ACS; W. K. Fortson to Coppinger, 22 April and 9 July 1890, Reel 134, 14 October 1890, Reel 135, ACS; H. A. Anthony to Coppinger, 7 June 1890, Reel 134, ACS; W. H. King, 3 October 1890, Reel 135, ACS; B. Tillis to Coppinger, 10 October 1890, Reel 135, ACS; W. H. Westbrook, 19 October 1890, Reel 135, ACS; J. W. Polk to Coppinger, 24 November 1890, Reel 135, ACS.

25. John C. Long to Coppinger, 10 November 1890, Reel 135, ACS; James Dargan to Coppinger, 11 November 1890, Reel 135, ACS.
26. William Jones to Coppinger, 13 January 1891, Reel 136, ACS; W. D. Leslie to Coppinger, 17 January 1891, Reel 136, ACS; L. W. West to Coppinger, 22 April 1891, Reel 137, ACS; John R. Jimison to Coppinger, 13 August 1891, Reel 138, ACS.
27. W. H. King to Coppinger, 28 November 1890, Reel 135, ACS; James Dargan to Coppinger, 7 December 1890, Reel 135, 3 January 1891, Reel 136, ACS.
28. James Dargan to Coppinger, 9 January 1891, Reel 136, ACS; Yves Dargan to Coppinger, 14 February 1891, Reel 136, ACS.
29. Miles West to Coppinger, 21 February 1891, Reel 136, ACS; L. W. West to Coppinger, 22 April 1891, Reel 137, ACS; William S. Dooley to Coppinger, 13 April 1891.
30. W. A. Diggs to Coppinger, 19 February 1891, Reel 136, ACS; W. K. Fortson to Coppinger, 30 March 1891, Reel 136, ACS.
31. Abner Downs to Coppinger, 13 May 1891, Reel 137, ACS; W. H. King to Coppinger, 8 May 1891, 19 May 1891, Reel 137, ACS; D. H. Patterson to Coppinger, 26 May 1891, Reel 137, ACS; W. M. Jones to Coppinger, 6 July 1891, Reel 137, ACS.
32. Handbill, "Public Sale," in correspondence of 15 October 1891, Reel 138, ACS; W. M. Wilson to Coppinger, 6 November 1891, Reel 139, ACS; W. A. Diggs to Coppinger, 31 October 1891, Reel 138, ACS; W. A. Diggs to Coppinger, 9 November 1891, Reel 139, ACS.
33. See the account of the confusion in New York City during February 1892 in Redkey, *Black Exodus*, 113–26. The emigrants' arrival in Liberia is described in E. E. Smith to Fendall, 19 April 1892, Reel 140, but located with the letters of 27 June 1892, ACS.
34. Redkey, *Black Exodus*, 134; W. D. Leslie to Reginald Fendall, 1 April 1892, Reel 139, ACS; L. J. Allington and A. J. Johnson to ACS, 2 May 1892, Reel 139, ACS; J. Shelton Leaphart to ACS, 15 June 1892, Reel 140, ACS; J. R. Jimison to ACS, 7 July 1892, Reel 141 (but located in the November 1892 section of correspondence), ACS; *Arkansas Gazette*, 11 March 1892. For more information about the black migration to Oklahoma, see Williamson, *The Crucible of Race*, 242–43.
35. Although the Morrilton *Pilot* ignored the 1892 black emigration, in the previous year, the paper had noted the earlier migration with a one-line entry on 13 February 1891, p. 11: "About forty negroes left this place Monday for Africa." See the *New York Times*, 24 February 1892.
36. *New York Times*, 22 and 26 February 1892. The records of the ACS show 1,301 applicants from Conway County between 1889 and 1891 out of

a population of 7,671 blacks in the county in 1890. The actual number of applicants is probably much higher. Hundreds of applications in 1890 and 1891 were on forms that did not identify the location of the applicants. The secretary usually cut off the postmark from the outside of the envelope and pasted it on the front of the form. Many of these fell off, leaving the location of the applicants a mystery. See Williamson, *Crucible of Race*, 230–31, for a discussion of white views of blacks.

37. W. K. Fortson to Coppinger, 9 July 1890, Reel 134, ACS; W. A. Diggs to Coppinger, 21 April 1891, Reel 137, ACS; John R. Jimison to Coppinger, 22 April 1891, Reel 137, ACS; James Harris to Coppinger, 4 December 1890, Reel 135, ACS; D. H. Patterson to Coppinger, 26 May 1891, Reel 137, ACS; B. T. Willis to Coppinger, 14 October 1890, Reel 135, ACS.

38. Alexander B. Smart interview, 18 February 1997. Smart's mother, Minnie Caroline Shaver, left Plumerville with her family for Liberia when she was only nine years old. Rogers's letter can be found in Atlanta *Voice of Missions*, February 1896, 3.

39. Morrilton *Pilot*, 14 April 1893; *Arkansas Gazette*, 7 and 16 April 1893.

40. For details of Landers's story, see the Morrilton *Pilot*, 14 April 1893; and *Arkansas Gazette*, 13 April 1893.

41. *Arkansas Gazette*, 27 May 1893; Marshall *Mountain Wave*, 4 May 1893; *Bits of Conway County Heritage*, 44.

42. Morrilton *Pilot*, 30 March 1894.

43. The *Pilot*'s threat of lynching against Thornton appeared on 7 April 1893. The paper's report of Thornton's lynching, under the headline "Looked Up a Rope," is so vivid and detailed that one suspects the reporter was part of the disguised mob. Morrilton *Pilot*, 21 April 1893. See also the report in the St. Louis *Globe-Democrat*, 20 April 1893. For Jeff Davis's role, see *Arkansas Gazette*, 27 April 1893. Davis is quoted in Dougan, *Arkansas Odyssey*, 311.

44. Morrilton *Pilot*, 28 April 1893; *Arkansas Gazette*, 21 and 22 April 1893.

45. The Thornton lynching may not have been the county's first. In November 1891, a traveler found the dead body of a black man hanging from a tree limb by a bridle rein. The man's neck was broken, and there were signs that he had been dragged for some distance. Morrilton *Pilot*, 13 November 1891. See the discussion of lynchings in Wright, *Racial Violence in Kentucky;* Tolnay and Beck, *Festival of Violence;* and Hofstadter, "Reflections on Violence in the United States."

46. The details about this lynching came from Poindexter Fiser, interview of 2 December 1992, Morrilton. Fiser explained that he was supposed to go with the group to do the deed. But he arrived a bit late, by which time the victim was hanging in a tree. C. Vann Woodward graduated from Morrilton High School in 1924. His recollection is described in his biography

by John Herbert Roper, *C. Vann Woodward, Southerner*, 16. See also the account in the New York *Tribune*, 10 December 1922.

5 Murder's Reward: Rule of the Fine-Haired Gentlemen

1. For information on Reid, see U.S. Congress, *Biographical Directory of the United States Congress, 1774–1989* (Washington, D.C.: Government Printing Office, 1989), 1704; for Jacobsen see Raymond Arsenault, "Charles Jacobsen of Arkansas: A Jewish Politician in the Land of Razorbacks, 1891–1915," in *"Turn to the South": Essays on Southern Jewry*, ed. Nathan M. Kaganoff and Melvin I. Urofsky (Charlottesville: University Press of Virginia, 1979), 55–75; on Carroll Armstrong, see Niswonger, *Arkansas Democratic Politics, 1896–1920*, 133; on Robert Leigh, see Morrilton *Arkansas Unit*, 1 August 1929, and *Handbook of the Arkansas River Valley*, 39–43.
2. Of the inner circle of Democratic leaders, only Charles Reid and Ben White diverged from the pattern of a second-generation Conway County elite. Reid, the son of a lawyer, moved to Conway County soon after the Civil War. White was a self-made man. Born in Conway County in 1852, he managed to save enough money as a small farmer to send himself to medical school in Nashville, Tennessee. He returned to Conway County to farm and practice medicine in 1881. *Historical Reminiscences of Conway County*, 100–101; Morrilton *Pilot*, 1 September 1892. John J. Beck found a very similar pattern for Rowan County, North Carolina. The leaders there in the development of a commercial town economy and culture in the 1870s and 1880s were members of an upper class that had evolved from the landed slave-owning class in antebellum days. He argues that economic changes in Rowan County were a managed transformation by which the elite kept control of the labor force. See John J. Beck, "Building the New South: A Revolution from Above in a Piedmont County," *Journal of Southern History* 53 (August 1987): 441–70.
3. The first electric light plant in Morrilton opened in 1891 and ran a light circuit through the center of town along Railroad Avenue. See the Morrilton *Pilot*, 27 November 1891. Morrilton did not get telephone service until 1899. *Bits of Conway County Heritage*, 28–29.
4. Alice French (pen name Octave Thanet), "Town Life in Arkansas," *Atlantic Monthly* 68 (September 1891): 333–34. See also her article published in the July 1891 issue, "Plantation Life in Arkansas," 32–49.
5. For a discussion of this view, see John W. Cell, *The Highest Stage of White Supremacy: The Origins of Segregation in South Africa and the American South* (Cambridge: Cambridge University Press, 1982); and Jack Temple

Kirby, *Darkness at the Dawning: Race and Reform in the Progressive South* (Philadelphia: J. B. Lippincott Company, 1972).

6. See, for example, Josiah H. Shinn, *The History of Arkansas: A Textbook for Public Schools, High School, and Academies* (Richmond, Va.: B. F. Johnson, 1905), 255–56. Shinn had been a school administrator in Morrilton before becoming state superintendent of public instruction and writing this work, one of the first school histories of Arkansas.

7. C. Vann Woodward, *The Strange Career of Jim Crow* (New York: Oxford University Press, 1955), viii; John E. McClure, *The Old South and the New* (Little Rock: n.p., 1891), 14, 28. Although neither Sheriff Shelby nor W. J. Stowers lived in Conway County during Reconstruction, both told a New York *World* reporter that Clayton's militia raped white women. New York *World*, 8 July 1889. For a discussion of Democratic mythologizing, see Paul M. Gaston, *The New South Creed: A Study in Southern Mythmaking* (New York: Knopf, 1970). See also Joel Williamson's discussion of common white images of blacks as oversexed and rape prone, in *The Crucible of Race*, 183–89, 306–10.

8. Morrilton *Pilot*, 16 September 1892.

9. John Mason interview; John Mason to Dallas Herndon; John Mason to Ernie Dean; Moose, "Civil War Reconstruction Days," *Bits of Conway County Heritage*, 39–44.

10. Although stories of the Clayton murder were well preserved among families of white Democrats, less oral lore has survived among the families who lost out in the struggle, white small farmers and African Americans. Joel Williamson, in *The Crucible of Race*, 226–28, calls the painful removal of blacks from politics in the Upper South in the early 1890s an "echo Reconstruction." Whereas Redemption in the 1870s had left blacks in the Deep South largely shut out from politics, the process was delayed about twenty years in the Upper South states.

11. Unable to find this book in an Arkansas library, I secured the book through interlibrary loan from a library in New York. W. Scott Morgan, *The Red Light: A Story of Southern Politics and Election Methods* (Moravian Falls, N.C.: Yellow Jacket Press, 1904). Morgan weaves the Conway County story with the story of Democratic triumph in Crittenden County through the narrative vehicle of his heroine, Eva Farley. She leaves "Morriston" after the congressional candidate is killed, and she joins relatives in "Critwell" County, where she falls in love with the leader of the county Alliance chapter. The last part of the book tells a similarly true account of political violence in Crittenden County.

12. *Biennial Report of the Secretary of State of the State of Arkansas* (Little Rock, 1895), 65–67; *Arkansas Gazette*, 7 September 1894.

13. Kousser, *The Shaping of Southern Politics*, 130; election numbers for

Conway County come from the *Biennial Report of the Secretary of State of the State of Arkansas*, 1890, 1892, 1894 (Little Rock, 1890–1895).

14. Curtis Barnes, interview of 2 February 1992; Mrs. Grant Reddig, interview of 17 October 1992; Beva Winningham, interview of 23 October 1992; Robert Morrow, interview of 22 October 1992. For a comparison with white Republicanism elsewhere in the Upper South, see McKinney, *Southern Mountain Republicans.*

15. George T. Bird military pension file, National Archives, Washington, D.C.; *Historical Reminiscences and Biographical Memoirs of Conway County*, 47; Maxine Barnes, interview of 2 February 1992.

16. See Hawkins's autobiography, *How I Stole Elections: The Autobiography of Sheriff Marlin Hawkins* (Little Rock: Rose Publishing, 1991); and the account of the opposition to the Hawkins machine by Gene Wirges, *Conflict of Interests: The Gene Wirges Story* (North Little Rock, Ark.: Riverboat Publishers, 1992). Wirges says on pp. 53–54 that over a ten-year period of Hawkins's rule, Conway County made the most traffic arrests but raised the least amount of fine money of all of Arkansas's seventy-five counties. Wirges charges that Hawkins and his associates stole the difference.

17. Wolfe, "Background of the German Immigration," 363–64; Koren, *The Serpent and the Dove*, 115–16.

18. *Twelfth Census: Population*, 495.

19. Koren, *The Serpent and the Dove*, 116.

20. James M. Woods, *Mission and Memory: A History of the Catholic Church in Arkansas* (Little Rock: Diocese of Little Rock, 1993), 187.

21. Koren, *The Serpent and the Dove*, 124.

22. Center Ridge *Conway County Banner*, 25 February 1904.

23. U.S. Manuscript Census Returns, Population Schedules, 1880 and 1900, Conway County, Arkansas.

24. *Arkansas Gazette*, 6 February 1889, 24 July 1889.

25. Cyrus McCullough testimony, CvB, 1938; Robert L. Pate testimony, CvB, 730; *Arkansas Gazette*, 25 July 1890.

26. Morrilton *Pilot*, 19 August 1892, 3 February 1893; and Conway *Log Cabin Democrat*, 10 February 1893, commenting on Leigh's editorial of 3 February 1893. The experience of Conway County supports C. Vann Woodward's views that the harsh radical racism of the 1890s was a departure from earlier days. See Woodward's *The Strange Career of Jim Crow* (New York: Oxford University Press, 1955). In contrast, Howard N. Rabinowitz argues that segregation of the 1890s was an improvement over the exclusion of blacks that had prevailed before. For Rabinowitz, *Plessy v. Ferguson* (1896) was a civil rights act. See Rabinowitz, "Segregation and Reconstruction," in *The Facts of Reconstruction: Essays in Honor of John Hope Franklin*, ed. Eric Anderson and Alfred E. Moss (Baton Rouge: Louisiana

State University Press, 1991), 79–97. In Conway County, blacks progressed from some segregation, within which they possessed real political power, to more segregation and exclusion from power. Woodward's argument about the relationship of agrarian populism and the rise of Jim Crow holds true for Conway County. The first attempt to force residential segregation in the county came in 1885, just months after the coalition of blacks and poor whites removed Democrats from office. Whites, dressed as the Ku Klux Klan, tried to force all blacks in the county to move south of the railroad line. For a close analysis of the theory and practice of radical racism in the 1890s, see Williamson, *The Crucible of Race*, 111–323.

27. Quoted in sketch of Charles Jacobsen in Williams, *Arkansans of the Years*, 3:165.

28. Indianapolis *Freeman*, 29 June 1895, printed in Willard B. Gatewood, "Arkansas Negroes in the 1890s: Documents," *Arkansas Historical Quarterly* 33 (winter 1974): 319.

29. For an introduction to the subject of political violence as it continued in the South, see Wright, *Racial Violence in Kentucky, 1865–1940;* Christopher Waldrep, *Night Riders: Defending Community in the Black Patch, 1890–1915* (Durham: Duke University Press, 1993); James R. McGovern, *Anatomy of a Lynching: The Killing of Claude Neal* (Baton Rouge: Louisiana State University Press, 1982); Howard Smead, *Blood Justice: The Lynching of Mack Charles Parker* (New York: Oxford University Press, 1986); and Brundage, *Lynching in the New South.* Tolnay and Beck's *Festival of Violence* debunks many myths and assumptions about lynchings through quantitative analysis. The authors nonetheless assume that lynchings occurred when whites felt threatened by blacks. They conclude that economic competition, particularly in cotton production, propelled lower-class whites to use lynching to weaken their poor black rivals. The Thornton lynching, like the rampage of lynchings that swept through Arkansas in 1892 and 1893, suggests just the contrary. Relatively prosperous white townsfolk, not poor farmers, turned to lynching after the real black threat had passed, when their position was so secure that they did not fear retribution.

30. James M. McPherson, *What They Fought For, 1861–1865* (Baton Rouge: Louisiana State University Press, 1994).

Bibliography

Archival Materials

Arkansas History Commission, Little Rock

Adjutant General's Office Papers, Boxes 1–3, 6–12.

African Methodist Episcopal Church, Arkansas Session Minutes, 1885–1890.

Correspondence Registers, Powell Clayton's Correspondence, 1868–1871.

James P. Eagle, outgoing letterbook, 1889.

Simon P. Hughes, outgoing letterbook, 1888–1889.

Individual File: John Madison [*sic*] Clayton.

Charles Lanman Collection.

Kie Oldham Collection, Box 2.

Small Manuscripts Collection, Box LXXII, No. 17.

Conway County Courthouse, Morrilton

Circuit Court Record Books, 1868–1893.

Circuit Court, Criminal Record Book, 1889–1899.

County Court Record Books, 1868–1893.

Indictments Record Book, 1887–1890.

Tax Assessment Books, 1887, 1889, 1890.

Duke University, Perkins Library

Jesse Turner Papers.

Library of Congress, Washington, D.C.

American Colonization Society Records, microfilm reels 132–41.

National Archives, Southwest Region, Fort Worth

United States v. Benjamin G. White, Cyrus H. McCullough, Russell Watson, William Durham, and William Palmer. Eastern District of Arkansas. Federal Court Case File CCR1022.

United States v. Charles C. Reed, James Lucas, and John O. Blakeney. Eastern District of Arkansas. Federal Court Case File CCR989.

United States v. Thomas C. Hervey, William T. Hobbs, and William Palmer. Eastern District of Arkansas. Federal Court Case File CCR986.

National Archives, Washington, D.C.

Contested Election: Clayton vs. Breckinridge, Committee on Elections, 51st Congress, 1889–1990. Four bound manuscript volumes.
Freedman's Bureau Records: Arkansas, Field Offices microfilm.
Military pension files for George T. Bird, Leroy Williams, Morton W. Williams, and Thomas Jefferson Williams.
Third Arkansas Union Cavalry, Descriptive Book.
Manuscript Census materials microfilms, Conway County, Arkansas
Population Schedules for 1850, 1860, 1870, 1880, 1900.
Agriculture Schedules for 1850, 1860, 1870, 1880.
Slave Schedules for 1850, 1860.

Stanford University Library, Special Collections

General Frederick Steele Collection, Box 2.

University of Arkansas, Special Collections

May Hope Moose papers.

University of Arkansas at Little Rock, Archives

John H. Rogers Family Collection, File 6.

Private Collections

Clarkia Turney, Morrilton, Arkansas. Hervey-Moose family papers.
Sheldon Bentley, West Lafayette, Indiana. Bentley family papers.

Newspapers

Atlanta *Voice of Missions*, 1893–1896.
Augusta (Ga.) *Chronicle and Constitutionalist*, 1882.
Center Ridge (Ark.) *Conway County Banner*, 1903–1904.
Charleston (S.C.) *News and Courier*, 1881–1882.
Conway (Ark.) *Log Cabin Democrat*, 1882, 1888, 1893.
Edgefield (S.C.) *Chronicle*, 1881–1882.
Fort Smith (Ark.) *Elevator*, 1886–1892.
Lead Hill (Ark.) *Bugle*, 1884.
Little Rock *Arkansas Democrat*, 1881–1893.
Little Rock *Arkansas Gazette*, 1852–1893.
Little Rock *Arkansas Mansion*, 1883–1884.

Little Rock *Daily Republican*, 1868–1869.
Little Rock *National Democrat*, 1863–1864.
Little Rock *Old Line Democrat*, 1860.
Little Rock *True Democrat*, 1860–1863.
Marshall (Ark.) *Mountain Wave*, 1893.
Morrilton *Arkansas Unit*, 1929.
Morrilton *Pilot*, 1890–1894.
New York *Press*, 1890.
New York Times, 1868–1893.
New York *World*, 1889–1890.
Pine Bluff (Ark.) *Commercial*, 1889.
Russellville (Ark.) *Democrat*, 1889.
St. Louis *Globe-Democrat*, 1887–1893.
Van Buren (Ark.) *Press*, 1868.
Washington Post, 1889–1890.

Interviews

Curtis and Maxine Barnes, 2 February 1992.
Emma Sue Beavers, 8 May 1992.
Gordon Earl Bentley, 7 October 1992.
Cecil and Edith Brown, 18 August 1993.
Robert Cruce, 18 December 1992.
Ruth Cupit, 15 February 1992.
Poindexter Fiser, 2 December 1992.
Hugh Goldsby, 18 December 1993.
Ken James, 28 March 1993.
Maxine Kelly, 12 April 1992.
James Malone Sr., 25 February 1994.
John Mason, audiotaped interview by Polly Church, 29 April 1978.
Wilma Medlock, 18 August 1993.
Robert Morrow, 22 October 1992.
Lela Overstreet, 16 August 1993.
Mrs. Grant Reddig, 17 October 1992, 28 February 1994.
Alexander B. Smart, 18 February 1997.
R. J. Stacks, 28 March 1993.
Mary Stallings Wilbourn, 24 February 1994.
Clarkia Turney, 6 January 1993.
Jack Willbanks, 24 August 1993.
Arlie Williams, 7 February 1992.
Beva Winningham, 23 October 1992.

Government Documents

Biennial Report of the Auditor of Public Accounts of the State of Arkansas for 1864, 1865, and 1866. Little Rock: Arkansas Gazette Printing, 1866.

Biennial Report of the Auditor of the State of Arkansas, 1887–1888. Little Rock: Press Printing, 1888.

Biennial Reports of the Secretary of State of the State of Arkansas, 1882–1896. Little Rock: various, 1882–1896.

50th Congress, 2d Session. House of Representatives. Miscellaneous Document No. 115. Washington, D.C.: Government Printing Office, 1889.

42d Congress, 2d Session. Senate Report No. 41, pt. 13. Washington, D.C.: Government Printing Office, 1872.

Historical Report of the Secretary of State of Arkansas. Little Rock: State of Arkansas, 1968.

Journal of the Senate of Arkansas, 1868–1869. Little Rock, 1869.

Journal of the Senate of Arkansas, 1871. Little Rock, 1871.

Ninth Census of the United States through *Eleventh Census of the United States.* Washington, D.C.: Government Printing Office, 1872–1895.

1990 Census of Population. General Population Characteristics: Arkansas. Washington, D.C.: Government Printing Office, 1992.

Report of the Adjutant General of the State of Arkansas. In *39th Congress, 2d Session, Senate Miscellaneous Documents.* No. 53.

Reports of the Supreme Court of the State of Arkansas. Little Rock: various, 1868–1893.

U.S. Congress. *Biographical Directory of the United States Congress, 1774–1989.* Washington, D.C.: Government Printing Office, 1989.

U.S. House of Representatives. *Digest of Contested Election Cases in the Fifty-First Congress Compiled under Resolution of the House, by Chester H. Rowell, Clerk to the Committee on Elections.* Washington, D.C.: Government Printing Office, 1891.

U.S. War Department. *The War of the Rebellion: A Compilation of the Official Records of the Union and Confederate Armies.* Washington, D.C.: Government Printing Office, 1880–1901.

Books, Articles, and Theses

Allsopp, Fred W. *History of the Arkansas Press for a Hundred Years and More.* Little Rock: Parke-Harper, 1922.

Anbinder, Tyler. *Nativism and Slavery: The Northern Know Nothings and the Politics of the 1850s.* New York: Oxford University Press, 1992.

Anderson, Eric. *Race and Politics in North Carolina, 1872–1901: The Black Second*. Baton Rouge: Louisiana State University Press, 1981.

Anderson, Eric, and Alfred A. Moss Jr., eds. *The Facts of Reconstruction: Essays in Honor of John Hope Franklin*. Baton Rouge: Louisiana State University Press, 1991.

Arsenault, Raymond. "Charles Jacobsen of Arkansas: A Jewish Politician in the Land of the Razorbacks, 1891–1915." In *"Turn to the South": Essays on Southern Jewry*, edited by Nathan M. Kaganoff and Melvin I. Urofsky. Charlottesville: University Press of Virginia, 1979.

——. *The Wild Ass of the Ozarks: Jeff Davis and the Social Bases of Southern Politics*. Philadelphia, Pa.: Temple University Press, 1984; Knoxville: University of Tennessee Press, 1988.

Ash, Stephen V. *Middle Tennessee Society Transformed, 1860–1870: War and Peace in the Upper South*. Baton Rouge: Louisiana State University Press, 1988.

Ayers, Edward L. *The Promise of the New South: Life after Reconstruction*. New York: Oxford University Press, 1992.

——. *Vengeance and Justice: Crime and Punishment in the 19th-Century American South*. New York: Oxford University Press, 1984.

Barjenbruch, Judith. "The Greenbacker Political Movement: An Arkansas View." *Arkansas Historical Quarterly* 36 (summer 1977): 107–22.

Barnes, Curtis. "History of the Hopewell Community." M.S.E. thesis, University of Central Arkansas, 1956.

Barnes, Kenneth C. "The Williams Clan: Mountain Farmers and Union Fighters in North Central Arkansas." *Arkansas Historical Quarterly* 52 (autumn 1993): 286–317.

Barney, William L. *The Secessionist Impulse: Alabama and Mississippi in 1860*. Princeton: Princeton University Press, 1974.

Bayliss, Garland Erastus. "Public Affairs in Arkansas, 1874–1896." Ph.D. diss., University of Texas, 1972.

Beck, John J. "Building the New South: A Revolution from Above in a Piedmont County." *Journal of Southern History* 53 (August 1987): 441–70.

Berry, Fred, and John Novak. *The History of Arkansas*. Little Rock: Rose Publishing, 1987.

Bessel, Richard. *Political Violence and the Rise of Nazism: The Storm Troopers in Eastern Germany, 1925–1934*. New Haven: Yale University Press, 1984.

Billings, Dwight B., Jr. *Planters and the Making of a "New South": Class, Politics, and Development in North Carolina, 1865–1900*. Chapel Hill: University of North Carolina Press, 1979.

Bishop, Albert Webb. *Loyalty on the Frontier, or Sketches of Union Men of the Southwest.* St. Louis: R. P. Studley, 1863.

Bits of Conway County Heritage. Morrilton: Daughters of the American Revolution, 1976.

Bolton, Charles C. *Poor Whites of the Antebellum South: Tenants and Laborers of Central North Carolina and Northeast Mississippi.* Durham, N.C.: Duke University Press, 1994.

Brandfon, Robert L. *Cotton Kingdom of the New South: A History of the Yazoo Mississippi Delta from Reconstruction to the Twentieth Century.* Cambridge: Harvard University Press, 1967.

Bromley, Mrs. J. N. *Biography of John W. Morris.* Marshall, Ark.: privately published, 1916.

Bruce, Dickson D., Jr. *Violence and Culture in the Antebellum South.* Austin: University of Texas Press, 1979.

Brundage, W. Fitzhugh. *Lynching in the New South: Georgia and Virginia, 1880–1930.* Urbana: University of Illinois Press, 1993.

Bryant, Jonathan M. *How Curious a Land: Conflict and Change in Greene County, Georgia, 1850–1885.* Chapel Hill: University of North Carolina Press, 1996.

Burnham, W. Dean. *Presidential Ballots, 1836–1892.* Baltimore, Md.: Johns Hopkins University Press, 1955; New York: Arno Press, 1976.

Burnside, William H. *The Honorable Powell Clayton.* Conway: University of Central Arkansas Press, 1991.

Burton, Orville Vernon. *In My Father's House Are Many Mansions: Family and Community in Edgefield, South Carolina.* Chapel Hill: University of North Carolina Press, 1985.

——. "Race and Reconstruction: Edgefield County, South Carolina." *Journal of Social History* 12 (fall 1978): 31–56.

——. "Ungrateful Servants? Edgefield's Black Reconstruction: Part 1 of the Total History of Edgefield County, South Carolina." Ph.D. diss., Princeton University, 1975.

Campbell, Randolph B. *A Southern Community in Crisis: Harrison County, Texas, 1850–1880.* Austin: Texas State Historical Association, 1983.

Carter, Dan T. *When the War Was Over: The Failure of Self-Reconstruction in the South, 1865–1867.* Baton Rouge: Louisiana State University Press, 1985.

Cartwright, Joseph H. *The Triumph of Jim Crow: Tennessee Race Relations in the 1880s.* Knoxville: University of Tennessee Press, 1976.

Cell, John W. *The Highest Stage of White Supremacy: The Origins of Segregation in South Africa and the American South.* Cambridge: Cambridge University Press, 1982.

"The Civil War Letters of John Patterson." *Pulaski County Historical Society Review* 6 (1958): 31–35.

Clayton, Powell. *The Aftermath of the Civil War in Arkansas.* New York: Neale Publishing, 1915.

Clinton, Catherine, and Nina Silber. *Divided Houses: Gender and the Civil War.* New York: Oxford University Press, 1992.

Cobb, James C. *The Most Southern Place on Earth: The Mississippi Delta and the Roots of Regional Identity.* New York: Oxford University Press, 1992.

Cohen, William. *At Freedom's Edge: Black Mobility and the Southern White Quest for Racial Control, 1861–1915.* Baton Rouge: Louisiana State University Press, 1991.

Conway County, Our Land, Our Home, Our People. Little Rock: Historical Publications of Arkansas, 1989.

Crenshaw, Martha, ed. *Terrorism, Legitimacy, and Power: The Consequences of Political Violence.* Middletown, Conn.: Wesleyan University Press, 1983.

Current, Richard Nelson. *Lincoln's Loyalists: Union Soldiers from the Confederacy.* Boston: Northeastern University Press, 1991.

——. *Those Terrible Carpetbaggers.* New York: Oxford University Press, 1988.

Davis, Ronald F. L. *Good and Faithful Labor: From Slavery to Sharecropping in the Natchez District, 1860–1890.* Westport, Conn.: Greenwood Press, 1982.

Degler, Carl. *The Other South: Southern Dissenters in the Nineteenth Century.* New York: Harper and Row, 1974.

Demby, James W. *Mysteries and Miseries of Arkansas, or a Defence of the Loyalty of the State.* St. Louis: privately printed, 1863.

Dillard, Tom. "To the Back of the Elephant: Racial Conflict in the Arkansas Republican Party." *Arkansas Historical Quarterly* 33 (spring 1974): 3–15.

Dirck, Brian. "Witt's Cavalry: An Arkansas Guerrilla Unit." *Faulkner Facts and Fiddlings* 36 (1994): 63–76.

Dougan, Michael. *Arkansas Odyssey: The Saga of Arkansas from Prehistoric Times to Present.* Little Rock: Rose Publishing, 1994.

——. *Confederate Arkansas: The People and Policies of a Frontier State in Wartime.* Tuscaloosa: University of Alabama Press, 1976.

DuBois, W. E. Burghardt. *Black Reconstruction in America.* New York: Russell and Russell, 1935.

Durrill, Wayne K. *War of Another Kind: A Southern Community in the Great Rebellion.* New York: Oxford University Press, 1990.

Elkins, F. Clark. "The Agricultural Wheel: County Politics and Consolidation, 1884–1885." *Arkansas Historical Quarterly* 29 (autumn 1970): 152–75.

——. "Arkansas Farmers Organize for Action, 1882–1884." *Arkansas Historical Quarterly* 13 (1954): 231–48.

English, Alpha Talley, ed. *Menifee: Past and Present.* Menifee, Ark.: Women's Civic League, 1976.

Fellman, Michael. *Inside War: The Guerrilla Conflict in Missouri during the American Civil War.* New York: Oxford University Press, 1989.

Fink, Leon. *Workingmen's Democracy: The Knights of Labor and American Politics.* Urbana: University of Illinois Press, 1983.

Finley, Randy. "The Freedmen's Bureau in Arkansas." Ph.D. diss., University of Arkansas, 1992.

——. *From Slavery to Uncertain Freedom: The Freedmen's Bureau in Arkansas, 1865–1869.* Fayetteville: University of Arkansas Press, 1996.

Fitzgerald, Michael W. *The Union League Movement in the Deep South: Politics and Agricultural Change during Reconstruction.* Baton Rouge: Louisiana State University Press, 1989.

Flynn, Charles L., Jr. *White Land, Black Labor: Caste and Class in Late Nineteenth-Century Georgia.* Baton Rouge: Louisiana State University Press, 1983.

Foner, Eric. *Reconstruction: America's Unfinished Revolution, 1863–1877.* New York: Harper and Row, 1988.

Fredrickson, George M. *The Black Image in the White Mind: The Debate on Afro-American Character and Destiny, 1817–1914.* New York: Harper and Row, 1971.

French, Alice. "Plantation Life in Arkansas." *Atlantic Monthly* 68 (July 1891): 32–49.

——. "Town Life in Arkansas." *Atlantic Monthly* 68 (September 1891): 332–40. Written under pen name Octave Thanet.

Gaither, Gerald H. *Blacks and the Populist Revolt: Ballots and Bigotry in the "New South."* Tuscaloosa: University of Alabama Press, 1977.

Gaston, Paul M. *The New South Creed: A Study in Southern Mythmaking.* New York: Knopf, 1970.

Gatewood, William B. "Arkansas Negroes in the 1890s: Documents." *Arkansas Historical Quarterly* 33 (winter 1974): 293–325.

Gillette, William. *Retreat from Reconstruction, 1869–1879.* Baton Rouge: Louisiana State University Press, 1979.

The Goodspeed Biographical and Historical Memoirs of Central Arkansas. Chicago: Goodspeed, 1889.

Goodwyn, Lawrence. *Democratic Promise: The Populist Movement in America.* New York: Oxford University Press, 1976.

——. *The Populist Movement: A Short History of the Agrarian Revolt in America.* New York: Oxford University Press, 1978.

Gordon, Fon Louise. *Caste and Class: The Black Experience in Arkansas, 1880–1920.* Athens: University of Georgia Press, 1995.

Graves, John William. *Town and Country: Race Relations in an Urban-Rural Context, 1865–1905.* Fayetteville: University of Arkansas Press, 1990.

Green, James R. *Grass-Roots Socialism: Radical Movements in the Southwest, 1895–1943.* Baton Rouge: Louisiana State University Press, 1978.

Grimsley, Mark. *The Hard Hand of War: Union Military Policy toward Southern Civilians, 1861–1865.* Cambridge: Cambridge University Press, 1995.

Hackney, Sheldon. "Southern Violence." In *Violence and Culture in America: Historical and Comparative Perspectives,* edited by Hugh Davis Graham and Ted Robert Gurr, 387–401. Washington, D.C.: Government Printing Office, 1969.

Hahn, Steven. *The Roots of Southern Populism: Yeoman Farmers and the Transformation of the Georgia Upcountry, 1850–1890.* New York: Oxford University Press, 1983.

Handbook of the Arkansas River Valley along the "Valley Route" between Van Buren and Little Rock. Chicago: C. S. Burch, 1887.

Harrell, John Mortimer. *Arkansas.* Vol. 10 of *Confederate Military History.* 12 vols. Atlanta: Confederate Publishing Company, 1899.

———. *The Brooks and Baxter War: A History of the Reconstruction Period in Arkansas.* St. Louis: Slawson, 1893.

Harris, J. William. *Plain Folk and Gentry in a Slave Society: White Liberty and Black Slavery in Augusta's Hinterland.* Middletown, Conn.: Wesleyan University Press, 1985.

Hart, Roger L. *Redeemers, Bourbons, and Populists: Tennessee, 1870–1896.* Baton Rouge: Louisiana State University Press, 1975.

Hawkins, Marlin. *How I Stole Elections: The Autobiography of Sheriff Marlin Hawkins.* Little Rock: Rose Publishing, 1991.

Henningson, Randy. "Upland Farmers and Agrarian Protest: Northwest Arkansas and the Brothers of Freedom." M.A. thesis, University of Arkansas, 1973.

Herndon, Dallas T. *Centennial History of Arkansas.* 3 vols. Chicago: S. J. Clarke, 1922.

Historical Reminiscences and Biographical Memoirs of Conway County, Arkansas. Little Rock: Arkansas Publishing Company, 1890.

Hofstadter, Richard, and Michael Wallace, eds. *American Violence: A Documentary History.* New York: Knopf, 1970.

Hogue, Wayman. *Back Yonder: An Ozark Chronicle.* New York: Minton, Balch, and Company, 1932.

Hyman, Michael R. *The Anti-Redeemers: Hill-Country Political Dissenters in the Lower South from Redemption to Populism.* Baton Rouge: Louisiana State University Press, 1990.

Johnson, Michael P. *Toward a Patriarchal Republic: The Secession of Georgia.* Baton Rouge: Louisiana State University Press, 1977.

Jones, James K. "Was Clayton's Murder a Political Crime?" *North American Review* 48 (1889): 287–93.

Kirby, Jack Temple. *Darkness at the Dawning: Race and Reform in the Progressive South.* Philadelphia: J. B. Lippincott, 1972.

Koren, Henry J. *The Serpent and the Dove: A History of the Congregation of the Holy Ghost in the United States, 1745–1984.* Pittsburgh: Spiritus Press, 1985.

Kousser, J. Morgan. *The Shaping of Southern Politics: Suffrage Restriction and the Establishment of the One-Party South, 1880–1910.* New Haven: Yale University Press, 1974.

Leslie, James W. *Pine Bluff and Jefferson County: A Pictorial History.* Virginia Beach: Donning, 1981.

Lewis, Elsie Mae. "From Nationalism to DisUnion: A Study of the Secession Movement in Arkansas, 1860–1861." Ph.D. diss., University of Chicago, 1946.

Mandle, Jay. *The Roots of Black Poverty: The Southern Plantation after the Civil War.* Durham: Duke University Press, 1978.

McCaslin, Richard B. *Tainted Breeze: The Great Hanging at Gainesville, Texas, 1862.* Baton Rouge: Louisiana State University Press, 1994.

McClure, John E. *The Old South and the New.* Little Rock: n.p., 1891.

McKenzie, Robert Tracy. *One South or Many? Plantation Belt and Upcountry in Civil War–Era Tennessee.* Cambridge: Cambridge University Press, 1994.

McKinney, Gordon B. *Southern Mountain Republicans, 1865–1900: Politics and the Appalachian Community.* Chapel Hill: University of North Carolina Press, 1978.

McKnight, O. E., and Boyd W. Johnson. *The Arkansas Story.* Oklahoma City: Harlow Publishing, 1955.

McPherson, James M. *Battle Cry of Freedom: The Civil War Era.* New York: Oxford University Press, 1988.

———. *What They Fought For, 1861–1865.* Baton Rouge: Louisiana State University Press, 1994.

McReynolds, Nina. "A Town That Disappeared: Lewisburg, Arkansas." M.S.E. thesis, University of Central Arkansas, 1958.

Merkl, Peter H. *Political Violence and Terror: Motifs and Motivations.* Berkeley: University of California Press, 1986.

Moneyhon, Carl H. "Black Politicians in Arkansas during the Gilded Age." *Arkansas Historical Quarterly* 44 (autumn 1985): 222–45.

———. *The Impact of the Civil War and Reconstruction on Arkansas: Persistence in the Midst of Ruin.* Baton Rouge: Louisiana State University Press, 1994.

Morgan, W. Scott. *The Red Light: A Story of Southern Politics and Election Methods.* Moravian Falls, N.C.: Yellow Jacket Press, 1904.

———. *History of the Wheel and Alliance and the Impending Revolution.* 1891; New York: Burt Franklin, 1968.

Nieburg, H. L. *Political Violence: The Behavioral Process.* New York: St. Martin's Press, 1969.

Niswonger, Richard L. *Arkansas Democratic Politics, 1896–1920.* Fayetteville: University of Arkansas Press, 1990.

Painter, Nell Irvin. *Exodusters: Black Migration to Kansas after Reconstruction.* New York: Knopf, 1977.

———. *Standing at Armageddon: The United States, 1877–1919.* New York: W. W. Norton, 1987.

Paisley, Clifton. "The Political Wheelers and Arkansas' Election of 1888." *Arkansas Historical Quarterly* 25 (spring 1966): 3–21.

Paludan, Phillip Shaw. *Victims: A True Story of the Civil War.* Knoxville: University of Tennessee Press, 1981.

Perman, Michael. *The Road to Redemption: Southern Politics, 1869–1879.* Chapel Hill: University of North Carolina Press, 1984.

Potter, David M. *The Impending Crisis, 1848–1861.* New York: Harper and Row, 1976.

Pyle, Jennifer Marie. "Two Decades of Agricultural Activism in Arkansas." Ph.D. diss., Stanford University, 1967.

Rabinowitz, Howard N. *The First New South, 1865–1920.* Arlington Heights, Ill.: Harlan Davidson, 1992.

Rable, George C. *But There Was No Peace: The Role of Violence in the Politics of Reconstruction.* Athens: University of Georgia Press, 1984.

Ransom, Roger L., and Richard Sutch. *One Kind of Freedom: The Economic Consequences of Emancipation.* Cambridge: Cambridge University Press, 1977.

Rector, Charles J. "Lily-White Republicanism: The Arkansas Experience, 1877–1928." *Ozark Historical Review* 22 (spring 1993): 49–68.

Redkey, Edwin S. *Black Exodus: Black Nationalist and Back-to-Africa Movements, 1890–1910.* New Haven: Yale University Press, 1969.

Reidy, Joseph P. *From Slavery to Agrarian Capitalism in the Cotton Plantation South: Central Georgia, 1800–1880.* Chapel Hill: University of North Carolina Press, 1992.

Reynolds, Thomas J. *The Pope County Militia War.* 1908; Little Rock: Foreman-Payne, 1968.

Roots, Logan S. "Assassination as a Political Argument." *North American Review* 48 (1889): 280–86.

Roper, John Herbert. *C. Vann Woodward, Southerner.* Athens: University of Georgia Press, 1987.

Royster, Charles. *The Destructive War: William Tecumseh Sherman, Stonewall Jackson, and the Americans.* New York: Alfred A. Knopf, 1991.

Rubenstein, Richard E. *Rebels in Eden: Mass Political Violence in the United States.* Boston: MacDonald, 1970.

Russell, Marvin Frank. "The Republican Party in Arkansas, 1874–1913." Ph.D. diss., University of Arkansas, 1985.

Saloutos, Theodore. *Farmer Movements in the South, 1865–1933.* Lincoln: University of Nebraska Press, 1964.

Schwartz, Michael. *Radical Protest and Social Structure: The Southern Farmers' Alliance and Cotton Tenancy, 1880–1890.* New York: Academic Press, 1976.

Shapiro, Herbert. *White Violence and Black Response: From Reconstruction to Montgomery.* Amherst: University of Massachusetts Press, 1988.

Shifflett, Crandall. *Patronage and Poverty in the Tobacco South: Louisa County, Virginia, 1860–1900.* Knoxville: University of Tennessee Press, 1982.

Shinn, Josiah H. *The History of Arkansas: A Text-Book for Public Schools, High Schools, and Academies.* Richmond, Va.: B. F. Johnson, 1905.

Singletary, Otis. "Militia Disturbances in Arkansas during Reconstruction." *Arkansas Historical Quarterly* 15 (1956): 140–50.

——. *Negro Militia and Reconstruction.* Austin: University of Texas Press, 1957.

Smith, Charles Spencer. *A History of the African Methodist Episcopal Church.* Philadelphia: AME Church, 1922.

Staples, Thomas S. *Reconstruction in Arkansas, 1862–1874.* New York: Columbia University Press, 1923.

Summers, Mark W. *Railroads, Reconstruction, and the Gospel of Prosperity: Aid under the Radical Republicans, 1865–1877.* Princeton: Princeton University Press, 1984.

Thomas, David Y. *Arkansas and Its People.* 4 vols. New York: American Historical Association, 1930.

Thompson, George H. *Arkansas and Reconstruction: The Influence of Geography, Economics, and Personality.* Port Washington, N.Y.: Kennikut Press, 1976.

Thompson, Wesley S. *"The Free State of Winston": A History of Winston County, Alabama.* Winfield, Ala.: Pareil Press, 1968.

Tindall, George Brown. *South Carolina Negroes, 1877–1900.* Columbia: University of South Carolina Press, 1952.

Tolnay, Stewart E., and E. M. Beck. *A Festival of Violence: An Analysis of Southern Lynchings, 1882–1930.* Urbana: University of Illinois Press, 1995.

Trelease, Allen W. *White Terror: The Ku Klux Klan Conspiracy and Southern Reconstruction.* New York: Harper and Row, 1971.

Waldrep, Christopher. *Night Riders: Defending Community in the Black Patch, 1890–1915.* Durham: Duke University Press, 1993.

Walz, Robert B. "Migration into Arkansas, 1834–1880." Ph.D. diss., University of Texas, 1958.

Wayne, Michael. *The Reshaping of Planter Society: The Natchez District, 1860–1880.* Baton Rouge: Louisiana State University Press, 1983.

Wiener, Jonathan M. *Social Origins of the New South: Alabama, 1860–1885.* Baton Rouge: Louisiana State University Press, 1978.

Wheeler, John McDaniel. "The People's Party in Arkansas, 1891–1896." Ph.D. diss., Tulane University, 1975.

Williams, Fay. *Arkansans of the Years.* Vol. 3. Little Rock: C. C. Allard, 1953.

Williamson, Joel. *The Crucible of Race: Black-White Relations in the American South since Emancipation.* New York: Oxford University Press, 1984.

Wirges, Gene. *Conflict of Interests: The Gene Wirges Story.* North Little Rock, Ark.: Riverboat Publishers, 1992.

Wolfe, Jonathan James. "Background of German Immigration." *Arkansas Historical Quarterly* 25 (1966): 151–82, 248–78, 354–85.

Woodman, Harold D. "Sequel to Slavery: The New History Views the Post-Bellum South." *Journal of Southern History* 43 (November 1977): 523–54.

Woods, James M. *Mission and Memory: A History of the Catholic Church in Arkansas.* Little Rock: Diocese of Little Rock, 1993.

——. *Rebellion and Realignment: Arkansas's Road to Secession.* Fayetteville: University of Arkansas Press, 1987.

Woodward, C. Vann. *Origins of the New South.* Baton Rouge: Louisiana State University Press, 1951.

——. *The Strange Career of Jim Crow.* New York: Oxford University Press, 1955.

Woodward, Earl F. "The Brooks and Baxter War in Arkansas, 1872–1874." *Arkansas Historical Quarterly* 30 (winter 1971): 315–36.

Worley, Ted. "The Arkansas Peace Society of 1861: A Study of Mountain Unionism." *Journal of Southern History* 24 (November 1958): 445–56.

——. "Documents Relating to the Arkansas Peace Society of 1861." *Arkansas Historical Quarterly* 17 (spring 1958): 82–111.

——, ed. "The Diary of Lieutenant Orville Gillet, U.S.A., 1864–1865." *Arkansas Historical Quarterly* 17 (spring 1958): 164–204.

Wright, Gavin. *The Political Economy of the Cotton South: Households, Markets, and Wealth in the Nineteenth Century.* New York: W. W. Norton, 1978.

——. *Revolutions in the Southern Economy since the Civil War.* New York: Basic Books, 1986.

Wright, George C. *Racial Violence in Kentucky, 1865–1940: Lynchings, Mob Rule, and "Legal Lynchings."* Baton Rouge: Louisiana State University Press, 1990.

INDEX

Adams, Edward W., 25–26, 28, 30, 35, 66
Adams, Robert J., 66
Adcock (physician), 54
Africa, 45. *See also* Liberia
African Americans: Catholic missions to, 45; disarmament of, 25–26; emigration to Arkansas, 33, 38–43, 60–61; political divisions among, 35, 66, 98; political organization of, 43, 57, 95; and Reconstruction violence, 22, 25–30. *See also* Liberia; Lynchings; Oklahoma: emigration to
African Methodist Episcopal Church, 120, 165 n.57, 165 n.59
The African Repository, 107
Agrarian populism, 46, 164 n.51. *See also* Agricultural Wheel; Brothers of Freedom; Farmers Alliance; Grange movement
Agricultural Wheel, 3, 5, 52, 71, 92–93, 123, 131; black membership, 173 n.14; founding of, 47; growth in 1880s, 56; merger with Brothers of Freedom, 48, 56, 164 n.51; merger with Farmers Alliance, 102; newspaper, 51; political activity, 56–57, 61, 65, 166 n.3
Agriculture. *See* Coffee cultivation; Cotton cultivation; Subsistence agriculture
Alexander (investigator), 71, 74
Allgood (physician), 138
Allnutt, W. D., 76–78, 80, 124, 133–40
American Colonization Society: emigration from Arkansas, 94, 105–12; and emigration from South Carolina, 39–40
American Party, 11
Anaconda mortgages, 49–50
Arkansas Democrat, 81, 83
Arkansas Gazette, 81, 83
Arkansas General Assembly. *See* Disfranchisement; Segregation
Armstead, Enoch, 67, 71, 88
Armstrong, Carroll, 120, 127, 139; as chairman of county Democratic Party, 64; as chairman of state Democratic Party, 119; and Clayton murder, 76, 80; and Confederate veterans organization, 122; at congressional hearing in Little Rock, 92; and mob attacks in Morrilton, 97
Augusta, Georgia, 41
Azor (ship), 107

Baker, George W., 62
Baker Hotel, 88
Baptist Church, 120
Batesville (Independence County), 16, 59
Baxter, Elisha, 35–36
Bell, John, 11–12
Benedict, Henry, 11
Benedictine order of monks, 43
Benjamin, Mason W., 66, 84, 142–43
Bentley, George: killing of, by brother, 72; in Reconstruction battles, 25, 30; as sheriff, 47; and theft of ballots, 69–70
Bentley, Oliver T., 79–90, 117, 119–24, 140, 170 n.39; and Clayton murder, 76, 79–80, 84–85, 170 n.42; and Clayton murder trial, 113, 115; early life, 72; and killing of brother, 72; and mob attacks in Morrilton, 66, 97; and theft of ballots, 68–71
Berry, James H., 46
Bird, George T., 125
Bird, William M., 125
Bird, William T., 125
Bismarck, Otto von, 44
Black River, 120
Black's store, 115

Blakeney, John O., 67–68, 88–89, 97
Bole, Thomas, 53
Boston Mountains, 7
Bradley, Adam R., 74
Brazelton (black politician), 57
Breckinridge, Clifton R., 76, 95, 136; and congressional investigation, 91–92, 173 n.6; in congressional race of 1888, 65–66; in congressional race of 1890, 98–99, 104; response to Clayton's murder, 81–82; speeches in House of Representatives, 86, 168 n.22
Breckinridge, John C., 11–12
Breeden, Pompey, 30
Brooks, Joseph, 35–36
Brooks-Baxter war, 35–36
Brothers of Freedom, 47–48, 50–51; founding of, 47; merger with Agricultural Wheel, 48, 56; and political activity, 52
Bryan, N. D., 42
Burchfield, Thomas, 25
Bush, E. D., 61
Butte, Montana, 112

Cadron township, 8
Caldwell, Henry C., 67, 88, 95, 171 n.50
Capital Hotel, 84
Carroll, George W., 9, 14
Casey, James, 30
Cate, William H., 70, 93
Catholic Church, 43–46, 126–27
Catholic Point (Conway County), 45
Center Ridge (Conway County), 61, 97–99, 102, 124–25
Chester, Pennsylvania, 61
Chism, Elijah, 68, 87
Christenberry, Gus, 84
Churchill, Thomas, 46
Civil War, 14–21; and political violence, 2, 131. *See also* Grand Army of the Republic; Sons of Veterans; United Confederate Veterans
Clarion (newspaper), 96
Clarksville (Johnson County), 124, 135
Clayton, John Middleton: arrival in Arkansas, 23; early life, 61; and election of 1888, 65, 70–71; murder of, 1, 74–81, 122, 131–40, 145; political career, 61
Clayton, Powell, 7, 61, 65, 98, 113, 122; and Brooks-Baxter war, 35–36; as governor, 23–32; and murder of brother, 81–84; as Republican leader after Reconstruction, 60, 95; testimony to Committee on Elections, 92
Clayton, Sarah Anne, 60
Clayton, William H., 80–81, 84, 90
Cleveland, Grover, 101, 104
Cleveland (Conway County), 80
Clinton (Van Buren County), 20, 169 n.33
Coblentz, Benjamin, 36
Coblentz, J. H. (Harry), 53, 62, 76–77, 89–90, 124, 126, 166 n.6
Coffee cultivation, 112
Columbia County, 26
Congress. *See* United States House of Representatives
Constitutional Union Party, 11
Conway, Elias, 12
Conway (Faulkner County), 70; back-to-Africa movement in, 111; black Catholic school in, 45, 126
Conway (political family), 10–12
Conway County: black emigration from, 94, 105–12; black emigration to, 33, 39–43, 60–61; black population in, 38, 129–30; boundary changes, 33; foreign emigration to, 43–46, 126–27; in Great Depression, 125; interracial cohabitation in, 28, 127–28; landscape, 7–8; planter persistence in, 23–24; secession meetings, 12–13; settlement, 7, 9; slaves, 8–9. *See also* Agrarian populism; Cotton cultivation; Subsistence agriculture

Conway County *Tribune*, 61
Conway Mounted Rifles, 14
Cook (undertaker), 139
Cooper (Congressman), 136–37, 139
Coppinger, William, 108–11
Cotton cultivation, 8–9, 48–51, 56
Cox, Thomas, 90, 172 n.56
Crawford County. *See* Van Buren
Cunningham, C. H., 57
Cunningham, George S., 83–84, 90, 119, 141–44, 172 n.55
Curtis, Samuel, 16–17

Damascus church, 102
Danforth, Keyes, 26
Dardanelle (Yell County), 172 n.55
Dargan, James, 107–9, 111
Davis, Jeff, 115, 119, 173 n.10
Dearing, Spencer, 41
Delaney, Jennie, 173 n.10
Democratic Party: in 1850s, 10–12; leadership in Conway County, 55–56, 117–19; reorganization, 31. *See also* Armstrong, Carroll; Old Hickory Club
Des Arc (Prairie County), 47
Diggs, W. A., 108
Disciples of Christ Church, 16, 120, 153 n.24
Disfranchisement: of African Americans and poor whites, 60, 99–101, 103–5, 124, 127; of former Confederates, 22; in South Carolina, 40
Douglas, Stephen, 11
Douglass, Frederick, 128
Downs, Abner, 105
Duncan, J. W., 21
Durham, William, 89

Eagle, James P., 61, 64–65, 82, 87, 96, 98
Edgefield County (South Carolina), 39–42, 107, 129, 160 n.12
Education: Catholic schools in Morrilton and Conway, 44–45, 126–27; Freedmen's Bureau school, 22. *See also* Shinn, Josiah H.
Egan, William P., 31
Elections: in 1860, 11; in 1872, 34; in 1874, 35; in 1880, 46; in 1882, 46; in 1884, 52–53; in 1886, 52, 57–58; in 1888, 61–72; in 1890, 96–97, 124; in 1892, 52, 102, 104–5, 124; in 1894, 52, 105, 124; in 1920, 125
Emigration. *See* Immigration; Liberia; Oklahoma: emigration to
Eugene, Oregon, 89
Eureka Springs (Marion County), 81
Evans, W. J., 22

Farmers Alliance, 96, 101–5, 123–24; merger with Agricultural Wheel, 102, 173 n.14. *See also* People's Party
Farmer's movement. *See* Agrarian populism
Faulkner County, 36, 98, 100, 164 n.51; creation of, 33. *See also* Conway; Greenbrier
Fayette County (Tennessee), 33
Featherston, Louis, 70–71, 93
Federal court (Little Rock), 71, 74, 88–91
First Arkansas Infantry Battalion, 16
First Arkansas Regiment, 15
Fishback, William M., 61–62
Fitzgerald, Edward (bishop), 44–45, 126–27
Fizer, N. B., 96
Ford, John, 91
Forrest City (St. Francis County), 166 n.5
Fort Smith (Sebastian County), 15, 43, 81; Whig sentiment in, 12
Fortson, W. K., 107
Freedmen's Bureau, 22
French, Alice, 120–21, 170 n.41

Galloway, George, 154 n.30
Garland, Augustus, 26, 36
Gary, Martin Witherspoon, 39

Germantown (Conway County), 94, 107
Germany: emigration to Arkansas from, 43–46
Gibbon, John J., 30–31
Gill, John W., 29, 31, 36
Gillet, Orville, 20
Gordon, Anderson, 10, 16, 19, 24–25, 29, 35, 37, 122
Gordon, Fon Louise, 38
Gordon, Susan, 10
Grand Army of the Republic, 97, 102, 124
Grange movement, 53
Grant, Ulysses S., 16, 28, 35–36
Gratten, A. G., 97, 173 n.5
Gray, Richard J., 86–87, 96, 103
Greeley, Horace, 35
Greenback Party, 46, 52, 61
Greenbrier (Faulkner County), 114
Greenville County (South Carolina), 42
Gregory, John C., 31
Griffin, George, 98
Griffin, George W. (sheriff), 47
Griggs, Lafayette, 57
Guerrilla warfare, 18–20
Guthrie, Oklahoma, 90

Halbrook, T. J., 53, 102
Hall, J. H., 103
Hammond, John, 40–41
Hanna, William S., 60, 98, 100
Harding, Warren G., 125
Hardy (Sharp County), 123
Harrod, J. H., 61, 70, 91
Hawkins, Marlin, 125, 179 n.16
Hawthorn, J. W., 54
Haynes, Henry, 62
Hays, Ransom, 67, 71, 88
Helena (Phillips County), 17
Henningson, Randy, 52
Henry, Eugene B., 25, 31, 35, 37, 66
Henry, Thomas T., 151 n.12
Hervey, Thomas C., 63, 83, 119–20; attack on black legislator, 58–59; attempt to stuff ballot box, 57–58; early years during Civil War, 59; as election judge, 67–68, 70; as sheriff and county judge, 117–18; trial for election fraud, 88–89
Hervey family: in Civil War, 20
Hesper (ship), 26
Hickey, Frank, 112–15, 118
Hill, Samuel, 167 n.16
Hinds, James, 26
Hinkle, Anthony, 27–28, 154 n.30
Hinkle, William R., 25, 31, 34, 158 n.60, 159 n.2
Hobbs, William T., 67–68, 72, 88
Hofstadter, Richard, 2
Holy Ghost Fathers, 43–45, 126–27
Hooper, Thomas, Jr., 82, 114
Hooper, Thomas, Sr., 82; Klan activity, 28; murder of, 29, 37
Horton, Neil Hobbs, 169 n.35
Hot Spring County. *See* Malvern
Howard, Elizabeth, 19
Howard township, 70, 91, 98, 103–5, 127; creation of, 42. *See also* Menifee; Plumerville
Hughes, Simon P., 53, 57, 61–62, 70

Immigration: of African Americans, 33, 38–43, 60–61; of foreigners, 43–46
Independence County. *See* Batesville
Ironclad Oath, 22
Italy: emigration to Arkansas from, 45

Jackson, Joe, 28
Jack-the-Ripper letters, 7, 82, 114, 70 n.39
Jacobsen, Charles, 103, 118, 129
Jefferson County, 60, 74, 104, 124. *See also* Pine Bluff
Jimison, John, 108
Johnson, Robert W., 11–12
Johnson County, 47
Johnsonville, Liberia, 111, 147
Jones, Allen, 58

Jones, James K., 81
Jones, William, 108
Jones, W. M. D., 128
Jordan, W. J., 96

Kansas House of Representatives: condemnation of election fraud in Arkansas, 81, 170 n.37
Kearney, William, 34
King, Bryant V., 151 n.12
Kissire, John, 102
Knights of Labor, 50, 61
Knights of Pythias, 120
Know-Nothing Party. *See* American Party
Kousser, J. Morgan, 103, 124
Ku Klux Klan, 2, 125, 127, 130–31, 180 n.26; and C. Vann Woodward, 4; murder of John Matthews, 37; night riding in 1885, 53–55; organization in Conway County, 23; and Reconstruction violence, 25–30
Kurtz, John, 20

Lacey, John F., 92, 173 n.6
Landers, Charles N., 112–14
Landers, J. S., 114
Landers, S. N., 74
Langley, Isom P., 99
Laurens County (South Carolina), 42
Lawson, William, 40–41
Lee, Sallie, 105
Leigh, Robert, 119, 129–30
Lemoyne, G. W., 14
Leslie, W. D., 94, 108, 110
Lewis, Alvin, 28–29
Lewis, Wash, 28–29
Lewisburg, 16, 36, 59, 130, 167 n.16; Confederate troops raised in, 14; as county seat, 34–35; decline of, 34; description of, 9; federal garrison at, 17–21; Freedmen's Bureau in, 22; illustration of, 10; Reconstruction violence in, 25–31; Republican rally in, 35
Liberia, 147; emigration from Conway County to, 94, 105–12, 129, 175 n.36; emigration from South Carolina to, 39–40
Liberia (ship), 108, 110
Lick Mountain township, 9, 60–61, 79, 97–99, 102, 108. *See also* Catholic Point; Center Ridge
Lincoln, Abraham, 11–13
Lincoln Club, 121–22
Lincoln County. *See* Varner
Lipscomb, Anthony, 105
Little Rock, 26; Frederick Douglass in, 128; lynching in, 110; Whig sentiment in, 12. *See also* Federal court; United States House of Representatives: investigation by Committee on Elections
Little Rock–Fort Smith railroad, 34, 38, 43, 167 n.16
Lonoke County, 164 n.51
Lucas, James, 67–68, 71, 83, 88–89, 97
Lynchings, 110, 114–16, 176 n.45, 176 n.46, 180 n.29

Macune, Charles W., 102
Maish, Levi, 138
Malone, A. D., 1, 77, 117, 122
Malvern (Hot Spring County), 112
Marienstatt monastery, 43–45, 126
Martial law, 29–31
Mason, Eliza, 128
Mason, John, 58–59, 77–78, 80, 103, 122, 165 n.59, 169 n.33
Matthews, John L., 27–29, 37
McCain, W. S., 91
McClure, John, 74, 76–77, 91–92, 95, 121–22, 136, 170 n.42
McCraven, Mary Ann, 75–80, 99, 133–38
McCrory (Woodruff County), 110
McCullough, Cyrus, 77, 80, 89, 165 n.59
McFarlin, W. B., 166 n.2
McKendree College, 128
McKinley, William, 60
McLaughlin, J. B., 97
McPherson, James, 131

Memphis, Tennessee, 33, 45
Menifee, William L., 12–13
Menifee (Conway County), 42, 104, 145. *See also* Liberia: emigration to
Mersurado River, 111
Methodist church, 120
Middlebrook, Aaron W., 75–76
Militia: black company in 1885, 55; Democratic company in 1884, 53; in 1874, 37; and election violence in 1888, 62–63, 66–70; in Reconstruction, 26–30, 79, 82, 98, 122, 130, 178 n.7
Militia Claims Commission, 31
Miller, Harry, 66
Miller County. *See* Texarkana
Moneyhon, Carl, 23
Monrovia, Liberia, 110–11
Moore, Mary, 33
Moore, Nathan, 29, 31
Moore, Sam, 33
Moose, Eleanor Wood, 122
Moose, William S., 118
Morgan, William, 22
Morgan, W. Scott, 123, 178 n.11
Morning Star Church, 148
Morrilton, 41, 57, 87, 92, 117, 120, 129–30, 147, 167 n.8; Catholic emigration to, 43–46, 126–27; Confederate veterans in, 122; cotton weighing in, 102; as county seat, 34; as Democratic stronghold, 55; founding, 34; growth in 1880s, 48; mob attacks in, 66, 97; political rallies in, 61–62, 65; racial violence in, 46–47, 114–15. *See also* Liberia: emigration to
Morrilton *Headlight*, 57, 68
Morrilton *Star*, 57–58, 62
Murphy, Isaac, 21–22

New York City, 107–10
Norman, R. L., 99
Norwood, C. M., 61, 64–65, 96

Oklahoma, 90; emigration to, 110, 129
Old Hickory Club, 70
Oxford, Mississippi, 62

Palmer, William, 67, 88–89
Parks, W. P., 46
Pate, Charles, 79–80, 84, 99, 103, 113–14
Pate, Robert L., 63, 82, 88, 99, 140, 169 n.33; attempt to stuff ballot box, 57–58; and Clayton murder trial, 112–14; co-owner of saloon, 73, 79; as election judge, 98; and lynching of Flannagan Thornton, 115; and murder of Clayton, 78–80, 84–85, 170 n.42
Pate (Confederate guerrilla), 18
Patterson, John, 20
Patterson (juror), 140
Peace societies, 15, 152 n.22
Pea Ridge (battle), 16
Peel (sister of Robert Pate), 99
People's Party (Populists), 101, 104–5, 124
Perry, Robert, 28
Perry County, 15, 26; agrarian populist movement in, 52; boundary changes, 33; murder of John Matthews, 37. *See also* Perryville
Perryville (Perry County), 37, 110
Petit Jean Mountain, 125
Phillips County. *See* Helena
Pine Bluff (Jefferson County), 75–76, 81, 128
Pinkerton Detective Agency, 72, 84. *See also* Wood, Albert
Plumerville, 1, 84–85, 87, 92, 97, 99, 104, 110, 117, 120, 129–30, 165 n.59, 167 n.8; black emigration to, 42; election fraud in, 57–58, 63–64, 67–70; murder of Joe Smith, 87–88; shooting of Charles Wahl, 73–74. *See also* Clayton, John Middleton: murder of; Liberia: emigration from Conway County to
Poll tax. *See* Disfranchisement: of African Americans and poor whites

Pope, James, 66
Pope County, 36; agrarian populist movement in, 52, 164 n.51. *See also* Russellville
Port Hudson, Louisiana (battle), 18
Prairie County. *See* Des Arc
Presbyterian Church, 120
Preston, John, 11
Pulaski County. *See* Little Rock

Quitman (Van Buren County), 18

Raiford, Sam, 42
Railroad coach law, 100
Railroads, 172 n.56; line laid through Conway County, 34, 43; state subsidies for, 35–36. *See also* Little Rock–Fort Smith railroad
Reconstruction, 21–32
Rector, Henry, 12
Reid, Charles C., Jr., 76, 103, 121, 177 n.2; alibis for Clayton murder, 85; and Clayton murder trial, 113; and election violence in 1888, 67–68; and theft of ballots, 69–70; trial for election fraud, 71, 88–89; as U.S. Congressman, 118
Reid, Charles C., Sr., 167 n.16
Republican Party, 71; corrupt officials, 31; and 1860 election, 11; failure to protect black interests, 95–96; internal divisions within, 34–36; national committee, 60. *See also* Lincoln Club; Militia: in Reconstruction; Clayton, Powell
Richmond, David, 87–88
Roberts, Green, 62
Rockefeller, Winthrop P., 125
Rogers, Green, 147
Rogers, John A., 170 n.37
Rogers, N. M., 112, 147
Roman Catholic Church. *See* Catholic Church
Roosevelt, Franklin Delano, 125
Russellville (Pope County), 43, 52, 115, 135
Ryan, Abraham H., 17–19
Sacred Heart Church, 126
Sagg (juror), 140
St. Francis County. *See* Forrest City
St. Joseph Colony, 43–45
St. Joseph of Cluny sisters, 44, 126–27
Saline County, 77
Sandlin's store, 115
Sater, Jared, 82
Scott County, 87
Sebastian County. *See* Fort Smith
Secession movement: in 1850–1851, 11; in 1860–1861, 12–14
Secret ballot. *See* Disfranchisement: of African Americans and poor whites
Sectionalism: upland-lowland split, 11–15
Segregation, 127. *See also* Railroad coach law
Senegal, 45
Seymour, Horatio, 28
Sharp County. *See* Hardy
Shaver, Minnie Caroline, 176 n.38
Shelby, Marcus, 66–67, 72, 80, 82–83, 87, 89
Sherman, Texas, 113
Shiloh (battle): Arkansas troops at, 15
Shinn, Josiah H., 178 n.6
Shorter College, 165 n.58
Simms, John, 68, 73, 75–76, 79, 117
Sirait, Thomas, 148
Slack, W. D., 46
Small, George W., 97, 99, 173 n.6
Smith, C. J., 96
Smith, Joseph, 85–87, 145
Smith's drugstore, 70
Snipes, T. C., 96
Solgohatchia (Conway County), 65, 67, 96, 105, 108
Sons of Veterans, 97, 124
South Carolina: black emigration from, 39–43, 107, 129
Southwest City, Missouri, 82
Spears, Pleasant H., 53–54
Speer Hotel, 71, 91, 120

Springfield, 9, 15, 65, 67, 97–98, 108, 125, 167 n.8; as center of agrarian populist movement, 56, 96, 103, 164 n.51; removal of county seat from, 34–35; Republican militia from, 26–27; secession meetings in, 12–13
Stallings, Samuel J., 13–14, 151 n.12
Standlee, Robert H., 11
Steele, Frederick, 17
Stobaugh, Ananias, 153 n.24
Stobaugh, Frank, 98, 125
Stout, W. C., 50
Stowers, W. J., 62, 64–65, 83
Streeter, A. J., 61
Strub, Joseph, 43–45
Subsistence agriculture, 9
Subtreasury plan, 102

Tacoma, Washington, 90
Taylor, G. H., 63
Taylor, Warren, 69–72, 88–90, 92, 172 n.55
Taylor, William, 102
Tennessee, 45; black emigration to Arkansas from, 33, 39
Tenth Arkansas Infantry, 15, 18, 21
Texarkana (Miller County), 110
Thanet, Octave. *See* French, Alice
Thies (boardinghouse owner), 45
Third Arkansas Cavalry, 17–20, 27
Thomas, A. D., 34–35, 158 n.60, 159 n.2
Thompson (prosecutor), 24, 31
Thornton, Flannagan, 114–15, 118, 127, 130
Thurmond, Strom, 160 n.12
Tillman, Ben, 160 n.12
Toombs (preacher), 148
Trower, G. E., 57–59, 165 n.58
Turner, Benton, 34–35
Turner, May, 129

Umphlett, L. B., 29
Unionists, 53; during Civil War, 15–17, 79, 152 n.22; in Reconstruction, 28–31; as a Republican block, 34, 47, 61, 97, 124–25
Union Labor Party, 100, 124; in 1888 election, 61, 70; in 1890 election, 96–97; as party of the Agricultural Wheel, 57
Union township, 104. *See also* Springfield
United Confederate Veterans, 122
United States House of Representatives, 95, 168 n.22, 173 n.6; investigation by Committee on Elections, 91–92; request for investigation of Arkansas election, 81; testimony before Committee on Elections, 133–40; vote declaring Clayton winner in election, 92; vote declaring Featherston winner in election, 93. *See also* Breckinridge, Clifton R.
University of Arkansas, 118

Van Buren (Crawford County): Whig sentiment in, 12
Van Buren County, 15, 21, 79, 153 n.24; agrarian populist movement in, 52, 164 n.51. *See also* Clinton; Quitman
Vanderbilt University, 68
Varner (Lincoln County), 110
Violence, 72–74, 92, 130–31; in Edgefield County, South Carolina, 39; postwar raids, 22; and Reconstruction, 24–31; street fights in Morrilton, 46; theory about, 2. *See also* Guerrilla warfare; Ku Klux Klan; Lynching; Militia
Voting. *See* Disfranchisement

Wahl, Charles, 67–68, 72–74, 77, 84, 89–90, 124, 126, 128
Walley, Bert, 80
Ward, Charles, 68
Ward, W. H., 48, 83
Washington township, 96. *See also* Solgohatchia
Watkins, Robert, 88
Wellborn township, 8–9, 23–24, 34, 62, 105; Confederate sympa-

thy in, 14. *See also* Lewisburg; Morrilton
Wells, Walter P., 69–71, 76, 85, 89, 91, 97, 103, 119
Whig Party, 10–12
White, Benjamin, 63, 70, 88–89, 119–21, 177 n.2; attack on black legislator, 58–59; and Clayton murder trial, 112–13; and lynching of Flannagan Thornton, 114–15; as sheriff, 103, 117–19; and shooting of Charles Wahl, 73–74
White County, 164 n.51
Wilson, Emzy, 150 n.2
Wilson, J. Ormond, 110
Wilson, W. M., 109
Wilson's Creek (battle), 25
Williams, Frank, 99
Williams, Galloway, 99
Williams, Nathan, 17, 154 n.30
Williams, Thomas Jefferson, 16–18, 99, 103, 125, 151 n.12, 153 n.24, 154 n.30, 157 n.49
Williams, Web, 102
Williams family, 16–18, 79; in Republican militia, 27, 98–99
Winburn, Jesse, 62
Witt, Allen R., 18, 21
Womack, E. H., 77–78, 133–40
Wood, Albert, 84–86, 145, 170 n.42
Wood, William T., 69–72
Woodruff County, 134, 164 n.51, 166 n.5. *See also* McCrory
Woodward, C. Vann, 121, 123, 179 n.26, 180 n.26; adolescence in Morrilton, 4; historical works, 4; and lynching in 1920, 116, 176 n.46; views on planter persistence, 23, 120
Wooten (cotton gin owner), 128

Yell County, 37, 83. *See also* Dardanelle

Zion Hill Church, 54

Kenneth Barnes is Associate Professor of History at the University of Central Arkansas and the author of *Nazism, Liberalism, and Christianity: Protestant Social Thought in Germany and Great Britain, 1925–1937.*

Library of Congress Cataloging-in-Publication Data

Barnes, Kenneth C.
Who killed John Clayton? political violence
and the emergence of the new South, 1861–1893 /
Kenneth C. Barnes.
p. cm.
Includes bibliographical references and index.
ISBN 0-8223-2058-4 (acid-free paper). —
ISBN 0-8223-2072-x (pbk. : acid-free paper)
1. Southern States—Politics and government—1865–1950.
2. Political violence—Southern States—History—19th century.
3. Clayton, John M., 1840–1889—Assassination.
4. Political parties—Southern States—History—19th century.
5. Racism—Political aspects—Southern States—History—
19th century. I. Title.
F215.B29 1998
976.7'051—dc21 97-37573